SECURITY AND POLITICS IN SOUTH AFRICA

CRITICAL SECURITY STUDIES

Ken Booth, SERIES EDITOR
UNIVERSITY OF WALES, ABERYSTWYTH

SECURITY AND POLITICS IN SOUTH AFRICA

The Regional Dimension

PETER VALE

LYNNE
RIENNER
PUBLISHERS

BOULDER
LONDON

Published in the United States of America in 2003 by
Lynne Rienner Publishers, Inc.
1800 30th Street, Boulder, Colorado 80301
www.rienner.com

and in the United Kingdom by
Lynne Rienner Publishers, Inc.
3 Henrietta Street, Covent Garden, London WC2E 8LU

Library of Congress Cataloging-in-Publication Data
Vale, Peter C. J.
   Security and politics in South Africa : the regional dimension / Peter Vale.
      p.   cm. — (Critical security studies)
   Includes bibliographical references and index.
   ISBN 1-58826-115-8 (alk. paper)
   1. South Africa—Politics and government—1994–   2. National security—South Africa.
3. Africa, Southern—Politics and government—1994–   4. National security—Africa, South-
ern.
I. Title.   II. Series.

DT1975.V35 2003
968.06'5—dc21

2002029167

British Cataloguing in Publication Data
A Cataloguing in Publication record for this book
is available from the British Library.

Printed and bound in the United States of America

∞ The paper used in this publication meets the requirements
   of the American National Standard for Permanence of
   Paper for Printed Library Materials Z39.40-1984.

   5   4   3   2   1

Contents

Acknowledgments

M any assisted in the writing of this book. Ken Booth, Maarten de Wit, and Larry Swatuk deserve particular thanks: in their own way each helped keep me on the intellectual straight-and-narrow despite an obvious determination to falter. Jackie Kalley, who has been my longest professional associate, worked on the bibliography, endnotes, and index, literally years after she first told me that I should write this book. Some willing (and several unwilling) colleagues and friends read various chapters and made sound suggestions. My appreciation goes to John Barratt, Diana Gibson, Heather Jacklin, Guy Lamb, Khabela Matlosa, Isabelle Masson, Philip Nel, Saliem Patel, Leon Pretorius, Christopher Saunders, Maxi Schoeman, Marion Ryan Sinclair, and Paul Williams. Larry Swatuk read the entire text in a nearly final draft and made suggestions that turned a jumble of words and ideas into an argument. Comments from two anonymous referees helped to tighten the text—a process that was smoothed by Richard Purslow, Shena Redmond, and Jon Howard. Tony Holiday, Alf Stadler, and Tony Morphet were always willing—day and night, I seem to remember—to answer a call on one or another philosophical and social theoretical point; Colin Darch did the same when I was following a point on the region. And an old friend, Don Maclennan, allowed me to draw the epigraphs from his 1971 antioratorio on Oskar Wolberheim (Don Maclennan and Norbert Nowotny, *In Memoriam: Oskar Wolberheim*). Newer friends Mervyn Shear, Henk van Rinsum, Hetty Winkel, Berthe Schoonman, and Harry Voorma willed me on. Maxime Reitzes gave me access to her archive on migration issues. Engela Remke of Nasionale Boekhandel in Cape Town hunted down the near-lost files on Anthony Harrigan's book. Three librarians, Ellen Tsie (University of the Western Cape), Joan Rapp (University of Cape Town), and Joanne Paul (St. John Vianney Seminary, Pretoria), willingly assisted when I desperately needed a reference. During my forced two-year exile in senior management at the University of the Western Cape, Isobel Pontac not only showed me what to do but also kept alive the idea that I might one day return to the real thing. When I finally did, it was Weiland Gevers who offered me refuge in the Graduate School of Humanities at the University of Cape Town.

*   *   *

Three southern Africans shared the daily toil of writing, and this book is for them. I know, however, that Louise, Beth, and Dan will not mind sharing it with those who walk the region's streets, its valleys, and its hills worrying where to shelter or feed or clothe—in short, where to secure themselves and their families.

Weeks before the final assault on the manuscript, I lost an older brother. What Alan Stilwell Vale would have made of all this, I am not sure. We differed on most things but none more so than what constituted politics, security, community, and, I now realize, family. What I do know is that his early perambulations in the region opened up a place called southern Africa before my very impressionable young eyes. My fascination with it has never dimmed. This book—the one he always wanted to see—says a belated thank-you.

Prologue

In a work that is long on theory, I want to begin with a few words of practice. There are no easy choices in southern Africa. However one views it, however upbeat the moment or dismal the mood, southern Africa seems an awfully troublesome region; because so, it will not be easy to bring either security or community to its people. To be candid, the magnitude of all this has come slowly to me. And to add confession to this early frankness, understanding the enormity of what faces the region and its people would not have happened if I had not changed my reading habits.

During the 1980s, as the struggle to end apartheid intensified, I had foreseen another future for southern Africa—a future in which states would prosper and, through them, a regional community would grow. Informed by the hope that the ending of apartheid promised, I then reasoned that a series of quick and complimentary solutions for the region would deliver southern Africa from the nightmare of destruction it faced. In those particular tea leaves, the prospects for regional peace and security seemed to be naturally folded within the debates that were carrying the battle to end apartheid.

South Africa's reemergence into the regional community, I frequently argued, would register a kind of zero-hour—a moment from which all the region's people (and the national states that seemed to both cradle and carry their lives) might begin to interact through routines of international behavior—routines that I reasoned had been brutally pushed aside by cross-border war, as well as the other forms of self-mutilation and chronic insecurity that were associated with the successive last stands of minority power in southern Africa. The anxious years of waiting, of planning, and of hoping could not, I then hoped, have been in vain—a strong, confident South Africa could halt the region's downward spiral—and around this, economies would grow, democracy prosper, education flourish: the

1

region's people, as Isaiah so triumphantly proclaims—would beat their swords into ploughshares.

The fact that this future southern Africa has not materialized is obvious. In contrast to order and progress, the region appears to have collapsed inward and, so it often seems, sprawled outward: the debris, many of my countrymen (both black and white) believe, has spilled onto South Africa's pavements—Zambian trinkets, Swazi mats, Basuto hats: even in a neighboring street of gentle Muizenberg, where most of this book was written and where the likes of Cecil John Rhodes, the region's great champion of imperialism, once bathed and where (a brief century ago) he died, I hear only Lingala, a language of Africa, certainly, but of a place that, conventionally speaking, is said to lie at some distance from the core focus of this book: southern Africa.

This evidence forced me to ask different questions about the region and its possible futures. As I asked these, I recognized that my old reading habits, because they were fixated by the idea that states were the natural order of southern African things, offered no clues to a sustainable and nonviolent way forward. In this reading, the region seemed destined to repeat the patterns of violence that had produced the destruction associated with colonialism and apartheid. The established scripts, and their ready champions, offered an opening only to one version of southern Africa's present, as well as a particular kind of future: indeed, their every statement appeared only to confirm the first of three lessons of policy analysis—old understandings reproduce past mistakes.

It was in a quest to avoid the horror of these mistakes in my own understanding of the region that I turned a corner and began to read about people rather than states. This journey has taken me away from looking at southern Africa as a community to be organized around a preselected ontology, to viewing it as a mélange of people caught by competing pressures in a quickly changing world. In this reading, the borders that separate one southern African state from another are more incidental than real—more obstacle than the facilitator of peace and progress. They also make no sense—which is why, when states try to reassert them, as they frequently do, southern Africa's people simply pass them by in a time-honored regional way—they walk across dry riverbeds or barren fields. It was as visiting scholar at the Chr Michelsen Institute in Bergen, Norway, that my mind on these matters was finally made up. From that moment, I read less mainstream international relations literature and more social theory: I have never looked back or regretted my decision to turn the corner.

In the chapters that follow, I have set down the understandings that I have gleaned from this change in reading. Aficionados of international relations, and its theory, will gather that I have come to occupy a position in critical theory. My overarching goal is to point to the immanent capacity (i.e., operating within a realm of discourse) for change in the realization of human potential that the idea of security and community offers to southern Africa's people. Collaterally, I have tried to pursue three intellectual goals. First, to help critical theory take a more empirical and policy-oriented turn, so as to answer one of the most frequent and damaging charges against it. Second, to engage with the process of ongoing anticolonial and antiracist struggle in southern Africa. And third, to insert the "utopian" aim of helping to recast the idea of security as an emancipatory project rooted in a conception of regional community that makes those humans who most need security its primary referents, rather than states and their makers. These are ambitious goals. The text exercises a profound critique of South African approaches to security-making both before and after the demise of apartheid; my purpose is to suggest that they are ahistorical, derivative, and bound up with highly forced narratives of state-based sovereignty. They strongly tend, therefore, toward continuity at a time in which change in South Africa and the region has been on every lip. As the argument matures, it offers pointers toward a different and more hopeful vision of community and security in the region.

As South Africa has engaged the region in the aftermath of apartheid, my worst fears seem to have been realized. The country seems to have reverted to type: put simply, old patterns of authority have reasserted themselves. This is a central theme in the book. The thinking that now fashions South Africa's choices in the region appears to be captured by the same ideas that promoted the apartheid government—in the name of Christian values and Western civilization—to nearly destroy southern Africa in the 1970s and 1980s. True, the nonsense of a Soviet total onslaught, the blinding Cold War ideology that first inspired, and then legitimized, apartheid's security establishment, is no longer heard; and yes, South Africa is nominally at peace with each of its neighbors, but its near obsession with state security has not ended. Understanding why there has been more continuity than change in southern Africa has also been a primary motive in writing this book.

If these views appear perverse or the supporting judgments sound harsh, I want to soften them somewhat: no small part of South Africa's choice is located in the power of experts whose opinion on a topic—in this case, South Africa's security options in the region—influences a particular policy direction. It is no secret that essentially the same voices that constructed the strategic discourses that underpinned apartheid's destabilization of southern Africa continue to fan the country's preoccupation with regional security. Let me provide the first of many examples that will be offered before the final page is turned. At an academic gathering in September 1998, I heard an earnest man from an officially sponsored military think tank present a paper on security dilemmas in Africa. Corroded by prejudice and riddled with the binaries reminiscent of the apartheid years, his argument looked backward to an age when militaries were thought to be instruments that advanced civilized and European values on this continent. His approach ignored, I fear, the old truth attributed to Abraham Maslow—if your only instrument is a hammer, every problem is a nail!

This brings us back to the change in my reading.

The cues to the establishment of a political region in southern Africa were not grounded in local knowledge. Rooted in early-nineteenth-century approaches to knowledge, the making of southern Africa was fueled primarily by the British experience of foreign places that supported the discourses that sustained its power. Southern Africa was made by British ways of knowing—by county and country life, by high tea and high table, by the consciousness of class. In every possible way, the British made modern southern Africa what it is because they governed it in a way no different from New England, Nova Scotia, or New South Wales. I recognized this during the year I spent with my family as the UNESCO-Africa chair at the University of Utrecht in the Netherlands. Surrounded by Dutch culture, its rich language, its gentle people, and its alternative understandings of Africa, especially in the south, I drew my readings in theory closer to my residual interest in southern African matters. But the real impact of the colonial legacy I have just described was still to come.

This happened during an early-morning run in central Harare, the capital of Zimbabwe. In an inner-city park, a memorial plinth has been erected to commemorate African soldiers who fell in World War I—below a bas-relief of an African face under a fez (an early King's African Rifleman, perhaps?) these seven words are written: "We lived and died for our King." The British, of course, were not alone in compelling locals to fight their wars: it is difficult to think of any one country in southern Africa where local people—black, brown, white—were not pressed into the service of respective European kings—Portuguese, Belgian, German. The story of southern Africans who were lost in the cause of Europe's international relations remains to be told.

But the fight for sovereign nationalism was to partially feed the twin ideals of self-determination and freedom—death in the cause of one's own was preferable to death in the service of foreign kings and because states—no, national states—were the naturally occurring way to emancipation.

By the time this happened, however, South Africa was already an established and powerful state. The Act of Union in 1910 that created South Africa ended the prospect that southern Africa could be a place without European-style borders. As it did so, it opened the understanding—an ontology—that a regional community could only be built around national states irrespective of whether one (i.e., South Africa) was more powerful than those that were to follow. This point is repeatedly made in these pages, so much so that it may well be that I have succeeded only in writing the same chapter in seven different keys. Not a bad fate this, considering that the great blues guitarist Eric Clapton was once accused by *Rolling Stone* magazine of rewriting the same song over and over again!

I now know that history in southern Africa, with its many aspiring nationalisms, is not a linear process. Settled and seemingly ageless time lines all too often hide framings—comparative and other—that need to be recognized, if explanation—let alone freedom—is to follow. So it is worth inserting this chronological fact for the first of a number of times: South Africa—the state that has anchored southern Africa's state system—is only eight years older than South Africa's first postapartheid president, Nelson Mandela. If all this suggests that we have a dearth in our understanding of the relevance of local and other history, my new reading will not have been in vain. This draws upon the second rule of policy analysis: sound policy options often follow new understandings.

Can this be done in southern Africa?

The relationship between knowledge and political organization is a powerful thread in social theory, and in southern Africa this has finally come to be recognized. Again and again in these pages I turn to an increasingly impressive body of work that is delivered, I must add, by a younger generation of scholars. They are all, however, at some distance from policy work, in southern Africa and elsewhere, that remains trapped by boundaries, both national and epistemological.

This explains why policy analysts, ever since South Africa formally shed the legacy of apartheid, have proffered so few new ways of understanding southern Africa. Most of these have reproduced the conflicting political goals that mark the region's past; by contrast, some have hidden and deeper agendas. The most prolific (and influential) are those who seek to build southern Africa through its economic prospects. A series of country ratios—gross national product, balance of payments, gross domestic product, and rates of return—is often employed to assess the region's prospects for incorporation into the market that is at the core of globalization discourse. As we will see, the technical rationality offered by these economic codes is a poor substitute for understanding southern Africa's rich tapestry of peoples and the social relations that pattern their lives. Ratios can certainly help us understand this other southern Africa—unhappily, however, the ones that matter most are not to be found in the business pages of the dailies. These other indices—human development, comparative poverty indices, cross-regional food production, water usage, infant mortality (to cite five of at least a dozen)—are more likely to be chalked on a pockmarked blackboard in a nongovernmental organization that is starved of foreign and local funding.

This is the third policy lesson: unlearning what we take for granted is always painful. States in southern Africa will not easily fade—they will remain cardinal to understanding the region well into the twenty-first century. But they are no longer what the grand narratives promised them to be—indeed, the region is not what I once thought it would become. This is not a word game: making policy is a desperately serious business with an awesome responsibility. In the pages that follow, I look closely at how South Africa has exercised its responsibility in the development of a policy on migration. This is an unhappy chapter because it tells how the rituals of the region's past make and remake a troubled present. I also look at a defining moment in the politics of the region: South Africa's 1998 intervention in Lesotho. Far from being a decisive act to secure order and regional stability, as Pretoria's policymakers triumphantly claimed, this seems to be the first desperate act of a decaying social order; it mirrors, I believe, the region's past as its future. In analytical and policy circles there should be no alarm about this development—after all, there can be no end to history, despite ambitious claims to the contrary. But the time has come to understand the direction in which the tide of southern African affairs is moving, and to do this one must reinvent a common history and cultural identity, redirect social priorities, and (to use a metaphor much loved today) reengineer institutions. The search for alternative forms of community, of rediscovering the past, of making the new—this is the subject of Chapter 6.

To say that southern Africa is in crisis is not the same as speaking the Quaker's truth to power. I also now know that we cannot build southern Africa by emulating European and other models—indeed, building regionalism by comparison has produced much of the current pain. Southern Africa can make a new future by looking beyond the bad habits that have made for a violent past, an unhappy present, and a gloomy future. To turn the page is to know that it is possible to make a new southern Africa because the region's glass, to use a metaphor to which I will also return, is half-full.

1

New Beginning

A s the first step in our analysis of security in southern Africa, let us recall Oskar Wolberheim:

> One day last spring he entered my house
> With a branch in his hand. He was no dove,
> And he was carrying an aloe branch.
> He said good morning quietly,
> Sat down at my table and cut the aloe
> Into little cubes. Using my milk and sugar
> He made himself a breakfast dish.
> And I could not ask him how he had enjoyed it
> Because the aloe juice had deprived him
> Of the power of speech.
> —quoted in Don Maclennan and Norbert
> Nowotny, In Memoriam: Oskar Wolberheim

In this book I explore the ideas that surround security in the region of southern Africa during the early twenty-first century. The frame that guides it is *critical*, hence the name of the series   Critical Security Studies—under which this book appears. To critically engage security and its problematique (in southern Africa and elsewhere) ignites deep-seated epistemological (how we know what we know) and ontological (the way we understand something) concerns, and in every word and each sentence in this book, it is difficult not to trip over these issues. To privilege conceptual ideas, as I already have and will continue to do throughout this writing, signals a major departure from other studies that join (or carry) in the same text the idea of security as well as that of southern Africa. Conceived or contrived in (sometimes near) the tradition of positive scholarship, this work is primarily concerned with the management, manufacture, and control of security in southern Africa. In sharp contrast, this book suggests that both a technocratic and management preoccupation with security conceals deep-seated relations of power. My concern is to uncover these in order to promote the idea of a people-centered discourse on the twin issues of security and community in southern Africa.

Three policy issues preoccupy the other—in these pages I call it "realist," "orthodox," or "traditional"—approach to the issue of security in southern Africa and, indeed, elsewhere: (1) how to reinforce the threat perceptions of the central security referent, the individual nation-states; (2) how to husband, or increase, the public resources devoted to maintaining security; and (3) how to manufacture new sites of security in order to maintain and enhance the position in public life of security professionals. These three policy issues reveal an interesting conjuncture of contemporary political life: on the one hand, the deepening lack of faith—in southern Africa, but elsewhere, too—in the core organizational features of the international; and, on the other, the increasing power of neoliberal economics that have had the effect of cutting state budgets—again in southern Africa and elsewhere. But they also show the power afforded to epistemic communities to make the discourses that continuously fashion state practice. It will quickly become clear that this book is concerned both with critiquing the regimes of truth that guide this immature science (to couple two phrases from Michel Foucault) as well as with the knowledge practice it adopts. My goal is to point to the immanent capacity for change in the realization of human potential that the idea of security and community offers to southern Africans.

Given the divergence in goals between this and orthodox books on this topic, many will come to read this as a book about the politics of security in southern Africa. Here in the foothills we must be very clear about this. If there is no end to history, as the arguments in this book show, the domain of politics is never settled or fixed. Because so, the purpose of theory is the ceaseless interrogation of what "counts as politics, of what is to be included in the domain of the political."[1] The book is written in a robust spirit that is both inquisitorial and, when viewed from the orthodoxy, certainly subversive: as a result, the techniques it uses (and the tools used to illuminate the practical points it often seeks to make) will not readily be applauded, or appreciated, by those in the security business for whom the idea of security is driven by the banal routines of legislative power or is politely hidden behind the rituals of state-sanctioned violence. An open-minded appreciation of what this book is about must begin with what history so powerfully teaches but which too few in the business of orthodox security studies seem unwilling to learn: critique is not taboo. Indeed, if there are lessons to be learned from the immediate past in southern Africa, especially in the 1970s and 1980s, one is that critique is central in any search for change, especially change that champions justice. Put prosaically, the purpose of critique is to facilitate discussion of all social and political options in order to open "up the possibility of transcending contemporary society and its built-in pathologies and forms of domination."[2]

As we have noted, in writing this book, I have pursued three intellectual goals. I wanted, first, to help critical theory take a necessary empirical turn: unless it does, and with great urgency, it will remain vulnerable to the "yes, but" syndrome—the realist taunt that continues to threaten the postpositive turn in international relations notwithstanding the significant inroads that this approach has made since the mid-1980s. The life and times of security in southern Africa provide an excellent case study: the policy issues around security and its alternatives are still (perhaps only momentarily) crystal-clear. The topic offers, therefore, a rich seam of discourse that if carefully mined can make important points about the relations between power and knowledge. With further reflection, these lessons may reach beyond the spatial openings offered by the idea of southern Africa. There is another side to this, however: whether critical theorists welcome it or not, contestations in the house of security are won and lost on issues of policy. However esoteric and attractive critical security studies may look on the written page, it must eventually address this central question: Security for whom? This book is intensely interested in the practical end of security—particularly in searching for alternative communities and in advancing the ideas of emancipation through considerations afforded by security.

To the second goal: this book aims to do more than cast a critical eye on security and its polity outcomes in southern Africa. Conscious of Edward Said's telling indictment of critique's silence on issues of racist theory and anti-imperialist resistance, I want to use southern Africa as a test case to suggest that there are ways to draw critical security studies closer to this third-world battleground (which is the label I use for the time being).[3] Throughout the book, therefore, I've consciously tried to engage the critical with the idea of a ceaseless anticolonial and antiracist struggle that continues way beyond the victory over apartheid in South Africa. There is, however, no doing this without a continual engagement with the project of history. The plain truth is that, until the postpositive turn, understanding the historical location of the idea of security in southern Africa has been totally absent from debates around the region, its ways, its future. The pages that follow consciously try to correct this.

These are two ambitious goals, to be sure. If the cumulative enterprise fails to deliver on them, I hope that the argument will, somehow, manage to strengthen the "message" (borrowing from Richard Wyn Jones, who followed Theodor Adorno) that critical security studies offers humanity in this bleak moment.[4] At a time in which the starving in Zimbabwe's Mashonaland, or those freezing in a Cape winter, are knocked off the front page of the newspapers in the region's richest state by a run in something called "securities" on the Johannesburg Stock Exchange, the idea of security, as currently articulated, obviously offers no comfort to the great bulk of the region's people. This is why, perhaps, those in the business of studying security should ask themselves what their business is about. They won't, of course. So the final intellectual goal is utopian: the hope that the issue of security can come to be not the protection of possessions, or the provision of weapons to protect those who are licensed to kill, but rather protection of those who are increasingly the most vulnerable to the way in which the globalized world has come to be constructed—"the poor, the disadvantaged, the voiceless, the unrepresented, the powerless."[5] This explains why—although rooted in, and compliant with the rituals of, academia—the message in this particular bottle is aimed at southern Africa's powerful and statist elites and the organic intellectuals that both feed and serve them. Those located on the region's margins know the message. As David Korten, the development economist, has suggested, those "who live ordinary lives far removed from the corridors of power . . . have the clearest perception of what is happening, but they don't speak out."[6]

For far too long, southern Africans have been the objects of the false-laid plans of colonialists, the crackpot ideas of capital, and the sinister ideologies of empire- and state-builders, each of which has been served by faithful battalions of security specialists. Entrapped within the closing discourses of progress, the region's people—most removed from the "non-rational authority of custom and tradition" and often cowed by the "revealed truths of dogmatic religion"—have handed their hopes for security, their very futures, to grotesque hands: all too often, to be mere coincidence, their hopes have been enslaved by the self-perpetuating codes of control and domination that characterize orthodox approaches to securing southern Africa.[7] By endlessly raising questions, and by continuously contesting the analytical currency of orthodox security studies, this message hopes to break a destructive cycle by delivering an entirely new perspective on security in southern Africa. In this there is a risk, to be sure; to succeed, it involves speaking truth to power by speaking of the everyday. Notwithstanding the utilitarian ethic and reductionist understandings of politics that bedevil our times, there can be no compromise with this

issue. Intellectuals, critical and otherwise, owe "society historically sea-
soned thoughts on profound issues of politics, life and the state—thoughts
conceived, as Günter Grass often [says] of his own work, knowing that
the dead are watching closely."[8]

Understanding and explaining security in southern Africa (but elsewhere, too) is largely exempt from close intellectual scrutiny.[9] The dominant organizational paradigm in international politics—the nation-state—
has largely closed off and controlled interest in only one rendition of the
idea of security for the reasons all too commonly advanced under the banner of state security. To draw a metaphor that has peppered the critical literature in international relations closer to the region, states in southern
Africa have patrolled local intellectual interest in security as vigilantly as
they have patrolled their borders. This ongoing reliance on surveillance as
a means to politics and knowledge is certain to have a considerable effect
on how this book will be received. This issue has been much on my mind,
and I return to it frequently in this chapter.

Many readers, especially in South Africa, will believe that some point
of judgment about the sanctity of national (or regional) interest has been
violated. They must know, however, there can be no serious inquiry into
security in southern Africa without bringing into question every truth,
trope, and turn, which until now have been hidden by the sheer banality of
what on this issue has been called common sense or the normality-as-
silence that traditional security theory has come to represent.[10] Not surprisingly, therefore, Zygmunt Bauman's indictment of sociology suggests
its many silences are "its . . . loudest voices."[11] So, too, on security in
southern Africa. With careful reading, however, I hope that the overtly
political appellation that this book will initially enjoy, particularly in policymaking circles, will fade as those who make policy seek more comprehensive, more inclusive approaches to the idea of security.

To reiterate a point that runs throughout the foregoing: however con-
fusing it initially seems, critical theory is integral to a political process,
and the purpose of this book is to show this.[12] So yes, indeed, this *is* a
political book, but political only in the status quo reading of the term. In
all other readings, the book sets out to offer a deep-seated analytical
insight into issues of security in southern Africa. Given the traditional
nervousness of policymakers about academic books on security—especially those that appear to be too critical or, worse perhaps, too theoretical, I want to begin elsewhere; the very obvious framing provided by the
time sequence of history seems to be a good alternative venue.

But first, a few more words on organization. The balance of this chapter is concerned with locating the idea of security within poststructuralist

theory. Chapter 2 explores renditions of southern Africa through this theoretical approach; my purpose is to situate South Africa and the region within an alternative explanation of history. Chapter 3 continues on this trajectory; my interest is to draw alternative renderings of the region's security forward to the present moment. Chapters 4 and 5 are moments where poststructural renditions meet policy: my initial concern is with South Africa's encounter with migration, whereas Chapter 5 deals with South Africa's fateful 1998 invasion of Lesotho. In Chapter 6, I explore the idea of community—especially alternative forms of community—in southern Africa, and in Chapter 7 I return to consider some unresolved issues in the poststructural study of security in southern Africa. In a brief Afterword, I have tried to anticipate some of the more obvious criticisms that will be raised against the book, which brings me to explain the reasons why I wrote it. The driving force behind this project and its construction is the simple weight of the numbers so loved by orthodox security studies: roughly 30 million people are living with HIV and AIDS in southern Africa, and the number is growing; in one corner of the region (Angola), the infant mortality rate stands at 193.72 deaths per 1,000 live births; in South Africa, there are 4.5 million registered handguns, and in 1995 the United Nations Crime and Justice Information Network reported that 6.6 percent of the population of sub-Saharan Africa were victims of so-called sexual incidents during the year. These figures clearly suggest that the region has been ill served by its states and their makers; it is time for a new beginning.

A New Beginning

International society is decidedly different from what it was in the 1980s. In southern Africa, this change has been predicated on a number of issues, but none has been more prominent than the formal ending of apartheid. The great celebration over that event masks the fact that it was not isolated, however: it was neither an insular moment in the life of the region nor, indeed, a single moment in international history. Rather, the ending of apartheid is integral to a pattern of developments that has seen, respectively, a region of states and a region of people (keeping these two apart is important to the entire argument in the book) respond to the tectonic shifts associated with what has come to be colloquially called "global change." But here is the first of innumerable paradoxes about security that run through these pages: even though apartheid—once described as the most important threat to regional security—has ended, nevertheless "threats to security continue to proliferate."[13]

This global change has proved to be a complicated process, one that is impossible to predict, impossible to understand, impossible to control: constantly on the move, it challenges perceptions and impressions. Because every moment seems suddenly so different, and the unexpected appears to be the only constant, making sense of what seems initially so much nonsense seems near impossible.[14] As a result, managing global change (and its impact) is an ongoing endeavor that appears to require ceaseless revision and, above all, a willingness to learn. Like many things in academic life and in the practical world of international politics, this is easy to say yet devilishly difficult to act upon. Thus while theoreticians and practitioners have come to realize that change is slippery, most do not recognize that their own capacity to engage with it is endless. Understanding why this is so is central to the many ideas embedded in this book: for our immediate purposes, however, three compacted reasons stand out.

First off, neither academia nor the policy end of international politics has demonstrated a capacity to anticipate change, let alone adequately explain its immediate impact.[15] Second (and this explains the first reason), academic training all too often rests on the belief that the lifeworld of the international (or the regional or, indeed, the national) consists of receiving stable ontologies and massaging them, rather than understanding that the social has constructed a particular configuration. And third, understanding and coping with time in its analytical and spatial dimensions have proved nearly impossible. Is change to be understood diachronically (measured against a past condition) or synchronically (measured against the simultaneous condition of other categories of people); and what structures change—instantaneous (or clock) time, conjunctural (or medium-term) time, or what Fernand Braudel calls the "*longue durée*"—change in the structures of thought?[16] These suggest why the analytical eye has been unable to capture the unanticipated impact of change, as well as why the same eye fails to explain why the surprising and the unexpected offer the only secure conceptual horizon.

There are deep questions of knowledge—its sociology, its construction—at work here, and these require, in the context of the central problematique of the book, some early and conceptual markers. Using the insights proved by social theory, the search for an explanation of change in southern Africa must probe the understandings that first conceived, then helped to form, a series of national security states in southern Africa. These have privileged the idea of states and their security and that—in their theory and practice—situate South Africa above other states in the region. Why this is so is central to the production of knowledge—especially the circumstances under which knowledge-claims around security in the region are and can be made. This is not coincidental, of course. It was Immanuel Kant, in his *Critique of Pure Reason*, who suggested that what we know and the conditions under which this knowing came about are inexorably tied. As Richard Devetak has put the same point, "Knowledge is always, and irreducibly, conditioned by historical and material contexts."[17] Within the southern African academy, with the successive holding power of colonialism, racism, and nationalism, this has had a particular importance: an importance that all too often has overlooked the power that South Africa has in the making of the region. Indeed, writing about security in southern Africa has almost entirely been lodged within closed scholarly contexts in a comparatively rich and privileged country. Small wonder, then, they believe that the facts underlying security are regarded as settled and that the resulting policy outcomes are entirely predictable and unproblematic.

For all the illumination it purportedly sheds on the international (and therefore the social), the vocabulary of orthodox strategic studies provides a dim light when it comes to understanding the direction of regional change or even, on considered reflection, the condition of the present. Not for nothing did Ken Booth famously observe that our work is words, but our words don't work anymore. The search for new words, however, has proved both onerous and time-consuming and has not, at the time of this writing, generated impressive shifts, certainly not the breakthroughs that will lead to Alexis de Tocqueville's ideal of a new science for a new age. The result is a preference (on the part of scholars and policymakers alike) to remain rooted in both the speech and the action associated with the words that work for the powerful—to remain within the comfort represented by continuities, rather than engaging in the search for new notions that might lead to different ideas, different interpretations, and so deliver different policy outcomes. In short, there is little real incentive to search for new theoretical mappings: in southern Africa, especially in South Africa, nowhere is this preoccupation with sameness more pronounced than with the idea of security. The resulting allure accounts for security's permanent character in a southern Africa that has, certainly formally, undergone immense political change; why this is so is, of course, the central point of disputation in the pages that follow. Like its twin, sovereignty (to which the same disputations will frequently turn), security runs like a golden thread in the debates (and the many nondebates) that continue to shape the affairs of the region. But, and this is the reason for the book, vain is the search for evidence of even a momentary hesitation about the concept of security—or the single impulse that ponders and problematizes the application of sovereignty.

This is a good place, therefore, to set out a few procedural markers, some of which, for these immediate purposes, have been purloined from the historian Tim Keegan.[18] There is little doubt that the postpositive move in international relations has helped to unsettle orthodox approaches to knowing the world.[19] This has permitted a proliferation of new, and quite refreshing, ontological claims to be made in the names of both international relations and security. Whatever the benefits of these—and their fruits are profusely scattered throughout this book—the techniques of academia continue to reveal important limitations—the obsession with approved gurus and their texts being one; another is "the virtual obsession with [particularistic] language" (as Rex Gibson describes it).[20] I have tried to be conscious of these but recognize that the genre of academia, even though it seeks to promote change, must invariably mean the maintenance of scholarly rituals, if not language. The real-world challenge is to prevent these from neutering the power of new ideas, new words, or—as in the case of this book—new ways of viewing old things.

This brings us to a discussion of critical theory and critical security studies: What? How? When?

One Way Out . . . and In

What remains of this chapter is intended to briefly guide the reader through some of the debates about the impact of social theory on the academic study of international relations, especially as they touch upon security. Social constructivist approaches to theory have produced a compelling explanation in the unfolding story of post–Cold War international knowledge. The growth of interest in constructivist approaches to understanding the global, in these changing times, has finally generated both light and heat in the study of international relations. The predilections of the young (and some not so young) to experiment with the international, or simply to think again about the world, have helped international relations partially escape the narrow confines of realist dogma that has been "complicit in the creation and recreation of international practices that threaten, discipline and do violence to others."[21]

As global change has demonstrated, we clearly live in disruptive times, but not all social, political, and international theory is critical; in fact, most is not. Unlike most other theories, however, critical theory is primarily concerned with outcomes, in particular with the justice and the happiness of individuals and communities. To seek these goals in the same breath as understanding and explaining security seems to present another paradox: Why is it that the one concept in social science—security— which should ideally make for the comfort and safety of individuals and communities, is so quintessentially associated with the *ultima ratio* of politics, violence, and war?[22]

However it is defined with the discourse of regular politics, and whatever the urgency attached to it within the discourses of the state, the very life of security—its ordering, its surveillance, the violent license it offers statecraft—is neither inevitable, natural, nor, very often, necessary. Like much else in life and politics, security is a social construct: a product of specific historical processes, a series of ideas and practices that have created a received, not a predetermined, end. This constructivist approach to theorizing draws on a sociological chain enunciated in the mid-1960s by Peter Berger and Thomas Luckham: "Society is a human product. Society is an objective reality. Man is a social product."[23]

As an approach to understanding international politics, constructivism emphasizes "the impact of ideas. Instead of taking the state for granted and assuming that it simply seeks to survive, constructivists regard the interests [including security interests], and identities of states as a highly malleable product of specific historical processes."[24] To deploy this particular explanation is purposeful: the source in which it appears, the liberal U.S. journal *Foreign Policy*, helps to reinforce the earlier contention that the ideas upon which this book is carried are neither particularly anarchist nor, indeed, iconoclastic. They belong in a respectable line of critical inquiries into initially international relations and, more recently, into security studies.[25] As with most other inquiries, this work shares the goal of understanding the shifts that have changed the world. However, by adopting a critical framing, it wants more—it wants to both understand and to change the very world it seeks to analyze. This is a familiar chime in social inquiry: popularly attributed to the younger Karl Marx's eleventh encounter with Ludwig Feuerbach, in international relations it was highlighted by Mark Hoffman in his groundbreaking late 1980s article on the "inter-paradigm" debate.[26]

What critical security studies offers, therefore, is not a neutral or value-free interpretation of security in southern Africa: it suggests instead that this particular goal is not possible or, indeed, desirable. Rather, critical inquiry is "both descriptive and constructive in its theoretical intent: it is both an intellectual and a social act."[27] Without real transformation, a critical analysis suggests there can be no security in southern Africa because what is today called security (even in the jubilation of the post-apartheid moment) is temporal and primarily geared to further the advantage of the already advantaged. Furthermore, a critical investigation into security believes that every discarded stone (foundation and other) on the path to building community in southern Africa must be examined. So, any real understanding of the discourses and the practices of security in southern Africa (or any corner of the world, for that matter) means looking at everything again; or, quite simply, it means looking at everything for the very first time through critical eyes! In Craig Calhoun's words, the task of critical theory is to subject "concepts, received understandings, and cultural categories constitutive of everyday life and public discourse to critical theoretical reconsideration" in order to interrogate the "prevailing order of social and political modernity through a method of immanent critique."[28] Its goal? To "advance a systematic and radical critique of society, demystifying how power, position and privilege relate to class, group and personal inequalities."[29]

But why bring critique, security, and southern Africa together in this fashion?

As Ken Booth and I noted, in an essay that in many ways is the precursor to this book, "multiracial Zimbabwe, independent Namibia and South Africa all attest to elasticity in racial questions in a part of the world in which—for centuries—race was the single most determining factor."[30] But celebration of this victory has been partial: the region remains poor and impoverished, its peoples trapped by both the ideas of politicians and the practices of security state makers. In contemporary southern Africa, therefore, security remains a slave to the preordained limits of a state system that is partial, lopsided, and entirely inappropriate to the needs of the region's people. By contesting the conceptual elements—like political control, state integrity, and regional order—that underpin thinking about the existing regional structure, critique offers, as we shall see, the potential to overcome what Sheldon Wolin has called "dystopia"—the very antithesis of utopia.[31]

Rather than affirming the routines associated with promoting control and power in southern Africa, therefore, this book is imbued with a spirit of questioning; with searching for new explanations for events on the ground; with reexamining all that appears both quite ordinary and well understood in the debates on security in southern Africa. Whatever the mainstream suggests (or fears), such scholarly adventure is never perverse, especially in times of great change; intellectual risk-taking (to intentionally borrow a noun that the economistic discourses have purloined, canonized, and used to so nearly poison life in southern Africa) is

central to the public role of intellectual inquiry. So, in contrast to the con-
formations offered by the security specialists who write on the topic, this
book will show why the idea of security in southern Africa should be a
permanently contested term—and suggest why security has open, not
closed, meanings.[32] The intellectual and political preoccupation of the
book is not therefore with legitimation and consolidation of knowledge;
quite the contrary, it is with Walter Benjamin's brushing against the grain
of history.

My intention is to move beyond positivist framings of the region and
its security. But what is positivism, and why move beyond it? For posi-
tivists, there is only one objective truth to be discovered, empirical reasoning is the correct form of reasoning, and finally there can be a distinction between observer and observed. Postpositivists reject this: reason
both silences and marginalizes; instead of reason constructing the world,
the world is socially constructed. As a result, it is not possible to divide the
observer from the observed. Theories construct the facts of the social
world, and truths are socially defined. As for rationality, this cannot be
transcended but is a historically learned activity. It is, therefore, not possible to examine security without examining the state and, indeed, the idea
of sovereignty that underpins the state. This brings us to the idea of community, which is a fundamental issue in this discussion. A central problem
for the study of security and, indeed, southern Africa is why the meaning
of security is tied to specific forms of political community.[33]

In the pages that follow, I move between different moments of postpositivism and thus want to make it clear into which house this book fits.
My point of departure is postpositivism, but the text moves easily between
three strands of this critical theory: postmodernism, constructivism, and
neo-Marxism. In this way, the text is aligned to the generic understanding
of critical theory as it has emerged in the United States, but many of the
arguments draw on the work of the Frankfurt School in its traditional and
contemporary setting. In this way, the work is associated with critical theory in the emancipatory tradition. Certainly this universal, even cavalier,
approach to theory will offer ammunition to critics. So this must be made
clear: although drawing heavily on theory, this is not a book on theory but
a book that offers critique to the discourses of security in South Africa.

Whatever the custodians of knowledge on (and over) security tell and
foretell, and whatever their memories recall, history is not a linear
process—it is invariably contested. In southern Africa, I will suggest, the
telling of history and the construction of a security-conscious region dominated by security-minded states have largely been one and the same
thing.[34] States and the making of their security appear to have been the

region's central historical project: in their keeping of this ontological faith, these states have produced great violence in a relatively short space of time. This violence (as we shall come to see) has primarily been driven by contestations over what determines respectively national and regional security. In this process, however, southern Africa's people have seldom been the beneficiaries; all too often they have been victims. To understand this conundrum, we must recognize that integral to all security is the question of community: Who has it? How to build it? How to make it? Who is in it? And as apartheid South Africa so empathically showed throughout the region in the 1970s and 1980s: How to break it?

Knowing Security the Southern African Way

In the 1980s southern Africa was caught in a cruel war. South Africa's embattled minority was determined to export their state's search for security (to borrow a metaphor once used in a title by Deon Geldenhuys) to the farthest corners of the region.[35] The result was destabilization, the generic term for apartheid's ghastly campaign that was waged both on its neighboring states and on southern Africa's people; it was a terribly destructive moment in the region's short, but very violent, recorded history. Once apartheid had ended, it was quite reasonable for politicians to promise (and the region's people to expect) a peace dividend—but today, significant corners of southern Africa are still at war.[36] Two examples make the point that the role of conflict in the region remains both compelling and tragic. In the Democratic Republic of Congo (DRC), notwithstanding a formal cessation of hostilities, fighting continues; and throughout South Africa—the region's strongest and most security-conscious country—bloody conflict sporadically flares among competing social groupings as well as among rival political factions. Terrible structural violence continues to be visited throughout southern Africa, and invariably the suffering is unequal; the unemployed, the homeless, the sick, the women, and the children—those with no voice in the mainstream fashioning of society are at the sharp end. This outcome is not a coincidence or, indeed, inevitable. It is the result of the way in which the region has come to understand and to practice the idea of security.

Although statist logic suggests that so-called peace dividends are an inevitable part of peacemaking, the failure to initiate deep-seated social change in the wake of peace illustrates that peacemaking is all too often concerned with security as a means to order. This is not to suggest that the idea of what constitutes understandings of security within mainstream thinking has stood still: as Simon Dalby, J. Ann Tickner, Ole Wæver, and many others have observed, the idea of security has taken on a host of new forms.[37] Such mutations, however, are primarily directed at maintaining the status quo and, especially, the state as the central referent—not at changing the social order in an emancipatory direction.

For some in the business of security studies in southern Africa, security has mutated vertically, for others, horizontally. But every expansion, each inflation, any twist of the term "security" draws its practice closer to conditions under which security, and the discourses that nourish it, can be managed and manipulated.[38] Simultaneous with this procedure, the policy process that guides security is closed off from open and public contestation by calls to nationalism, or nation-building, or national interest. The formula is as simple as it is effective: conventional perspectives on security seek out ways to control the ideas and institutions concerned with the very object—security—upon which they seek to pronounce. In postapartheid southern Africa, the primary, but not exclusive, locus of this particular controlling concern with security continues to be the geospace known, and called, South Africa.[39] Given this, well may we ask: What has changed in southern Africa in the aftermath of the ending of apartheid?

Patterns of conflict in the region are increasingly characterized by intrastate as opposed to interstate conflict. However, a critical questioning around this microissue suggests a different interpretation of this "reality," or this "new development," than that which is conventionally offered. A genealogy of the origins of the region's state system, which is my central task of Chapter 2, suggests that the interstate violence in southern Africa that so dramatically characterized the apartheid years may have only been a variant of what some have called "domestic" violence. The search for security in the region, this view suggests, has only superficially involved states and their contrived insecurities. In fact, interstate conflict in the region, even during the apartheid years, may only have been epiphenomenona because states-qua-states were imposed on what we have come to call "the region." By showing that the region's subordinate state system (an appellation first used by Larry Bowman) is not "a timeless and essential secret," but that its essence was "fabricated in a piecemeal fashion from alien forms," the region can be shown to be a single polity.[40] As a result, all conflict in the region can be considered domestic. There is more here in the constructivist vein: the inverse suggests that the search for interstate security in southern Africa has been constitutive of the development of, successively, individual states and the region's state system.

There is no social-science trick at work in the generation of a paradox that suggests that southern Africa's search for security has invariably been about the conditions of domestic politics; indeed, a central preoccupation of critique is to make strange, by offering alternative interpretations, events that are accepted as commonplace. This example parallels Ann Tickner's assertion that U.S. president Ronald Reagan's Strategic Defense Initiative, "with its vision of global destruction, made it abundantly clear that the state, even the United States, could no longer assure the security of citizens within its own boundaries."[41] Equally so, and drawn closer to the task at hand, the central source of insecurity for the majority of southern Africans was the power of the state that practiced apartheid—yet this was the very state that set the conditionalities for the formation of southern Africa's state system. So apartheid South Africa's insistence that it was insecure, and its resulting fight for security, became a source of insecurity to the majority of its own citizens and to the people of the region.[42] The state system—in the name of South Africa's minority—waged war on the region's people. The complicity of orthodox security studies in this is clear: where they might have legitimately been subversive in support of the interests of ordinary people, they sought to sustain political order and, through this, particular forms of state power.[43]

Traps, Tricks, and Tropes

In order to understand the power of this paradox, it is necessary to turn to the sociology of knowledge and ask what shapes our understanding of what constitutes "reality." For most of those preoccupied with the security debates in southern Africa, if they get here at all, this is a queasy moment, one at which few, it seems, are willing to pause. After all, in a region in which the obvious seems so real, the search beyond the ordinary, the everyday, and the commonplace is usually both uncomfortable and discomforting. Quite simply, however, there is no appreciation of the complexities of security in southern Africa (and the search for its future forms) without understanding the process that creates our understandings of the world and, in this case, southern Africa and its security. To change the world, as critical theory attempts to do, we must therefore engage the intellectually demanding task of how it is that we know—and why we know. Let me deliberately superimpose two metaphors in order to stress that this is often said but rarely done. Security studies and social theory are two worlds: uncomfortable bedfellows in which one seldom asks questions of the other.

Why? An answer has been provided by Robert Cox in his celebrated series: "Theory is always *for* someone and *for* some purpose"; and in his

less celebrated embellishment, "we need to know the context in which theory is produced and used; and we need to know whether the aim of the user
is to maintain the existing social order or to change it."[44] To accept this is
to accept that theory is both time-bound and, equally important, purpose-
bound. One stream, what Cox (following Max Horkheimer's analysis) calls
"problem solving theory," is preoccupied with maintaining the existing
order; the other (Horkheimer's term for this was "critical theory") is that
theory is integral to change. For the first, the bustling and seemingly urgent
business of state security—with its institutionalizing, its defending, its managing, its controlling—the main theoretical preoccupation is (in that most
fatal of all analytical phrases) to let the facts speak for themselves.[45] But
because this particular construction of reality hides the innumerable values
and deep-seated prejudices that make for both established knowledge and
establishment knowings about the world, it is never enough for the second.
So for critical theorists, the facts alone are never, ever enough—especially
in a field like security, with its rituals of power. And this—the closed world
of security—is the well that waters critical security studies.

Rooted in the quasi-Marxist origins of critical theory, the technique of
critical security studies is clear: the destabilization of the hegemonic discourses on security.[46] In southern Africa this means questioning all the comfortable assumptions that have marked interpretations and understandings
of regional events, especially those that are always cozily grouped together
(and then silenced or controlled) under the heading of "security." Faithful
to its constructivist roots, critical security studies scrutinizes the origins,
practice, processes, and problems of orthodox security studies. By questioning all the taken-for-granted assumptions about the politics of security
in the region and the hand-me-down policy prescriptions, which have fostered discrimination and poverty in the name of security, critical security
studies shows why it is that security experts have engaged in histrionics
when, instead, they should have understood history. It also shows why, for
far too long, the politics of the region has been dominated by force, by
states, and by men when, instead, the organizing theme in the region ought,
perhaps, to have been the search for alternative community, the power of
imagination, and the agency provided by women.

With Antonio Gramsci, the purpose of critical theory is twofold: the
erosion of the legitimacy of the ruling historic bloc, and the development
of a counterhegemonic position.[47] To achieve this, critical security studies
relentlessly probes social knowledge and its politics. How do we know
things? Why do we know things? Who makes the "facts"? Whose interests are served by the ways in which a tale is told?

Toward Community and Emancipation

The central policy goal of critical security studies is to wrest control over the decisions that affect (or will come to affect) individual lives. There is no easy way to deal with this in southern Africa, no polite common-room prattle that will move along the text from the destruction wrought by the orthodox study of security to the next uncomfortable question: How can the region's people free themselves? Because the statist lens seems so resilient, it is easiest to use it to illustrate the cumulative destruction that has become the region's tragic fate. But this—used either illustratively or for comparative purposes—has the effect of drawing the region backward toward an unhappy past in which security was map-bound and all maps well secured around South Africa's hegemony.[48] However, a careful reading of history shows that innumerable interpretations of community and emancipation are intertwined in the region's past, and therefore their reinterpretation offers hope for its future. Because the dominant organizing principle in southern Africa has been states, many alternative interpretations lie close to the structuralism represented by states, but others, as we come to see, lie at some distance from structure.

Critical security studies seeks not only to identify and explain communities to be built in southern Africa but also to provide the means to arrive at them by helping people to gain more control over their lives. To achieve this, it believes that community and emancipation should be drawn closer together; this melding of structure and agency belongs in a work on security (more so, perhaps, than any other place in contemporary social theory) because profound experiences of insecurity continue to entrap individuals in false communities, not only in southern Africa (as its rich social history graphically illustrates) but throughout the world.[49] In these circumstances, coercion is offered as the only path to security: state power is therefore exercised in the name of making the world normal.[50]

To write about southern African security and its institutions in any other way but critically is to re-create the conditions of the region's unhappy past. This is why on a quick and superficial reading, this book (especially as it opens) appears to be preoccupied simply with challenging statist interpretations of the southern African region. As an elementary understanding of contemporary southern Africa suggests, traditional state-centered readings of the region and its ways leave much to be desired. As a result, and we shall come to see this, the mismatch between events on the ground and ways to frame them seemed destined to dog interpretations of southern Africa well into the twenty-first century. To change all this, however, critical security studies requires us to locate these paths in the context of their making.

By now it should be clear that this work is not a representation of the "frozen moment"—that single historical frame, so loved by the policy community primarily because it provides the platform upon which to model simple, and measured, management alternatives. No, this work is intended to stimulate further change, to allow the intervention of humans in the making of their own history, in short, to favor the force of agency over power of structure. Knowledge represents a powerful tool in the shaping of society and the building of alternative community; to change the world requires that we should think differently about it. If security is to mean something to those at the very margins of southern African society or if it is to alter patterns of power, then an alternative ontology must be constructed within which security serves the interests of people. This— the pursuit of the Enlightenment idea that some truths are better than others—is also a difficult move to make both intellectually and politically.

Therefore, even a casual reading of this text reveals an emancipatory face. The search for emancipation in the region lies beyond understandings that are grounded in the idea of sovereignty. In subsequent chapters, I draw particular attention to the practice of international relations in South Africa and southern Africa. The purpose is to suggest that politics at this level has reinforced statist interpretations, rather than offering multiple readings of community in the region. Although these comments finger metatheories like realism, they also show that "emancipation and security are . . . two sides of the same coin."[51] The centrality of the theme of emancipation in the unfolding of South Africa and southern Africa has been identified but inadequately developed at the theoretical level.[52] That is why I am interested in interrogating the juncture between emancipation and security in the hope of pushing out an understanding of the dichotomy between the celebratory side associated with the ending of apartheid and the declinist perspective that some now believe beckons both South and southern Africa.

This closes an initial circle by bringing us back to where we started: this book continuously probes prospects for the creation of a new ontology in which to locate and understand security in southern Africa.[53] The notion that there is an "objective" entity, a distinctive ontological structure, recognizable by realists, neorealists, and antirealists alike (to borrow now from a long-standing debate in the philosophy of the mind and philosophical logic), is problematic. But the least that must be said is this: if by "ontology" we mean what Aristotle meant—the study of Being-qua-Being—then we mean a thing or structure that was actualized via the workings of formal, material, efficient, and final causes. If we do mean this and are not merely playing fast and loose with an ancient term of art that has become fashionable once more in the social sciences, then we must recognize that the ontological structure of which we speak when we speak of southern Africa is radically unstable. Colonial history and colonizing cartographers have given the notion of southern Africa a form of sorts—and must therefore number among its formal causes. This history and this cartography live under the continual threat of subversion by the uncovering of our precolonial past by Africanist historiographers, by post-colonial experience, and by critical inquiry. Because of this, the ontology of southern Africa is rendered unstable by that which liberates the region or threatens to do so.[54] But as a careful reading of the pages that follow will suggest, there is more here than critique alone: there is a belief that there are working alternatives to the regional status quo.

Let me close this early ramble through the unfolding world of critical security studies with a summary of the epistemological concerns of the book—and another confession. This book directs critique both at the idea of security and at southern Africa, a region (and its derived polity) that has seldom, if ever, been subjected to deep-seated questioning. Through-out its writing, I have used the thieving-magpie approach to both research and explanation that, as Simon Schama so wryly observes, "may seem, superficially . . . to be new-fangled but in fact is very old fashioned."[55] This approach must be set against the realist approach—an approach in which the study of international politics is "treated as a domain of its own."[56]

Southern Africa is a pliable polity; without recognizing this, it will not be possible for the region's people to escape the legacy of their violent past or secure their future. Even orthodox analysts of southern African security seem to understand this, but for them moving beyond it represents formidable challenges. Disciplined by their desire to control and limited by their ontological focus, their statist efforts to widen and deepen the debate over security in the region, while remaining its gatekeepers, have led no farther than the creation of a "grab bag of different issue areas [which lack] a cohesive framework for analyzing the complementary and contradictory themes at work."[57]

In the pages that follow, answers are sought to a variety of questions intimately linked to security. And the search for answers to these questions lies beyond mainstream international relations scholarship; it lies in the territory of cultural studies, feminism, and environmental studies. A reader knowledgeable in the disciplinary routines of security studies will not take long to see that I have drawn more from these sources than from the reg-

ular fare of academic disciplines—strategic studies, international relations, political science, economics, and public management—commonly
associated with security issues. Resistance to drawing ideas in security
from outside a predetermined menu of controlling disciplines will
inevitably be rooted in traditional conceptions of social science that draw
on natural science. These claim that knowledge and knower must be separated in order to theorize properly on social issues. This hunger for a
value-free social science, in which "most, if not all, things are both know-
able and hence predictable," has powerfully influenced understandings of
security in southern Africa, a point confirmed by the establishment of a
separate academic subject called "military science" within the South
African security academe.[58] This branching-off of scholarly endeavor has
been the subject of many discussions. For Zygmunt Bauman, the special-
ization that follows leads to a "peculiar language and imagery" and "their
elimination from the core canon of the discipline" and to absolution from
the mainstream of scholarship.[59] This has happened in South Africa—a
condition, I hasten to add, compounded by the academic boycott against
the country during the apartheid years. But few, if any, moments in scholarship, let alone life, are without their wider sociological entanglements,
and "military science," "security studies," and "international relations"
were polluted with social values as much as was the ideology of apartheid
upon which they were nourished.[60] This point—that apartheid's regional
strategy was political rather than intrinsically value-free or scientific—has
been continuously reinforced at hearings before South Africa's Truth and
Reconciliation Commission and has been reported, not always satisfacto-
rily, in its findings.[61]

The process of arriving at the "truth" of South Africa's own past has
also provided a mechanism for avoiding the real politics of the region. Let
me draw the issue out by referring to the six tasks that underpin South
Africa's Truth and Reconciliation Commission and ask a single and
uncomfortable question. First a listing of the tasks: to create a picture of
the nature, causes, and extent of human rights violations over a thirty-
three-year period; to grant amnesty in exchange for truth; to provide an
opportunity for victims to relate their side of the story; to rehabilitate the
dignity of victims; to report its findings; and to make recommendations on
the prevention of similar violations in the future. Now the question: Why
is it, with all that we knew and understood about the region, its history,
and its search for security, that mainstream international relations, realist
security studies, and military science were not called to testify before the
commission? It was, after all, these theories that brought apartheid to what
it was and that used apartheid's insecurities to sow destruction in southern

Africa. For the moment, I want to leave this issue, but as we draw closer to a conclusion in the chapters that follow, I want to come back to the culpability of ideas in the creation of politics.

But now it is time to turn the page and join in the critical discussion of security discourses in southern Africa that preoccupies the rest of this book. Before doing so, however, a playful conceptual note borrowed from the South African social theorist Tony Morphet's penetrating, but all too brief, discourse analysis of midcentury race relations in his native land: "If anyone thinks that they can glimpse Foucault and Derrida looking over my shoulder . . . (as I write) . . . they are correct; but I should say that they are at a considerable distance. It might have been a better . . . [book] . . . if they were closer."[62]

2

The South African Moment

I should explain that this is not
free association. There is in all
things a cost structure. Nothing is,
really, free. Take, for example, the
apparently gratuitous beauty of fish.
Some are this shape, some are that.
But if you put a fish this shape
On a mercator projection it becomes
A fish that shape, and vice versa.
And the transformation obeys an iron law.
—Oskar Wolberheim

This chapter interrogates the discursive formation that has permitted the establishment of states in southern Africa. Using the form of organization offered to politics by the experience of Westphalia, especially the idea of sovereignty, a particular social configuration took root in a distant corner of Africa. Within a short century following the creation of the region's first state, South Africa, the idea of region developed from geographical expression into an established institution that mimics political community and evinces a series of security concerns—most, but not all, of its own making. My method is to critique the series of narratives that rendered this state-centered configuration as a naturally occurring reality; in particular, my attention falls on three regimes of social ordering: knowledge production, sovereignty, and the politics of frontiers. These have offered, as the reader will come to see, powerful conceptual tools in stabilizing issues around what constitutes region and security and helped to establish South Africa as the first in a community of unequal states. Although much of the engagement in this chapter is with history, a careful reading reveals that its true métier is social theory.

Writings on (and of) southern Africa exemplify the familiar Foucauldian link between knowledge and power. How we know southern

Africa, how we remember its ways—indeed, how we anticipate its future—are a function of particular renditions of (and on) the region. Between apparently stable chronological markers, a grand narrative carries the idea of southern Africa toward a future pregnant with the promise of progress. In this well-authorized frame, southern Africa—historical experience, place of institutions, and home for eternity—is a function of the holding power of a narrative tradition that reflects a simple conceptual idea: the anarchy represented by innumerable unknowns can be tamed by rational ordering.

As an example of this unfolding, consider this account of the region's purported settled past, its apparent incontestable present, and the rationality promised to its future by a new regional cosmology that was penned by the Harvard historian Robert I. Rotberg.

> Southern Africa rotates around South Africa, and always has. From the early nineteenth century, when Shaka's Zulu warriors transformed the martial arts and the politics of the region, to the 1990s, when Mandela's diplomats and their initiates are given pride of place in all regional and international forums, apartheid-free South Africa calls the tune in the region. . . . Cecil Rhodes, the British imperialist, mining entrepreneur, and successful colonial politician, forcefully gave the region its current shape. By thrusting iron tentacles relentlessly northward from Cape Town into what are now Botswana, Zimbabwe, Zambia and Zaire, he tied the region's mining centres and population magnets together and bound them to the ports of South Africa. His conquest of Zimbabwe, his attempted conquest of Zaire and Mozambique, his successful assertions of economic suzerainty over Zambia and Malawi also forged links which . . . endure . . . in the administrative, legal and linguistic, educational, cultural, political, and economic structures of the region.[1]

It is unquestionably true that the region's incorporation, as a place called "southern Africa," into the unfolding processes of modernity was premised on the discovery of minerals and, equally so, that these were located in South Africa. But the site for this was Johannesburg, the region's place of gold—southern Africa's "industrial hub," as apartheid's propaganda machine liked to call it, rather than Cape Town.[2] Certainly the grand story of conquest and the civilizing mission propagated by speakers of English resided in Cape Town where Rhodes's presence lurks over the city; from the Devil's Peak, his bust broods over the path that looks northward to his famously proclaimed "hinterland"—a word that returns in a chapter preoccupied with the expansive energy of the imperial project.[3]

A core goal of this book is to address the security practices that have been unleashed by violent texts, like Rotberg's, on a current generation of regional state-makers. However, the book is also concerned with demonstrating that pathways—other than those that have been offered to the region by the grandeur of countries, estates, and funds represented by the likes of Cecil John Rhodes—to security are both possible and desirable in southern Africa.[4]

Our current purpose requires that we return to Rotberg, however. His construction of southern Africa reveals how understandings of nineteenth-century heroism continue to author southern Africa more than a century later. By placing, successively, the Cape of Good Hope, and then South Africa, at the epicenter of the region, his technique looks to the power of sovereign organization and the rationality of capital in erasing any uncertainties from the affairs of the region. In this fashion, the region's many complexities, including issues of race and class, are silenced. Given its ease of access, and its endless replications, this approach has profoundly influenced discourses on the region, not least those on security. The power of its hold on the latter explains why ritual thinking on regional security routinely offers up only three options. These revolve around one of the oldest concepts in international relations: the balance of power. In a form appropriately contrived for the region, "the mechanism of power balancing—stabilizing relations among states by maintaining power equivalences" around the hierarchical, geographic, and political of the region's principal player, South Africa, yields the following prefigured options:[5]

- South Africa's insecurity is a threat to the region.[6]
- South Africa will (and must) fill any security vacuum in southern Africa.[7]
- There can be no security guarantees in the region without South Africa's compliance.[8]

Reduced to these outcome logics, the region's security is the grim prisoner of the power that has been distributed by the founding narrative. So, southern Africa's search for security appears doomed to captivity by a single state—a state that ironically has often proved incapable of providing security to its own citizens.

The preservation of this condition—indeed, its very equation with the idea of order and progress—has been an article of faith in the discursive practice of regional security in southern Africa. As this is turned into policy, there was (and still is, it seems) no prospect for security except that

South Africa has to "lay down the law to others"—to borrow Emerich de Vattel's fatal phrase. Let me offer an example of this kind of thinking. In August 1998, in the face of the increasing instability in the Democratic Republic of Congo and the decision by Zimbabwean president Robert Mugabe to send troops to assist the DRC's embattled president, Laurent Kabila, the national director of the South African Institute of International Affairs, chastised South Africa's government for its "softly-softly" approach to the region and called for an initiative in the region to be backed up by South Africa's military and economic muscle.[9]

On reflection, we can readily appreciate the policy limitations afforded by this particular approach to the affairs of the region, but for now our interest lies with the world of ideas—especially ideas on security. The grim prognosis that set constructions of the region's security generate is the product of a particular literary device that insists that community can be achieved only by the timeless truth represented by sovereign states. To draw theorist Rob Walker closer to this tragedy-in-the-making is to recognize the light that his work continues to offer occasions like this and to highlight the frozen ontology within which debates on security in southern Africa continue to be represented. To repeat, as Walker might: conventional explanations of southern Africa and its future security remain anchored in "a celebration of a historically specific [accounting] of the nature, location and possibilities of political identity and community."[10]

Although prudence (not to mention the politeness associated with academic knowings over and in southern Africa) suggests that such pathways to knowledge are perhaps best left buried in anonymity, I must add a few critical observations. The damage done by equating southern African security with the maintenance of states runs far deeper than the limits of producing, and endlessly reproducing, a series of routinized speculations over the region's prospects for security. Unfortunately, the translation of this theory into practice suggests the complicity of scholarship in the perpetuation of state-sponsored violence. Any hope that the ending of apartheid might end the ritual of close (and, most often, closed) collaboration between scholarship and this violence was destroyed with the rise and flourishing of new sites of security knowledge in (and upon) southern Africa, especially in postapartheid South Africa. As we will see, such institutions (and the security professionals who serve them) have shown little inclination to offer fresh accounts of the passage to security in the region or even to engage in sustained critique of existing ones. Indeed, if anything, this new (but very old) work has shown an urgency to dismiss—even undermine—any alternative renderings of the region's security.[11]

Ironically, given the scope of South Africa's destruction of the region in the 1970s and 1980s, this reinvention of South Africa's past as the hope for the region's future has been done with the connivance of Northern Hemisphere states that have willingly provided funding for the development of policy positions for the postapartheid region. But—and again ironically—this same voice of foreign authority continues to believe that violence is integral to (and inevitable in) southern Africa, especially when it comes to matters of security. A collection edited by Bill Gutteridge and Jack Spence, two established (and establishment) figures on the affairs of region, especially its prospects for security, illustrates the far too many outside constructions of southern Africa's future as its past, as well as the far too few voices of intellectual contestation, either local or foreign.[12] Intentionally I have highlighted these continuities, these contradictions: my political purpose is to finger the complicity of both foreign funding and scholarship in the perpetuation of texts of violence over, and on, the region. My analytical purpose, however, helps to draw the message of the book closer to the work of Zygmunt Bauman—especially his assertion (adopted here to fit the immediate conditions) that the past, present, and future of violence in the region has more to say about the discourse over security in southern Africa than this particular discourse is able to add to our knowledge of the region.[13]

There is a little more here: although these constructions of security in the region have profound implications for theory, the power of the insight they promise over life-and-death policy matters is constantly at hand. As a result, their implications for this book, quite frankly, are overwhelming. Given all that has happened in southern Africa—especially the violence and deep shame over apartheid with its crude and cruel rationalized categories—the boundaries and borders that mark discourses on the region's security can never be the subject of sufficient problematization. This explains why this book (and this chapter) almost obsessively challenges the accepted canons in, and around, the idea of southern Africa, especially as they touch upon security.

Although the notion that southern Africa is naturally nested within sovereign states was formalized during the fading years of the nineteenth century, this drawing of interstate boundaries was preceded by a nearly unending creation of further divides within states still under construction. Small wonder, then, that the politics of internal boundaries and their maintenance—by violence, more often than not—was to infect many of the debates on regional security that were to follow. Even a rudimentary understanding of the region and its politics suggests that contestation over the domestic affairs of individual states—South Africa, Namibia, and Zimbabwe are sound examples—was the normal state of affairs, not the exception. In truth, Hobbesian fatalism would stalk each of the region's states because, quite plainly, the anarchy said to be represented by the international was present in the internal affairs that were lived in each.

In order to understand the ambiguities inherent in the practice of southern African affairs, I want to turn to the promised regimes of boundary-making in the region—knowledge production, sovereignty, and the politics of frontiers—and show how they operate as mechanisms of control to sustain particular perspectives on regional security. In presenting these as a reading of both the past and the present, my goal is to open the way to future understandings of regional security and to suggest possible ways in which communities yet to be built might be realized in southern Africa. My chief technique is genealogical and my chief focus is sovereignty, but initially I want to begin somewhere else and will use a comparative frame.

Knowledge and Its Production

It is clear that Western culture has entirely cast understandings and scholarly interpretations of southern Africa: indeed, these ways of knowing the world have established the region's political, economic, and sociological ways.[14] In security matters, a potent text has been written by Anglo-American epistemes, which is why it is difficult to think of any interpretation of regional security that has not set out to imitate this work. Even limited exceptions, like the efforts by Dutch, German, and Scandinavian scholarship, to throw a fresh light on the region's search for security have been entirely sidelined by the self-referential power of Anglo-American discourses.[15] This mode of inquiry has relied upon the Comtean-type rationality: drawing lines and creating categories as a way to understand, to explain, and, indeed, to organize the region. This way of knowing was routinized by the production of knowledge that was carried by institutions constructed by both the promise and the pomp of imperial progress.[16] In southern Africa, these set out to identify and map the importance of an increasingly well-described geographic space—South Africa's Cape of Good Hope—which, like other parts of the empire, was the target of the attention of many Victorian scientists, including the evolutionist Charles Darwin, who visited the Colony (as the Cape Colony was commonly called) in the *Beagle* in 1836. The superimposition of science upon the project of empire effectively privileged one particular group within this space, that is, South Africa's English-speakers, who had ready access, through language and other cultural accruements, to the unfolding knowledge regime that was empire.

The power of this gaze, as Robert Rotberg has confirmed, silences all other narratives and sets the promise that the disciplined routines of knowledge would, with time, bring the region's far-flung corners toward the rationality represented by modernity. Cast in this same mold, a full half-century later, the study of security, much like the study of international relations in (and on) southern Africa, was fostered by a series of closed classificatory routines and the promise of salvation. These silenced dissenting voices because, like all forms of Orientalism, they were "resistant to all forms of internal and external criticism."[17] The result of this is plain: construction of the idea of security in southern Africa has silenced any deviation from the view that the region's proto-Westphalian state, the Cape of Good Hope, was a natural impulse toward a community of sovereign nation-states.

But a closer, more critical inspection of southern Africa suggests that the Colony's commanding place in the region was not preordained, not natural, or even rational: it was the product of the complex processes of an imperial bargain.[18] Indeed, as the greatly mourned Susan Strange might have suggested, it was integral to "the social, political and economic arrangements affecting global systems of production, exchange and distribution, and the mix of values reflected therein."[19]

Because this idea is central to the discussion that follows, it requires immediate embellishment. As in most imperial bargains, each party anticipated a gain, and each had something to lose if the bargain were to crumble. At its core was the region's nascent wealth, which could be extracted only by deepening the process of imperial engagement. But here lies the nub of all subsequent debates on the region's security: this was a risky undertaking. Southern Africa was located far from Britain and needed to be protected; in addition, defense then, as now, was an expensive business. Readily at hand, however, were South Africa's English-speakers, a community that was willing to provide this service in exchange for the spoils of local commerce and access to capital and markets in the metropole. Thus to defend the region's founding bargain, South Africans (as they would soon come to be called) were provided the license to arm in the interests of protecting the spoils of empire. Not surprisingly, they used these same weapons to defend themselves against those located on the other side of multiple frontiers.

In offering this alternative interpretation of the region and the discourses that founded it, rather than the regular diet of Victorian guts-and-glory, we have opened the way to the genealogy that will soon follow. Before doing so, however, I want to isolate the discourses that created the idea of southern Africa. Rather than confront the far-reaching implications of a founding bargain that excluded the majority and privileged a minority, the institutional culture that sustained interpretations of security in the region was closed off from considerations of the social. As a result, the practice of security in southern Africa turned on simple binaries, which have routinely reinforced processes of inclusion and exclusion: settlers were the privileged insiders, and natives—the majority—were the deprived outsiders in the place of their birth (to deliberately draw on the natal metaphor that flowed through the discourses of liberation). Stated differently, the dominant mode of security in southern Africa was structured to protect the interests of migrants to the subcontinent, not the residents within it. This idea will return to haunt this analysis in Chapter 4, as we shall come to see.

Given the confidence of its making, as Robert Rotberg expansively attests, it is not surprising that the question that follows from this—security for whom?—has never been central to security studies in southern Africa. The answer was thought to be self-evident: security was always for the powerful, the rich, and the enfranchised settlers. Thus efforts to understand and explain security in the region did not question the near-commonsensical holding power of the idea that destiny had commanded states to lead the affairs of the region. This has had a profound effect on the practice of regional relations: all of these, in all their myriad forms, were constructed to stabilize and further deepen the position of states in the region. The Southern African Customs Union (SACU), for instance, the region's longest-surviving interstate institution, buttressed South African power (and its wealth) in the region for close to a century.[20] By providing states with a secure source of income, participation in SACU also opened the door to the statehood that would come to its three minor partners, Bechuanaland, Basutoland, and Swaziland. The theory and practice of regional security in southern Africa have been profoundly one-sided: they have sought to legitimize the access of privilege to power and sanctioned the power of the powerful to set the terms of interstate relations.

Looking backward, of course, it is easy to appreciate the irony at work in these efforts to map, to frame, and to organize the region's many unknowns: as the region's tragic history has so graphically shown, South Africa's search for security has often been the root of the region's instability. We have twice noted this, and its persistence opens a core issue in contemporary international relations: If states dominate both theory and practice, who speaks for people?

Sovereignty's Sins

To offer an answer, our attention turns to the second regime of social ordering: sovereignty. As both theory and practice, the shorthand represented by sovereignty seems to legitimize the link between a stable and established system of states and a regional community backward through time. This, of course, is what provides the fantasy—again so eloquently presented by Robert Rotberg—that states offer the only plausible means to stability, community, and prosperity. Look closer, however, and an exceptionally dense political practice (to use a phrase from Rob Walker) reveals itself around the issue of sovereignty in the region.

The construction of southern Africa around the abstract legal claim offered by sovereignty, like much of the knowledge around its security, has been incidental, invented, and entirely based on imported ideas. Tragically, there is more than a semantic and conceptual word game at play here—how we have come to know sovereignty in southern Africa has determined the quality of regional community, and this all too often has offered the region's people only the most deadly of outcomes. To understand the role of sovereignty in the unfolding practice of southern Africa, both the old and the new, I will set down some fragmentary ideas about the development of the region in the promised rough genealogy that will run to the chapter's closing. By historicizing the concept of sovereignty, my purpose is to highlight mutations in the region's compulsion to use sovereignty at key moments in order to show how it was that the region got from the there-and-then to the here-and-now.

The accreditation of power through sovereignty in southern Africa was first mediated by the imperial task of governing colonies: sovereignty, in the case of the Cape of Good Hope and other colonial entities, was executed by instruments of governance that were formally presided over by the highest decisionmaking authority: the British monarchy. In this guise, sovereignty was mainly symbolic: deriving from the authority of the distant Crown.

As with many other terms used in political discourse, however, the understandings and uses of sovereignty were seldom stable. When the notion was first used in the governance of the region, two hundred years after the Treaty of Westphalia, it revealed how far it had migrated from its earlier symbolic use. In 1848, the British governor and high commissioner of the Cape, the "egocentric and bombastic" Sir Harry Smith, proclaimed the turbulent area across the Cape Colony's northern border as the "Orange River Sovereignty."[21] The proclamation brought under "the rule and government of Her Majesty" the tract of land between the Orange

River and its major tributary, the Vaal—this is the current South African province called the Free State. The purportedly high-minded purpose of the governor's action—to encourage political stability on the Colony's northern border—was prompted by pressure from Cape settler society who feared for the security of their fledgling state. For settlers, the immediate beneficiaries of the colonial bargain, "expansion of territorial commitments in the interests of . . . accumulation and prosperity," was "self-evidently the business of empire," but what lay beyond the border was always suspect, always the other, always a threat, especially because the move toward some form of self-government of the Colony was under way.[22] The governor's action further reflected the role that was played in the link between the relatively new features of modernity and the impulse to sovereignty by, among other things, print-capitalism, to appropriate a less familiar phrase from the acclaimed work of Benedict Anderson. Tim Keegan points out that those most intensely interested in the Orange River Sovereignty were "their own mouthpiece, the newspaper *The Friend of the Sovereignty* [which] faithfully [pushed] for a more militant, aggressive, aggrandizing commitment of imperial power on the frontiers of settlement. To *The Friend*, land settlement and capital investment were the twin pillars of development and progress in the temperate colonies."[23]

Although the Orange River Sovereignty was to last only six years, it provided a powerful conceptual and political vehicle around which a comprehensive—and increasingly violent—reorganization of social relations in southern Africa would take place. By importing the rulemaking that was increasingly associated with the idea of sovereignty as a contract between parties into southern Africa, Governor Smith shifted the formal practice of regional relations from premodern to modern—from this point onward, sovereignty in southern Africa was to reveal three complementary faces.[24] We must appreciate these in order to understand the power sovereignty has exercised in determining the security debates in the region.

One face of this was, in the contemporary sense, domestic: concerned essentially with the Crown's and, on self-government in 1853, the colonists' exclusive right to exercise authority over their own affairs. The other was international (again in the contemporary sense). Here the Crown used sovereignty to demarcate itself from others, providing the territory that made for the Orange River Sovereignty with an international legal personality separated from the Cape Colony and separate from that of other political units (to borrow a phrase from the historian Christopher Saunders). This brought the new legal entity into association with neighbors in a relationship that approximated a form of regional community.

The bivalency represented by these two forms of sovereignty is, of course, very familiar: sovereignty secures the domestic and defines the international. Because the argument in this chapter frequently returns to this inside-outside issue, we will leave it here for the moment and turn to the third sense of sovereignty as it applied to the Orange River Sovereignty. This was the use of the term "sovereignty" itself to define the direction of security discourses. Thus the Cape Colony, in the name of the Crown, would defend the sovereignty of "the Sovereignty." In this understanding, the term approximated the contemporary notion of hegemony—in this case, hegemony of the most powerful political entity according to which it alone had the right to author the rules of security and its making. This perspective was lodged in the cultural practice involved in setting the region's security discourse and would have profound consequences for all discursive practices on the region that were to follow.

Prior to the Orange River Sovereignty, southern Africa revealed no interstate community outside of the confines set by the immediate sovereign mission. The British had occupied the Colony for the second time in 1806. By midcentury, it was the most powerful political entity on the subcontinent, with its northern border, as we have just noted, formally ending at the Orange River. But an imperial project could seldom be static, and it is no surprise to learn that the Cape doubled its sovereign size during the nineteenth century. Too easily, too readily, and far too quickly it is forgotten that one person's frontier is another's home, and the endless replication of the frontier experience, to the north and the east, dislodged and dislocated people as modernity demanded order by demarcating and expanding into the hinterland.

On many "frontiers," then, separate Crown colonies were established in the second half of the nineteenth century: British Kaffaria (now South Africa's Eastern Province) was incorporated in 1866, Griqualand West in 1880 (the present Northern Cape Province), and Bechualand in 1895 (it achieved sovereign independence in 1966, calling itself Botswana). The present Lesotho (then called Basutoland) was annexed in 1871 but changed its status in 1884, eventually achieving independence in 1965. The territory called the Transkei was incorporated into the Cape in stages between 1879 and 1894. But the emerging regional form of southern Africa was wider than these manifestations of sovereign expansion that were anchored in the Cape Colony. There was also a series of states manqué dotted across the face of southern Africa: these included Portuguese and German entrepôts on the eastern and western coasts, and a semblance of political expression—in family and clan republics, mainly—which had developed among emigrant Boers from the Cape Colony. Dislodged by their opposition to the British, these republican entities were the culmination of the regional emigration that has come to be known generically as the "Great Trek." As such, statelets began to take shape in the late 1830s; they faced out and (most often) upon migrating Africans that had become categorized into "tribes." Were these interfaces and the resulting communities of a sovereign kind? It is hard to tell. Clearly, they were political units and "different groups competed for power. . . . The result was that . . . white factions interacted with black factions in a variety of ways."[25] By 1900, however, two of these polities, the Orange Free State Republic and the Transvaal Republic, had declared themselves fully sovereign and operated within the region's embryonic state system. Other places were reflected in the London Stock Exchange: the British South Africa Company was able to obtain an interest and ultimately administrative control in a substantial tract of land in the territory that would come to bear the eponymous label Rhodesia.[26]

Despite the detail I have offered here, my goal is not to provide fresh interpretation of the complex social and political relations that unfolded in nineteenth-century southern Africa; neither do I intend to offer a critique of the shifts in historiographical accounts of these events. My goal in setting down this genealogy, rather, is to suggest that "sovereignty [in Southern Africa] emerged over a considerable period and obviously must be understood in the context of the complex developments usually subsumed into stories about the rise of the modern state and of capitalism."[27] One further artifact promises to complete the finding that I immediately seek. The Wars of Occupation and Dispossession in southern Africa during the 1880s and 1890s were fought over who had the right to enforce the contractual conditions of the sovereign condition that was emerging in the subcontinent. It is not surprising, therefore, that the outcome—the collapse of black as well as Boer power—profoundly changed the constitutional form of the subcontinent. With primary resistance to white rule and colonial occupation at an end, the ever-tightening control of the British was the harbinger of a regional system—an international system manqué—that deepened under the influence of empire and would run until South Africa's declaration of a republic in 1961. Like many other state systems, more than simple geographic proximity constituted this one: it was engendered by political practice and revealed quite distinct principles of behavior. In this regard, its formal procedure was sovereign consolidation into empire through treaty and law, but its informal reach—through the power of economic incorporation and the impact of culture—would be equated with both community and security in southern Africa. But it was certainly not a process that would—to use a metaphor appropriate to the capacity of the British to assert themselves in the farthest corners of the globe—be smooth sailing.

"The struggle [that would] constitute South Africa as a tangible nation-state"—the Anglo–South Africa War—was fought between 1899 and 1902 and ended with the Treaty of Vereeniging that was signed in Pretoria on May 31, 1902.[28] This was another significant moment in the mutation of sovereignty: the formal agreement opened a regional fault line that would run between South Africa and its neighbors, an important divide that still endures. The decade of reconstruction leading up to union in 1910 established the essential administrative, ideological, and economic framework in which South Africa's domestic and regional authority was both confirmed and elaborated through the license afforded by the idea of sovereignty. After Vereeniging, sovereignty as a means both to state-making and, not surprisingly, to domestic legitimacy was extended in the region by its widening use in both common law and regional practice.

In addition, South Africa's security map was taking shape; the impulse to seal sovereignty and defend it by arms because the most powerful state enjoyed monopoly over the legitimate use of regional force (to twist Max Weber's famous definition) was ever-present. However, the full process of regional community, through the processes offered by sovereignty, was not complete; its heyday was to follow half a century later with the great independence movement of the 1960s. But the larger architecture was set; the Peace of Vereeniging followed by the Act of Union left South Africa as the first state among sovereign unequals.

Political theory has rightly problematized the idea of sovereignty as a mark and marker of international certainty: my current purpose is not, however, to offer fresh conceptual paths in this critique. What I mean to do is draw some of these ideas closer to what we have already noted about sovereignty in southern Africa. As we do so, it seems best to remember a lesson from the distinguished international lawyer Richard Falk: "there is no neutral ground when it comes to sovereignty."[29] We have already encountered sovereignty in its bland form: the right to exert authority within a specific geographical space by polities that have been called "states." Or to put it as a lawyer might: within determined geographical spaces, constructed authority exercises a legitimate right (backed by Max Weber's violence) in the cause of its national order and (in what has become an entirely different, but consequential, idea) to pursue its national interests. States exercise this *state sovereignty* up against the Hobbesian anarchy that purportedly operates at the regional or international levels where, realism suggests, justice and progress are not possible. Readers familiar with poststructural international relations theory will recognize that this is both the point and the power of Rob Walker's Inside/Outside metaphor that problematizes the quite arbitrary distinction that is drawn between order within states and the unruly, ungovernable realm said to exist in the world beyond them.[30] We have already alluded to the boundaries of race constructed within the states of the region, and they give the lie to the derived idea that southern African states were (and are) tranquil pools of political harmony. We must turn now to the other tier, that is, the relationship between sovereignty in the region and the development of capitalism.

As revisionist historians have shown, in southern Africa capitalism developed from a three-way relationship between the Crown, the Colony, and the muscle of coolie labor. This triad helped to consolidate South Africa's dominant position in southern Africa. In this reading, the fusion of British mining capital, U.S. technology, and African muscle drew a sleepy African backwater into the deepening complexity of late-nine-teenth-century modernity. Although both interpretations suggest something about capitalism, they say nothing about sovereignty. In an illuminating insight on the social construction of sovereignty in the same century, Alexander Murphy persuasively demonstrates that the discourse surrounding sovereignty showed a movement away from its being vested within the ruler toward the idea that it rested within the nation.[31] The chief beneficiaries of this particular mutation were, of course, the Latin American states, but the shift was to have a profound effect both on empire and imperial practice in southern Africa, especially as the idea transformed toward the Wilsonian principle of self-determination. To understand the effects of this, we turn to the neglected art of economic history.

Although the immediate prize in southern Africa was South Africa, the discovery of mineral wealth elsewhere in the region—the discovery of copper in what is now Zambia in the 1890s offers an instructive example—concentrated imperial ambition. Although the development of these economic interests increasingly drew upon this ambition, understandings of what kind of sovereign personality they might approximate constantly migrated between empire, capital, and what we might term "states-in-waiting." Modern Zimbabwe, as we have just noted, took initial shape as the British South Africa Company, which was floated by Cecil John Rhodes on the London Stock Exchange. The point here is that a succession of new states in the region were not born of natural ordering but were the products of constantly changing political, economic, and strategic considerations. This construction of similitudes to represent the essence of separate states each with a distinctive legal presence and international personality represents the cultural certainty of Westphalia in southern Africa and accounts for South Africa's long history of identification with minority-ruled European Westphalian manqué states in the region. Each of these, of course, to a greater or lesser degree established its own self-referential mystery and raison d'être, but each was authored by the heroic ideas of empire.[32] This fragmentary evidence suggests how the region's march toward modernity, although often marked by moments of uncertainty and divided loyalty, resolutely pursued the making of money. Stripped of the intrigues that seem to have engaged successive generations of imperial historians, a successful partnership between capital and the discursive techniques around sovereignty, and its application as a project of empire, reinforced a nascent sense that a state system could develop in the region.[33]

The beneficiaries of this immediate search for a community through the idea offered by empire, of course, were South Africa's English-speaking settlers. The region's indigenous people (for whom the modernization offered by colonialism, and the community it promised, were more curse than convenience) were almost entirely excluded.[34] Only for those who were co-opted and made partners was the English language a partial passport to the community of Europeans in Africa. It was not, however, the mirror of deep cultural kinship yet offered the only pathway to survival in a place that increasingly turned on the power of a cash economy that— happily for the wealthy and the culturally assimilated and the investors in London Stock Exchange—was organized around a single currency: the pound sterling.

Though they were excluded from this community "from above," they were drawn into another form of community. In order to understand this, we must highlight a social phenomenon that will appear many times in Chapter 5: migration as a feature of southern African life. To sustain their profitably, the region's mines—especially those located in South Africa increasingly drew upon cheap labor that was to be sourced throughout the region's many hinterlands. Again, of course, one person's hinterland was another's center of the universe.

Because of this, and the seemingly commonsensical way that it suggests the progressive modernization of the region, we should pause here to reflect on an issue close to the heart of this book. The critical historian and social theorist Ruth First—who was brutally slain by an apartheid bomb in 1982—suggested that this search for labor had visited great destruction on African family life and indigenous communities throughout the region. This disruption of the cognitive cosmos, as we will see below, is not unique. But no small part of the region's search for future security will be in finding ways to repair this damage.

Ironically, however, this migration of African people to Johannesburg's mines resuscitated a feature of premodern southern African life. During (and after) the Mfecane (the Zulu term for "crushing") that took place during the second and third decades of the nineteenth century, the region was patterned by the movement of its people in search of forms of association that were independent of the construction of the region by Western knowledge systems.[35] Although parceled into political units (Christopher Saunders again), in the minds of its indigenous peoples the region was free of borders in the sovereign sense. The deepening migrant labor system, therefore, strengthened, rather than weakened, a premodern understanding—based on memory, patterns of life, and cultural networks—that the place that was increasingly called southern Africa belonged to all its people irrespective of the disciplining routine of sovereignty, upon which settlers (and the empire, which protected them) continuously drew in order to provide an alibi for their deepening hold on the region's wealth. We are dangerously close here to one of the great unexplored myths of contemporary southern Africa: that indigenous people lived happily in an unexplored land of milk and honey, to use the famous biblical idiom. As the book closes, I briefly turn to the epistemological challenge this idea presents to a new generation of scholars.

The Closing of Frontiers

But what finally came to seal off southern Africa's first state from its unequals was not sovereignty with its constant mutations and many meanings; it was the closing of frontiers, the third of our regimes of boundary creation. And by way of completing the genealogy of sovereignty, we will address this issue. To do so, we must return to the region's earliest European settlers.

The philosopher Anthony Holiday records that "the first Dutch settlement at the Cape of Good Hope in 1652 took place one year after Hobbes had published The Leviathan."[36] Holiday's purpose is to suggest that settlers brought to the Cape distinctive understandings of their own superiority and a particular hostility to any world other than their own. As they situated themselves, their own cultural and knowledge practices—including the capacity for violence—were privileged over those of the brute other. This was not an experience exceptional to southern Africa of course, as

Tzvetan Torodov has argued; the same happened in North America.[37] What form this privilege was to take was based essentially on the social practices of distant Europe. There is a little more here, too. It is not simply that conquests, like this, disempower natives but, as Mohammed Bamyeh, notes, "the psychology of imperialism . . . reshuffles the cognitive cosmos of the adversary without offering a *stable* alternative in its place."[38]

Although the settlement of the Cape of Good Hope took place four years after the Treaty of Westphalia, state-making was not seemingly its original intent. Jan van Riebeeck, the servant of the Dutch East India Company (DEIC) who established the first settler mission on South African soil, proclaimed his goal to be one "in which the name of Christ may be extended [and] the interests of the Company promoted."[39] As was so often the case, the language represented by distance helped to locate this corner of Africa in the Dutch mind. This suggests that multiple objectives were woven around the single project of settlement, but it is not clear that the words "nation," "state," and even "sovereignty" were hidden behind van Riebeeck's pious intentions.[40] However, the techniques of administrative control that were first brought to bear on this distant Cape peninsula—"Africa's appendix" as the poet-journalist Anthony Delius was much later to call it—did offer an indication of the politics of control and state-making that would follow.

The Dutch preoccupation with frontiers was born of a logic that was both to structure the shape of the region as well as to set European understandings above the local. This serves to explain why the inclusion of the bearers of supposedly superior culture and ways, and the concomitant exclusion of the indigenous and peripheral, have been a constant theme in the politics—even in the politics of sovereignty as it took on a constitutional form—of first South Africa and then of southern Africa.

Unlike European frontiers, the creation of boundaries in South and southern Africa was not contingent on the notion of reciprocity. The indigenous people of South Africa (and later of the region) were, as innumerable accounts suggest, regarded by Europeans, at best, as children and, at worst, as savages. They could enjoy none of the privileges of insiders because they lay outside of the community experience of those who carry the mandate of sequentially the DEIC, the Dutch government, and the British Crown. Cast beyond this process of formal recognition, they could not enjoy any reciprocity, not even diffuse reciprocity. As David Chidester suggests, it was only their conversion to Christianity that provided them with a reciprocal community around which a form of sovereignty could be constructed.[41] Faced with the absence of reciprocity but firmly believing in the necessity of control, administrative systems developed a series of savage codes to deal with this unnaturally occurring situation. In South Africa, initially, and then throughout the region, Westphalian states perfected an array of brutal (and brutalizing) controls, each one associated with armed power—commando, magistrate, location, reserve, poll tax. These ritualized the power of settlers as insiders, even though they were outsiders, and denied the rights of natives, because they were not inside, but outside, community.

This absence of reciprocity raises a further artifact in our crude genealogy on sovereignty: this is drawn from the thesis of the U.S. historian Frederick Jackson Turner who first suggested that the closing of the American frontier in the 1890s would have violent effects on domestic politics. The essence of Turner's argument was portrayed in the 1990 movie *Dances with Wolves*, which graphically displayed the power, potency, and pathos involved in frontier relations. My immediate epistemological concerns are somewhat more focused than the comparative academic literature on this issue and lie beyond Kevin Costner's romantic portrayal of the American frontier.[42] It is best served by a discussion of the transmogrification of the idea of sovereignty by the control (and eventual closure) of frontiers in southern Africa. To appreciate the power of this for security discourses, we must draw closer to the work—entirely neglected by scholars of international relations and orthodox security studies—of the revisionist historian Martin Legassick, who following Turner advanced the idea that frontiers in southern Africa were neither entirely open nor completely closed: they did, however, come to experience an "open" phase and a "closing" one.[43] The latter was the moment of Westphalian closure—it confirmed lines of demarcation by establishing boundaries that in succession marked sovereignty and marked out the state.

But contingency was the rule, not the exception, so the frontier's open moment provided a glimpse of a community that might well have been. As David Chidester again notes, a "frontier zone [opened] with contact between two or more previously distinct societies and remains open as long as power relations are unstable and contested, with no group or coalition able to establish dominance."[44] These open moments were characterized by the absence of a single source of coercive authority, by relatively low population densities, by a fluidity in race relations, by pragmatic resort to policies of cooperation and mutual accommodation, and by clientage, rather than bondage, as the basis of labor relations.[45] In the unbounded environment, there was very little to enforce identity and, as if to intensify the violence of its closing, Legassick suggests that Trekboers were assisted in their adaptation to the local environment by the knowledge, skills, and labor of natives. This moment was well illustrated in *Dances with Wolves*, but that rendition also graphically displayed the violence of frontier closure when "a single political authority succeeds in establishing hegemony over the area."[46] This was when colonists,

> with the government [and Empire] at their backs, imposed hegemony over indigenous peoples and exerted a growing monopoly on productive resources, and as coercion increasingly became the basis of group relations and the organisation of labour. On the closing frontier, too, stratification within the ranks of the colonialists sharpened, with decreasing proportion being landowners, and growing numbers becoming property-less and dependent.[47]

The open frontier was a melting pot (to intentionally select a powerful social metaphor from the 1960s) across which trade, ideas, and marriage continued. Open frontiers were the continuation of premodern southern Africa, but modernization, by invoking sovereignty and the use of violence as a means to control, ensured its demise. Using Foucault's lights, we can be sure of one thing: the closing of frontiers terminated options that would certainly have yielded a different southern Africa than what we now know. What shape security and community would have taken in this *other* region we cannot be certain. What we do know is that the impulse toward the closing of frontiers was rooted in a range of pressures: the personal ambition of administrators like Sir Harry Smith, the interests of capital, and, of course, fears of further violence across borders-in-waiting.

It was also influenced by the calculations of European politics: a fear of competition from other states with imperial ambitions—the Dutch, the French, the Germans, and even the Portuguese. Subsequent accounts have made, in my view, far too much of this fear of the interests of other Europeans. From the second British occupation of the Cape, southern Africa was (to use a term that Sir Halford Mackinder might well have approved) a British sphere of influence. But inter-European conflict remained, nonetheless, a persuasive and influential factor that was to cast a long shadow over debates on security in the region well into the 1970s. It lay, for instance, behind the entirely overblown debate on the purported threat to British "vital interests" over their access to the naval facilities at Simonstown.[48] Infinitely more important than security at sea was the process of security-making within which insiders *and* outsiders were created at two different levels throughout the region: across new regional frontiers, and in the consolidation and incorporation of power and wealth within the confines of the newly minted states (each claiming sovereignty, each with its own currency, each with an understanding of security).

Few moments in political life, however, are as neatly fixed as this analysis suggests, and, to recall Richard Falk, we can always expect the unexpected from sovereignty. A separate interpretation (some have erroneously called it Calvinist) of the link between sovereignty and territory was not bound to spatial conventions.[49] The historian Rodney Davenport, in an essay on the life of Paul Kruger, the Boer leader and statesman, recalls how the

> Calvinism believed and practiced by the Trekboers, along the southern watershed on the Orange River, was valued as a shield against the threat of "re-barbarization," latent in frontier life. In its uncompromising adherence to biblical precepts, it provided a moral stiffening against danger and temptation. The sovereignty of the divine will, and its identification in the combined will of the faithful community, excluded the need for sentimentality in religion and gave a sobering legitimacy to whatever needed to be done for the nation of believers to survive as migrants in rough neighborhoods.[50]

I use this passage to build toward locating the very separateness (in their understandings of sovereignty, certainly, but also in the way they would initially conduct the politics of their community) of the region's Afrikaner people. Given their forty-odd-year hold on the politics of southern Africa, the case for this privileged attention is obvious. Afrikaners' search for community was based on an understanding of "*volks-eie*" sovereignty (belonging to themselves as a separate people) that drew all Afrikaners—irrespective of their spatial location—together and reached upward to God. The work of the historian Leonard Thompson suggests that the late 1870s, however, represented a pivotal moment in encouraging Afrikaners, scattered as they were by then throughout southern Africa, to think of themselves as distinct people with a common, but not necessarily territorially bound, destiny.[51] He notes that by the 1890s "Afrikaner clergy and intellectuals in various parts of Southern Africa were responding to the pressures of British Imperialism and mining capitalism by propagating knowledge of the historical achievements of their people and the virtues of their culture."[52] This moment in the forging of this particular understanding of sovereignty is linked to the influential work of the neo-Calvinist Abraham Kuyper—founder of the Free University of Amsterdam and later prime minister of the Netherlands—who substituted Congregationalist patterns of church and government for an all-powerful church, within which each community and each corporate body was to be "*soewerein in eie kring*" (sovereign in its own sphere).[53] The idea of this community was, certainly initially, not bound to the notion of a specific territory: "the socio-political effect of this idea was that each of these 'circles' or 'spheres of life' functioned on the basis of their own rights and laws, that they were largely self-sufficient, and therefore in many ways independent from the state."[54] Embedded in the idea that "isolation is our strength," these conceptualizations of the identity-forming purpose of boundaries were certainly more fluid even than those offered by the controlling dimension of sovereignty provided by empire.

In her persuasive deconstruction of apartheid discourse, Aletta Norval locates the moment when Afrikaner understandings of sovereignty shifted in toward the idea of a territorial unit as the source of identity. By casting the net of the development of Afrikaner sovereignty wider and more ambiguously than that previously on offer, she fingers the influence of romantic nationalism and national socialism in the 1930s as the moment when Afrikaner understandings of sovereignty migrated.[55] This, she suggests, closed Afrikaner power around the idea of the South African state. This interpretation casts a particularly critical light on the work of successive generations of Afrikaner historians who resolutely held the view that, from the moment van Riebeeck's settlers set foot on land, a closed and settled category of South Africans—Afrikaners—longed for a sovereign nation-state. Essentially my purpose here is illustrative: I want to suggest that the coincidence between sovereignty and community confirming its incorporation into the modern world, even in the powerful and influential discourses of Afrikaner nationalism, is not absolute. Two points follow from this: the idea of an Afrikaner nation, like other pre-Westphalian forms of social organization, was based partially in the power of the church and allegiance that Westphalian sovereignty sought to destroy in Europe; and consequently, nation-building in Africa has not always been the simple product of colonialism and imperialism—it has also grown out of theology.

First Among Unequals

The creation of the region's first Westphalian state—the Union of South Africa in 1910—proved a turning point for the region's history by offering it a distinct and secure constitutional form as well as the promise of progress. But rather than neatly settling the issues of southern Africa, the Act of Union deepened the ambiguities associated with sovereignty:

instead of completely closing the frontier, the act attached conditionalities that might apply on the possible incorporation of the three territories— then known as the High Commission Territories (Basutoland, Bechuana- land, and Swaziland; now Lesotho, Botswana, and Swaziland)—and also left open the possibility for South Africa's unstated ambitions to incorpo- rate what was then called the Rhodesias, both South and North (now, respectively, Zimbabwe and Zambia).[56] The very fact of union, therefore, laid out ambitions for a Greater South Africa—a southern African state that might well lie beyond the borders of the new union.[57] So, although the issue of South Africa as a state and, indeed, as nation appeared to be set- tled by law, the question of its sovereignty and its further expansion remained, for all intents and purposes, open. The frontier, in other words, was not closed; it remained open until the 1960s with the consolidation of apartheid and South Africa's withdrawal from the British commonwealth in 1961. The understanding of its openness was reflected in the political rhetoric throughout the 1940 and 1950s. Jan Smuts, twice South African prime minister and, until Nelson Mandela, regarded as the country's great- est statesman, frequently transposed the idea of "South" and "southern" Africa in his speeches right up until his death in September 1950.[58] In his earlier life he had been far more ambitious for the expansion of South Africa: in 1915, for example, he suggested that there was "now the prospect of the Union becoming almost double its present area."[59] Popu- lar writing in South Africa was replete with the celebration of these open frontiers well into the 1950s.[60] A long lineage of literature from Percy Fitzpatrick's celebrated book *Jock of the Bushveld* seemed to rejoice in this

> world not closed by bureaucracy, but still on the edge of lawlessness, with free characters moving through it impelled by their own strengths or weaknesses of their own personalities, larger than life characters . . . like Rocky Mountain Jack with his plain philosophy that "you kin reckon it dead sure thar's something wrong about a thing that don't explain itself."[61]

As we draw close to the end of a long and exploratory chapter, it seems necessary to explain how this frontier closed and point to a range of ambiguities that continued up to South Africa's participation in World War I—an event that was about the durability of the Westphalian system.[62] This formally placed the weapons of state in the form of an army—"the expression of the nation" to use (in what remains of this chapter) one of two phrases from John Ruggie.[63] From 1929, this minority, in the name of

South Africa's people, began to conduct its own foreign policy; they exercised international sovereignty for the first time. By this time, however, German South West Africa (now called Namibia) had, through the spoils of a war fought by South Africa on behalf of the British Crown, all but been formally included in the union. And Southern Rhodesia (now Zimbabwe) had, by dint of a 1926 referendum exercised by the Colony's tiny white minority, decided to strengthen the boundary between itself and South Africa. It took more than thirty years (1962) for the next Westphalian-type state in the region, Tanganyika (with the addition of Zanzibar, it is now called Tanzania), to emerge. By this time, however, the patrolling of South African borders—in all its meanings and with the manifold implications that would build toward violence—had already commenced.[64] The question of the assignment of South African soldiers elsewhere on the continent was to remain a cardinal issue until the 1980s. Through this, South Africa's own determination to play the role of an imperial state on the continent remained a temptation, but it was also, as Ken Grundy perceptively notes, a means of constructing nationhood.[65] To put the point differently, it was part of the Darwinian unfolding that dominions and other lesser forms of statehood would grow up—or, more properly—would be blooded by the experience of war.

In a fragmented piece written, probably, in the 1970s, Deon Fourie, who would be appointed the country's second professor of strategic studies, ominously points to the violent path that this search for order, for foreign and security policy, would take:

> There is really no great tradition of crisis management nor of using military force as an instrument of South Africa's own foreign policy. [The Republic] lacks a body of experience even precedent for decision taking in times of emergency or crisis as a consequence of [its] former complete dependency on the British government. The South African Defence Force has the capability but it is still not clear that it regards its capabilities as the primary means of responding to the country's problems.[66]

The promise of delivery by the ordering of policy has been a powerful means to regulate sovereignty and borders in the region. Mainstream security discourse within South Africa has used these to finally close the frontier. By this time, however, the gap between the region's first state, South Africa, and its unequals was central to all recognized debates on southern African security. But it was also reflected in another mirror: the sense of racial and cultural superiority that was constructed within the country came to be reflected in the relations between South Africa and its neighbors. This excerpt from a picture caption in a propaganda journal suggests the veracity of the idea of difference (and Other) that persisted and that feeds the idea that South Africa should command the region:[67] "The phenomenal expansion of economic activity since [World War II] has made South Africa the most advanced state in Africa. The vast wealth of her natural resources, developed with enterprise and initiative, has raised her living standards above those of any other African country and paced her among the industrialized nations of the world."[68] And so, as often happens in social theory, gendered cliché reinforces the point: all the region's maps were charted upon and, indeed, around South Africa, the wealth of its interests and the interests of its wealthy.

Drawing on David Campbell's work on the mutually constitutive character of foreign policy in both state-formation and the creation of national identity, the impulse to sovereignty and the violent politics of frontiers and their closings set the conditions for the region's states and a system we now know as southern Africa.[69] Put differently, and drawing from another theoretical thread, historical sociology, the other states in the region were defined not so much by an interaction of internal forces as by their external setting toward the state called South Africa.[70] As its self-image mutated, particularly during the apartheid years, primordial feelings of superiority and insecurity crossed both frontier and border. It is easy to provide examples; for now, however, the following two must do. The independence movement in southern Africa—which was seen as a moment of hope for southern Africans as well as the idea of regional community—was viewed by South Africa as a threat to regional security. And the intrusion into the region of Marxism—upon the independence of Mozambique and Angola—was regarded as deeply threatening by the same state even though in the region's (and its own) streets, and in the remotest villages, it was said to be the dawn of a new political age.

The Comtean theorists that constructed mainstream understandings of southern Africa and its security have seldom paused to reflect on the contingency in the creation of the region's states. This absence has yielded profound effects on South Africa's behavior in the region—as the tragic lesson of destabilization demonstrated. But the same lack of reflection weighs heavily on the region's future—even in the postapartheid period—because every moment of policymaking seems often finely balanced between the hope of control and an unknown future that is free of the only feature in the region's lifeworld that promised permanence: violence.

It may seem inappropriate, given South Africa's obsession with reconciling, to name names. But for these purposes—and because probably truth will elude us even as history is remade—we need to note that the main carriers of the idea that state and sovereignty were settled were the closed epistemic communities that will be introduced in Chapter 3. For now, we need to note that these communities strongly asserted apartheid South Africa's right to exercise its sovereignty within the international community when the idea of sovereignty turned, as it did after World War II, from state sovereignty to popular sovereignty.

These same groups were all too willing to play loose and fast with sovereignty when political expedience became an issue. This suggests that the notion of sovereignty in southern Africa, notwithstanding the permanence (not to mention the omnipotence) of South Africa's power in the region, is not stable. Grand apartheid's disassembly of South Africa, in the cause of creating the four separate "independent states" of Transkei, Venda, Bophuthatswana, and Ciskei, was a case of its instability in domestic security practice.[71] But it must also be recalled that South Africa proposed the secession of part of its territory, an area called Ingwavuma, to Swaziland in return for a concession over security.[72] Elsewhere in the region, this tendency to secession beyond established sovereignty (to coin a phrase) has been a constant theme. In his masterful book on the Angolan civil war, Ryszard Kapuściński reports on a prescient—given the country's subsequent history, I have chosen this adjective very carefully—dispatch he sent to Warsaw on November 11, 1975:

> Angola has been divided for the moment into two states with incredibly complicated borders that change almost every day according to which side launches an offensive today or tomorrow and what part of the territory is taken from the enemy. Now much will depend on which countries recognize the MPLA [Popular Movement for the Liberation of Angola] government or the FNLA-Unita [National Front for the Liberation of Angola] government, and at what tempo. So a new, diplomatic war for Angola has begun.[73]

And in Zambia, the fear of the secession of Barotse Province has been a constant theme in the country's politics, as has the fear of a secession of Matabeleland from Zimbabwe. So, for all its memory of stability, sovereignty has been, and will remain, a form of political currency—mutating, migrating, and mixing with history to reinforce preselected choices. As a result, it is easy to make this prediction: states and their making in southern Africa have not run their historical course. In the chapters that follow, I frequently return to this idea. For now, however, the lesson lies elsewhere.

If the closing of frontiers that have established a place called South Africa teaches anything, it is that the theory and practice of international relations is vastly different. Three stories from the region's twentieth-century history suggest why this is so.[74] Analyzing the notorious practice of "black-birding" at "Crooks' Corner" in what is now South Africa's Limpopo Province, Martin Murray writes that by the 1910s "competition had forced freelance poachers to push their illicit recruiting activities hundreds of miles northward. . . . Gangs of labour thieves staked out territorial claims to recognized labour routes, took up arms to protect business operations, and assumed virtual carte blanche sovereignty over large tracts of land."[75] Then, writing about the 1960s, a politician from the country now called Botswana, Michael Dingake—who served a fifteen-year sentence on Robben Island for furthering the aims of South Africa's African National Congress (ANC)—drew attention to a kind of regional community that defended the sovereignty claims of either colonialism or constructed states:

> Before political independence we depended very much on our South African brothers when we earned a livelihood in their economy. We were never subjected to subtle discrimination . . . except by the common enemy—the colour bar/apartheid state . . . our black brothers taught us how to survive, how to cheat the pass laws . . . we were welcome . . . in the ghettos, in the factories, in the schools . . . (our success is the product) . . . of the hospitality and magnanimity of our black brothers across the border.[76]

Finally, Allister Sparks, the acclaimed South African journalist, in 1996 described a small corner of the region's biggest city, where a whole community of (then) Zairians live in Johannesburg where French (probably Lingala) is the only language you hear on the streets.[77] In all three cases, the fact of borders and understandings of sovereignty appear palpably different. This explains why the region's maps (to deliberately return to the cliché) seem unable to hold the organizational dimensions of time and space through which sovereignty once confidently promised to deliver to southern Africans.

This chapter has sought to demonstrate how the production of knowledge frames and situates knowing in the service of power. What first facilitated the understanding that brought social theory to this recognition, however, was the critical turn in philosophy. As the story of the construction of southern Africa, its sovereignty, and its security has unfolded in this chapter, critical ideas have crisscrossed the narrative. But it was the historian of southern Africa Patrick Harries who, drawing on Émile Durkheim, pointed out that "boundaries were erected in order to restructure the African world in a way that would make it more comprehensible to Europeans."[78] We have seen how their constructions and their modes of production serve the cause of inclusion and exclusion; by excavating discourses over empire and state sovereignty, we have traced the successive development of administrative control and surveillance and seen how frontiers come to close; and we have used this to suggest that knowledge and sovereignty themselves close around an instrument much loved by security studies: firepower. Drawn together, these analytical pointers provide in southern Africa the license for what John Ruggie calls the "modern system of territorial rule."[79]

In order to do this we have strayed, quite purposefully, some distance from the closed rituals associated with mainstream security studies and the self-referential Anglo-American modes of knowing that produce a closed kind of knowledge both on the region and on its security. Rather than the constant reprocessing of familiar routines, I have tried to use a more adventurous suite of scholarly techniques drawn from contemporary social theory: genealogy, in particular, but also deconstruction and, even on occasion, counterfactual history. My purpose has not simply been methodological exploration for its own sake; rather, I have wanted to reveal the rich texture of southern African issues—in security, certainly, but elsewhere, too—that remain still to be unlocked by different techniques and by other ways of knowing the region. As we will come to see in later chapters, this alternative text—rather than the rituals associated with the grand narrative and state sovereignty—is where security lies for southern Africans. First, however, we must fulfill a promise made early in this chapter and investigate the influence that the Victorian narrative, in the manner of Robert Rotberg, has had on generations of state-makers in South Africa. To do so, however, requires that we turn the page.

3

Making South Africa's Security

*The politics mongers are now
Attacking the realm of bicycles.
It's the question of balance they
Are corrupting. You may think it's
Easy to ride a bicycle, but nobody
(I repeat, nobody) has yet explained
exactly how you do it. And that is
something that takes away my confidence.
It makes me vulnerable.
So I Don't want any old politician
Telling me how to ride a bicycle
When the art itself cannot be
Remotely described by the most
Learned of research scientists.
—Oskar Wolberheim*

This chapter probes the conversational rituals that condition South Africa's security behavior and the institutional practice that informs (and has informed) the country's thinking on issues of regional war and peace. This points to our destination: for all the celebration that accompanied the ending of apartheid, little has changed in the field of security in southern Africa. To be sure, the region is nominally at peace, and certainly the end of the Cold War has likewise ended South Africa's proxy war in the region. But far too many continuities in the guise of security trap the region in codes of unnecessary violence.

Truth and Truisms

Before turning to consider these issues, however, some words on both the texture and form of this chapter: on one reading, like the previous one, it will be considered too historical for any practical use in a time in which

the immediate—the now, the can-do, the must-happen—is on every political agenda. As is plain, however, the narrative that runs throughout the
course of this book is preoccupied with history. To insist on this in busy
times is not simply to reintroduce the inevitable and tired cliché (after both
Confucius and Marx) that those who ignore history are destined to repeat
its mistakes. Rather, it is to recognize that in quite astonishing ways the
contemporary script on South Africa and southern Africa—in security as
well as every other sphere of public policy—is entirely emptied of historical content. This is a function of the collective amnesia that has swept
across South African politics, notwithstanding the ritualized homage to
memory in the country's reconciliation process, in which the latter was
traded for telling the truth. But we must recognize that this absence of history, if anything, validates the practice of the present in the name of
progress and modernity. In all possible ways, policymakers and state-makers have institutionalized technocratic rationality by simply suspending
the past. Thus only by awakening the history that stalks southern Africa
can we be alive to the horror of the synthetic present. So, yes, this chapter, like its predecessor, is rooted in the thicket of history, but there is a tex-
tual difference: whereas that account was Foucauldian in nature, this is
more critical, more concerned with bringing the dark forces that have
shaped understandings of security in southern Africa closer to the light
offered by emancipatory practice.

If recognition of the importance of history is one entrée into the discussion that follows, another is the intrigue offered by the techniques of
policy and policymaking. As they have made the state and its security and,
simultaneously, service the institutional and conversational rituals that
reinforce it, South Africa's politicians and speechwriters have turned to
the diet metaphor to explain the why and the how of public expenditure
cuts.[1] Thus "belt-tightening," "scaling-down," "down-sizing," and "trimming excess fat" have become commonplace figures of security- and pol-
icy-speak.[2] The use of this rhetorical device as a means to politics *and* policy signals the ascendancy of neoliberalism in a country that ironically is
governed by a coalition that includes the Communist Party and a powerful trade union. This much seems obvious; what is less obvious is the role
that speech plays in the politics of security and state-making.

So metaphor offers a point of entry into the conversations that have
made security, especially in the emancipatory practice that must follow.
By using the idea that we are what we eat in a derivative sense, I want to
underline the message of this chapter for the broader idea. Physiologists
argue that the modification of human behavior is the key to the reduction
of body mass. Without changes in the way people live the pattern of their

lives, particularly what is consumed—why, when, and how—it seems impossible to permanently change body mass. They further suggest that unless children are taught correct eating habits, the prospects of their living happy, healthy lives are dimmed. These may be near-homilies associated with the body cult of the 1990s, but they point the way to policy and its making, especially in the area of security. Unless governments—not only in southern Africa but also elsewhere—change the way in which they conceive of security, they will not change their behavior: until they do so, they have little prospect of reducing their expenditures on security and in improving the security of their citizens. Following this logic, the way for governments to reduce budgets is to discover new ways of knowing the region, particularly in knowing new constructions of the region that are offered by alternative ideas around security and different forms of community. This looks and sounds very simple, but achieving these as policy goals is very difficult, primarily because the instructional practices of orthodox security studies and the institutions to which they gave life, and which now nourish them, provide a formidable holding power. If this is practice, I return to poststructuralist theory to make the next point.

The rooting of the political in both linguistics and semiotics has been well explored in the writing of Jacques Lacan, Jacques Derrida, and Michel Foucault, but the power of literary devices in setting both course and discourse in security studies is less developed. However, the insights offered by text were carried to international relations by Michael Shapiro and James Der Derian, who focused on "privileged forms of representation whose dominance has led to the unproblematic acceptance of subjects, objects, acts and themes through which the political world is constructed."[3] Within this world, metaphor plays a substantial role. Using a search metaphor, I want to straddle the past and the present of security in southern Africa by pointing to the continuities in the midst of change.

The search metaphor (we have already seen) was much used in southern African security discourse in the late 1970s and the early 1980s; interestingly, it has returned two decades later. In its early manifestation, it was associated with the closed circumstances that were presented and represented by minority white power in both South and southern Africa in the wake of the ending of colonialism. The notion of change also plays a role in its more recent appearance—particularly, the idea of "global change," with its endless horizons and boundless opportunities. Both uses, however, deploy the same literary techniques, even the same nomenclatures to advance their respective arguments. In both, too, the ideas of national interest and sovereignty play a pivotal role, and both come to use the anchor of authoritarian control to suspend any discussion of politics that threatens the status quo. Put simply, the search metaphor seems to reveal an unending quest to locate and privilege particular understandings of security in a world represented as predictable but caught, invariably, by unending and highly contested politics.

In order to build a platform of the ways in which security determines and influences the continuing pattern of violence and its ways, I turn now to the conversations that have held constant—in effect, kept stable—ideas on security in southern Africa notwithstanding the profound changes associated both with the ending of apartheid and with ubiquitous global change. Since 1990, South Africa—idea, ideal, and institution—was on every political lip. Because so, it has been difficult to look beyond, or delve beneath, the euphoria associated with the "ending of apartheid," or with "bringing South Africa home to the community of nations," or with South Africa's move from "pariah to participant"—or with any one of a host of banalities that celebrate, rather than interrogate, the "new" South Africa's international relationships and its security discourses. If anything, this euphoria was heightened by empty political rhetoric and its modern twin, media hype; drawn together, they have manufactured words like "miracle" and "wonder" to describe South Africa's transitionary politics. This conjunction has deepened the appeal of empty phrases like "example to the world." Not surprisingly, this lauding of South Africa's achievements has made the ending of apartheid a contemporary cliché— a celebration of the reassertion of the presence and personality of the South African state. But moving beyond this has been rendered difficult by the power of the personal image and the near-personalization of South Africa, its political process, and the peaceful outcomes that its settlement has come to represent. In pursuit of this particular form of substitution, Nelson Mandela was described (on the day of his inauguration) by CNN's Peter Arnett as "the last twentieth-century hero" and, four years later, by a radio talk-show host, Sally Burdett, as the "world's most charismatic leader."[4] This praise-singing in place of pointed and sustained debate— or, for our purposes, bunting (to use an apposite word) in place of theoretically informed critique has silently confirmed South Africa as the "inevitable" leader of southern Africa—as master of its immediate dominion.

The tone here suggests why transition left unchallenged South Africa's place in the making of the region's security discourse. As a result, the frame that guides thinking on regional security retards, rather than encourages, the long-term search for community in southern Africa. Given this, it is no surprise that the sovereign barriers between South Africa and its neighbors have been fortified by the ideological purpose of three distinct moments in twentieth-century thought: racial discrimination, capitalism, and the Cold War. Although each of these can be said to be the product of ways of explaining the immediate and the urgent, each has aimed to protect particular interests while championing the constantly expanding horizon associated with modernity. For much of what remains of the chapter, we will consider these aspects.

Tales of Difference

It is no surprise that the discourse of racial difference should play a role in the determination of South Africa's strategic purpose. But to understand its impact, we must look backward to the invention of the racial discourse upon which the politics of separation was forged and upon which the state called South Africa flourished.

Before doing so, a word about the present: notwithstanding the emotion attached to the idea of the "rainbow nation" (a trope to which we will often return), South Africa remains caught within the memory trap of race—and thus the social practices that this issue has nurtured. As a result, much of the political space within contemporary South African politics is still occupied by race; although the twentieth century has run its course, the color line, as W.E.B. Du Bois predicted in 1903, remains a core problem for the country and the region (as it does, incidentally, for the world).

In his remarkable book on the science of eugenics in South Africa, the historian Saul Dubow teases out the "eclectic" sources of South Africa's racial ideology: "Dutch neo-Calvinism, German Romanticism, Anglo-Saxon racial ideology [these] were all incorporated as [apartheid's] constituent elements."[5] As these threads ran through apartheid and its making, the power of security—discourse first, but inevitably practice—hovered over the discussions. The "othering" offered by racial discourse, as we have already seen, was present at the very creation of the South African state and has run throughout the country's history. This suggests that the link between race and security was more direct than derivative. The goal of nationhood—so central to the Afrikaners' discovery of themselves, their reworking of sovereignty, and their place in both Africa and the world—was a search for a community that could come to be accounted for in its racial purity and, eventually, in its cultural exclusivity. These were the headwaters of many theoretical and rhetorical tributaries, and they watered apartheid's thirst for a rational explanation of its wider role in the world. Was it, for example, simply a search for racial purity along the lines of ideology that had been practiced in Europe in the 1930s, or was it the

politics of white pragmatism in Africa, or was it integral to Western strategic interests in southern Africa?[6] In each of these settings, a security
argument was made and, indeed, sustained.

Whatever particular interpretation one prefers, an exacting thread is
central to this chapter: the politics of race in southern Africa and the practice of security were inexorably intertwined. In important ways, this was
encouraged by the feelings of embattlement that emerged from the hostile
international community that South African state-makers, security specialists, and diplomats faced during the country's slow (and sometimes
not-so-slow) slide into international pariahhood. And it was caught in the
title of a 1988 book on southern Africa issued by the International Institute for Strategic Studies, *The Defence of White Power*.[7] The near-univer-
sal hostility to South Africa's racial ideology and the prospects that
apartheid might be ended by force of arms became an overriding calculation of successive minority governments, as any reading of the archive
shows.

Not surprisingly, there was a violent twist to this: the politics of race
in South Africa was the politics of fear. As Debbie Posel, the social theorist, has put it, "in South Africa, associations of blackness with the 'primitive' and with violence, and the concomitant fear of the unruly mob,
[were] . . . deeply entrenched."[8] Although this fear factor was ever-present,
the fusion of race and security in South Africa was often expressed through
the vocabulary of cultural essentialism rather than the scientific racism that
might be tapped from, say, social Darwinism. Whatever the chosen origins,
the cumulative result was a drawing-together of the fear-driven racial politics of Afrikaner (and white) nationalism with the necessity of security—
personal, national, and international. The propaganda around South
Africa's defense policy, especially from the 1960s, was vitiated by exaggerated claims of the necessity—indeed, the imperative—of recognizing
that whites (especially Afrikaners) had a place, especially a secure place,
under the southern African sky. These invariably were linked to the romanticized fables embedded in dominant interpretations of Afrikaner history—
interpretations that were fed by the 1932 centenary celebrations of the
Great Trek and, particularly, by historical myths that were to be derived
from Afrikaner memories, especially through creations like the
Voortrekker Monument. There are many interpretations of the latter, but a
recent one juxtaposes two appropriate images. The "Voortrekkers [are pre-
sented] as pioneers of civilization; the Christian nation; imaging community; the unified nation; and the authentic nation. In contrast, the natives
are consistently presented as a warring barbarous rabble. While

Voortrekker soldiers stand in straight and ordered lines, natives are chaotic, undisciplined and unordered."[9]

Although these emotional appeals made political (and other) sense within the imaginings of the Afrikaner-centered state called South Africa, especially in its initial victory over English-speaking (read: British) hegemony in 1948, they were to be increasingly rendered obsolete as an unacceptable form of political discourse at home and abroad. But race as a means to security and security as a means to identity was an idea deeply ingrained in South Africa's very soul—more deeply, perhaps, than in any other place. This explains why, of course, legal and constitutional direction regulated race relations, place of birth, place in society, and even place of burial—indeed, the very essence of identity and security. Not surprisingly, therefore, as apartheid South Africa became increasingly militarized, security—particularly the security of the state—became an inevitable part of social practice. One powerful route to this was provided through white male conscription—a rite of masculine passage developed in metro-political security circles and very effective in outposts of Western power and thought.[10] Like everything else, impulses to security in apartheid invariably ran along the fault line of race, and responses to these upheavals were incessantly refashioned by security discourse.[11]

This confluence of race—the socialization represented by the idea of security and military security—was quick to create and cross international borders. As it did so, it mixed with realist understandings of security and the ever-ready license to kill in the name of a number of ideologies—nationalism and anticommunism were certainly the most important. Whites were defending the security of "their" homeland—a homeland that blacks had rendered insecure by their own determination to share its spoils. The central security divide within the country, therefore, even during the most "reformist" moments of National Party rule, remained Du Bois's color line. Even the incorporation of blacks in South Africa's military, a process that Ken Grundy, whose sensitive work on southern Africa sets him apart from all others who pursued the vocation of politics as science, presciently described as "soldiers without politics," was cast within a racial framing.[12]

It follows that race and security were invariably (to carefully choose a metaphor) two sides of the same political coin. Racial codes were transposed in the dehumanizing speech of war and othering perfected for both the purpose of killing and the routine gestures of national life. The practice of these politics in the heat of battle and in the mundane everyday affairs was socially debilitating.[13] As South Africa's Truth and Reconciliation Commission highlighted, pejorative and racially loaded epithets were invariably present at the very moment of social encounter and in every recollection of events.[14] In apartheid South Africa, security knowledge as racial knowing—irrespective of whether its goal was local, regional, and/or international—was created and invariably reinforced in what the writer Njabulo Ndebele has called the "psychology of maintenance":

> This was the . . . habit that made prejudice a standard mode of perception. . . . This . . . flourished in its crude aspects among members of the white, mainly Afrikaner, working class, for whom jobs were reserved in the police force, the army railways and harbours, the civil service, and small-scale farming. Ruling elites, in both the political and industrial sectors, satisfied that they had bought the compliance of the white electorate, gave a blank cheque to the military and law-enforcement establishments.[15]

This institutionalized process of maintaining domination (to use Ndebele again) came to be scattered across the face of southern Africa. The framing of security within the racial lenses in the country was referred throughout the region. The practice of discrimination and violence along racial divides was to be seen in many places, but if South Africa's was its perfection, the racial politics in the contest over places once called Rhodesia and South West Africa suggests how racial discrimination was regional and how slowly and how violent was its retreat as fears for security—personal, national, even international—deepened.

Tall and Epic Tales

What has gone before suggests, in the cause of race difference, that the mundane provided the license to construct further frontiers and further power and to perpetuate further violence at home and abroad. I want to use this idea of the everyday to introduce the narrative of Cold War in the making of South Africa's security discourse in southern Africa. It is abundantly clear that the Cold War was (and continues to be) an epic narrative—a tall tale. As such, it very easily played into the heroic accounts that South African settlers told and retold themselves in the securing of "their" country.

Before considering these tales, we must point out the disciplinary myths that helped to embellish security studies as a fixed point of knowledge. I am immediately interested in the idea that "security" is more properly "national security" and more accurately "state security"; my contention is that this is a construct of more recent vintage. By inserting this as both fact and opinion, I draw on the work presented by others in the emerging field of critical security studies who locate the origins of national security in the U.S. National Security Act of 1947—legislation that aimed to provide integrated policies and procedures for departments, agencies, and functions of the U.S. government relating to national security.[16] This interpretation is supported in a collection edited by Norman Graebner that aimed to broadcast the proceedings of a conference organized at West Point in April 1982 that focused on the "efforts of the Truman and Eisenhower administrations to come to terms with the consequences of the Allied defeat of the Axis powers and the ensuing failure of the victors to disentangle their interests in a militarily and politically divided world."[17]

The celebration of U.S. hegemony as exceptionalism at that time is well established in the lore of international relations: the discipline's regeneration sought to legitimize the importance of U.S. military and economic power throughout the world. This was, of course, the subject of Stanley Hoffman's important 1977 article on international relations as American social science.[18] He argued that the invention of the discipline helped the United States meet the demands of its foreign policy after World War II. The impact of these renditions of security, especially in its positivist form, systematically inculcated first and eventually emphasized the modernist longing for order upon which mainstream international relations scholarship, including security studies, has fed. My immediate concern is not, however, with following further this thread; rather, in pursuance of the objectives of this chapter, I want to critically locate "national security" as a tall tale in South Africa and trace the resulting impact on the discourse of regional security. In order to do this, we turn to the powerful insights that are to be delivered by deconstruction.

In 1965, the South African government–supporting publishing house, Nasionale Boekhandel, published a book by the U.S. strategist Anthony Harrigan.[19] Ordinarily his book, like many on the country's security and politics that were published at that time, should have stayed in well-deserved obscurity, but in excavating it for this specific purpose I want to show how its message offered apartheid South Africa a peculiar and attractive interpretation of thinking around the idea of national security. There are four further reasons for reappraising the book so many decades later. First, it was issued the same year that Rhodesia's white minority made their Unilateral Declaration of Independence—a moment of some anxiety for the white community throughout southern

Africa. Second, it was issued in the English language by a publisher whose list was mainly aimed at promoting Afrikaans, South Africa's other official language at that time; this suggests that its message was intended for wider international dissemination, which undoubtedly would have included free distribution abroad to make a propaganda case for minority rule in South Africa, a common practice during the Cold War.[20] Third, the book suggests how deeply the Cold War and its cultural representations spread from the United States and how effectively these had been taken up in minority-ruled South Africa.[21] Finally, the book's title (*Defence Against Total Attack*) captured an idea that with the passing of the years—but especially in the late 1970s and the 1980s—strongly resonated within South Africa's security circles. This was especially so with the proclamation of the Total Strategy—the political doctrine that guided official South Africa's security thinking during the presidency of P. W. Botha and that shaped South Africa's policy of destabilization in southern Africa.

The spirit of the Harrigan book, as well as the messianic response of South Africa's growing security establishment to its message (and others of the same ilk), is caught in a single sentence: "There is a world-wide significance to the struggle of the South African people to escape engulfment by barbarism, which has been the fate of most Europeans who have made their home in Africa."[22] To arrive at this conclusion, the author begins with the immediacy of the 1961 crisis in Congo and, thereafter, rehearses a set of routine and well-worn impressions on the nature of man, contemporary society, and plain pessimism. These are drawn closer to the holding idea of security in a line that reads: "A nation's security . . . is never permanently won because the world is permanently in convulsion."[23] The narrative banalizes the work of the existential philosopher Karl Jaspers, but the political and propaganda point is carried forward by some familiar devices used in realism—the timelessness represented by the Melian dialogue from Thucydides, for instance, and credential support (mainly in the form of disjoined quotations) from international relations scholars like James D. Dougherty and Harvard's Thomas C. Schelling.

These genuflections to academe aside, the text is redolent with crude racism and boorish anticommunism, which at that particular time characterized contributions to a variety of establishment defense journals in which, as Harrigan notes, earlier versions of the book had appeared. These include the North Atlantic Treaty Organization's *Fifteen Nations*, the *Australian Army Journal*, *Proceedings of the U.S. Naval Institute*, *Quarterly Review* (London), *Europa-Archiv*, and the *Royal United Service Institution Journal*. Looking back across the roughly four decades that separate that writing from this, it is still quite easy to judge Harrigan's work: although drawing upon the academy, it is patently not an academic text; its pseudoscientific setting has offered the patina of intellectual respectability to an immediate political text and a wider project that aimed to shore up the case for minority rule in South Africa by employing the legitimacy offered by the engineered body of knowledge that (all too recently) was called "strategic studies" and that in time would shade into security studies.

The license afforded by the emergence of the latter and its role as a means to the politics of state security for the white minority in South Africa becomes plain in his final chapter, which draws together the issue areas represented by eugenics, the idea of state, and the narrative of Cold War struggle in advancing the cause of modernity. Particular significance is registered in the country's "skyscrapers and modern highways," and these are drawn backward toward the foundational myths of Afrikaner ideology and identity—in particular the "[Great] Trek that was a march toward the fulfilment of South Africa's destiny for greatness."[24] In his effort to provide political opportunities for Afrikaner ideology at an increasingly embattled time, Anthony Harrigan contrasts the momentum offered by South Africa's quest for modernity against the "lesser breeds" represented in Africa and in southern Africa.[25] Harrigan's work, like most of the writing on security at the time, establishes three things: a bridge to history, a sense of place, and the permanence of threat.

It may seem unfair to single out this work by an American publicist instead of focusing on the work of South African writers who may, at the same time, have produced interpretations that were perhaps less ideologically directed.[26] Nevertheless, Harrigan's book is emblematic of the knowledge represented by embryonic security studies as well as international relations within apartheid South Africa. Not surprisingly, then, the book was glowingly received in South Africa. The daily propaganda broadcast *Current Affairs* described the book as a "timely reminder that we live on a world of hard realities."[27]

Once again it seems invidious to name names, especially because the finality of the grave has closed off opportunities for further exchange of views. To overcome this difficulty, I will refer to my own earlier judgment of the work that Harrigan inspired in South Africa, which I described as "boldly sectarian and crudely simplistic" where the cumulative impression is one of "archaic reasoning, unsubstantiated impressions and arcane deductions," where scholarship was characterized by its "vulgar anti-Communist message"—all of which demonstrates the missionary nature of international relations in South Africa.[28]

My purpose in reporting, lightly deconstructing, and then classifying this intellectually inauspicious body of knowledge has already been stated: it was crucial in transporting the post–World War II discovery and production of security knowledge from the United States to South Africa, where it was increasingly used to assuage the fears of the country's ruling white minority. Its impact on regional politics in southern Africa was devastating. For South Africa's minority, the idea of security came to be the one—perhaps the only—acceptable form of organization in regional affairs. By locating realism at the center of regional discourse, all alternative efforts to explain and expand understandings of social relations, especially of the cross-border variety, were silenced by the power of these Cold War interpretations. The result was the muting of competing narratives around regional security or, indeed, the region by the institutionalized practice of knowing. Within the authorization that this offered, the country's policy agenda was set; and within the same coda, "research and knowledge falling outside the Realist agenda was dismissed as 'unscientific' and not really as security knowing."[29]

We could safely end this discussion here, but I want to draw the immediate circle tighter around southern Africa. The construction of a total onslaught against the republic of South Africa as a discourse of regional security, as well as its role in setting the agendas for inclusion and exclusion, was so politically satisfying and so rich with the possibilities offered by positivist social science that pronouncing upon it was for many in South Africa (and in the metropoles of academic legitimacy) politically satisfying, intellectually engaging, and career-advancing.[30]

Local determination to advance this narrow, but apparently academically respectable, position that linked apartheid, the Cold War, and southern Africa was drawn together in 1977 in the creation of the Institute for Strategic Studies at the University of Pretoria (ISSUP). In a search for an "operational universe," a symposium launching the institute suggested that the "central concept in the modern study of interstate relations is national security, an inclusive concept which, apart from traditional 'defence policy,' also includes the non-military actions of a state to ensure its total capacity to survive as a political entity in order to exert influence and to carry out its internal and international objectives."[31] Two conceptual points are important: First, rather than follow the U.S. route to naming the epistemological project "national security," South Africa drew from the British roots of its educational system and called it "strategic studies"; second, the chief referent was with states and the needs of states.[32] The gathering in Pretoria was, however, not an endpoint in the making of knowledge on security in South Africa; it marked, rather, a moment in the development of public institution that further stabilized the discourse that came to govern South Africa's security. The book of the conference proceedings (*National Security: A Modern Approach*) was well received in South Africa: Fredrick Clifford-Vaughan of the University of Natal called it "a necessary and interesting book" and described the formation of a think tank on national security as a "worthwhile project."[33]

The two questions (one double-headed, the other contingent on the first) that few dared to ask was, what on earth would happen to this discourse once apartheid finally crumbled? And what accounts of the region and its security would then drive the countless personal and political knowledge-making agendas in universities and think tanks?

Tales of Change

South Africa's transition has addressed what the British writer Edward Mortimer considers to be the most urgent question of international affairs: how people who feel profoundly different from each other can live together without fighting. For all the celebration that has attended South Africa's answer to this question, however, all judgments must be interim ones. South Africa's future is far from settled; many corners of the country remain, as we have seen, caught in terrible violence, and South Africans are only now exploring a series of associations in which publics, programs, procedures, and politics will come to play their respective parts. The celebration over change in South Africa therefore seems associated more with liberation from the unhappy past than with belief in a secure future for the rainbow nation.

Like this book, this chapter is concerned with past and future: what comes between these two moments is the here and the now. South Africa's here-and-now is etched in the idea of change: this word—as both verb and noun—is in each and every one of the country's many political lexicons. It is therefore not surprising that the institutions that govern all aspects of South Africa's postapartheid life are subjected to all the contestations implicit in the idea of change and the threat posed by continuity. By extending the vote to all the country's citizens, the end of apartheid increased more than the number of those involved in formal politics: it appears to have changed the relationships between center and periphery, between state and citizen, between doctor and patient, between husband and wife, between parent and child. The result is a profound restructuring of formal relations within the country at the same time as it, certainly nominally, has opened opportunities to all. And yet for all the talk (and the reality) of change, there is a compelling consistency in the new South Africa, especially in the field of security. It looks like the old South Africa and—often far too close for political or analytical comfort—it seems to behave like it. In no small way this is because it defines its two key foreign policy objectives—security and wealth-creation—within the same neorealist-neoliberal paradigm, as did the National Party headed by F. W. De Klerk.[34]

In short, for all its change South Africa remains essentially the same. Interestingly, it has taken an anthropologist to point out that the continuities that made the South African miracle possible were afforded by the "resilience of administrative practices."[35] As a result, South Africa remains, as it was during apartheid and has been from the arrival of Dutch settlers, a controlling state. It would seem, however, that we arrived at our conclusion far too soon for theoretical or analytical comfort. The answer to only one question will allow us to pass this point: Why did apartheid end? Exploring this answer drives—with differing degrees of intensity— almost all the discourses that have driven the ubiquitous global change.

A beginning can be made by setting down, as have others, the reasons why apartheid ended.[36] Before doing so, a methodological note is in order: apartheid's ending certainly was no monocausal event. However, in order to follow the unfolding argument, it is necessary to distill five specific accounts of its ending to suggest the limitations of received knowledge, especially in security.

A first explanation links apartheid's ending with the collapse of the Berlin Wall, which proved to be a "historical instant" that changed "old verities."[37] After those momentous hours on Friedrichstrasse in November 1989, all previous positions were closed off and, mutatis mutandis, the way was cleared for the emergence of the new South Africa. Through this frame, South Africa—even though its problem was racial—was no different than a hundred post–World War II conflicts. In an age in which political discourses were driven by war and its making—a forty-five-year "peace" was called the Cold *War*—the solution to any protracted political problem could only be sought through violence.[38]

A second explanation suggests that political and military stalemate drove South Africa to change. This, too, is structuralist, but unlike the first, which is impressionistic, some empirical evidence can support this position. Although the minority's armed power had prevailed, its long-term prospects were poor. In crucial areas, changing technology had left South Africa's military farther and farther behind; as a result, the capacity to sustain a war, even (or especially) an African one, was faltering, as the

Battle of Cuito-Cuanavale showed; influential circles raised serious questions about the wisdom of continuing a war on the borders.[39] More seriously, the struggle for South Africa had delivered what South African strategists feared most: it had come home.[40] Increasingly, the battle was fought on the streets of the country's dusty townships, rather than through the gun turrets of those weapons that the minority, despite sanctions, was able to export. Equally, there was no hope that the majority could prevail. New forms of surveillance had overtaken the idea of wars of national liberation with their roots in the romance of the Cuban experience. Then, old allies—the Soviets more than anyone else—appeared to face changing priorities. If there had been doubts about the direction of perestroika, it was glasnost with its nearly watertight agreement over the division of the world into spheres of interest—especially after the October 1986 Reykjavik Summit—which confirmed that things could never be quite the same again. As the bipolar world ended, therefore, it was inevitable that peripheral conflicts, like the one over apartheid, would also draw to a close.

The next explanation advances the importance of the Cold War as a thread but specifically focuses on the southern African region. As the 1980s ended, this view runs, the euphoria over the liberation of Zimbabwe had given way to disillusionment: the power of successive structural adjustment programs had ensured that the government was able to deliver neither governance to the international community nor tangible benefits to its citizens. Then, South Africa's long-running destabilization was counterproductive to Western interests, which were, certainly officially, intent on stabilizing the region through monetarism and on promoting a multilateral regional project known then as the Southern African Development Co-ordination Conference (the precursor to today's Southern African Development Community, or SADC). And following again upon Reykjavik, it became clear that the issues around Namibia, contrary to the mythologies of the minority, were quite easy to resolve. The multiparty constitution under discussion for that country offered insights into what, with sufficient goodwill and sound timing, might happen within South Africa itself.

Benefiting from hindsight, a fourth explanation points to the advancing years of the then-imprisoned Nelson Mandela and his colleagues. Although the great unspoken of formal South African politics, their continued imprisonment became perhaps the single most important mobilizing issue in international politics during the late 1980s.[41] The arguments made for their release and, concomitantly, against apartheid—both domestically and abroad—were far more persuasive than those that South Africa's minority government could muster as, in the cause of anticommunism, it protested its innocence even to doughty anticommunists like Ronald Reagan and Margaret Thatcher.[42]

The final explanation returns to the notion of stalemate but moves away from a structural base associated with states and political structure toward the idea that there was, as the 1980s ended, increasing fluidity within the global system. A regime of international trade (and other) sanctions had blunted South Africa's international competitiveness, and its ever-depleting exchequer was pressed to respond to the security requirements of what was effectively government by decree. The strength of this view rests on the understanding that South Africa's economy was open even though its politics was closed. At a time when the ideology of the market was rampant, and fortunes were won and lost on the belief that greed was good, few countries, even geographically distant South Africa, could survive without access to the elixir of monetarism. This argument highlights why the infamous Rubicon speech of August 1986 was so important in hastening apartheid's end. This was the failure of South African president P. W. Botha to deliver political reform in a speech to the National Party in Durban, after promising to do so, which caused first Chase Manhattan and then other banks to call up the country's access to foreign loans.[43]

The latter account suggests that the South African state, however repressive and obdurate, had ironically lost the ability to set its own security agenda. The old emphasis on geopolitics was waning, and new items were being drawn to the surface of global politics. In a crude theoretical frame, these were to be called "globalization" and were driven by the quickening tempo of, among other issues, technology, financial flows, and communications. As a result, accepted political processes and long-held political agendas, like anticommunism, appeared overtaken by new concerns that, it seemed, no longer accepted the view that the state was the centerpiece of international society.

These five explanations help frame the "giveness" of the past and embed further mythologies as to why it was that apartheid ended. The point is not only to locate the importance of change in the unfolding of this chapter but also to suggest the limitations of these approaches. Appreciating this establishes a platform upon which to understand the impact of change on southern Africa's future; but to move in this direction requires a parallel set of understandings: these touch on security.

Experience suggests that the obstacles to change lie in the trap of immediate memory. This seems to explain the initial determination of South Africa's entrenched minority to hold on to power despite an obviously changing international agenda in which threats to their security ironically deepened even as the global system seemed more open. The international isolation that they experienced deepened a sense of paranoia and had the effect of shrouding the country in a culture of secrecy and suspicion. With traditions of authoritarianism close at hand and effective control over propaganda, the government ensured that South African society was locked within Max Weber's administrative cage that was controlled by securocrats, as the political scientist Willie Breytenbach famously called them.[44] As the name suggests, these bureaucrats were cued by a militaristic discourse that fed on anticommunism, known as the "Total Onslaught."[45] To achieve the policy goals fed by this construction of their reality, South Africa's government became highly centralized. Elaborately constructed intergovernmental committees ensured that few aspects of public policy escaped the close scrutiny of (and control by) government.[46] Where this approach to public management faltered, as it did during the civic resistance of the 1980s, individuals and political organizations were banned under successive states of emergency.

South Africa's own strain of anticommunism, like many others, was a manifestation of the exceptional circumstances that South Africa's minority faced, but the bridge to history, a sense of place, and the constructed threat settled its permanence.[47] In its daily life, however, the threat was both commonsensical and reduced to Njabulo Ndebele's idea of system maintenance. By the mid-1980s, the Total Onslaught had penetrated the "very stuff of everyday life, familiar assumptions, mundane practices and beliefs."[48] This rendered security concerns to the everyday, and this everyday included subjecting schoolchildren to a better understanding of the threats to their own and state security.[49]

And yet within less than a decade the South African miracle had been achieved. Looking backward, we may ask, Why did this obduracy, this passion for apartheid's security, matter so little?

The increasing international fluidity to which we have referred helps to locate an answer and simultaneously provides another point of departure for a wider argument. The growth of the idea of globalization in international relations was not a sudden development. In a not uncommon case of the cart of practice leading the horse of theory, it was clear, even in the midst of the Cold War, that states could no longer control each and every international activity. As Hayward Alker notes, "The equal and absolute juridical and territorial sovereignty of each nation-state seemed a unit constituting principle out of phase with a world of 'super powers' and 'satellites,' multinational corporations with budgets greater than many states' [gross national product], UN peacekeeping forces, International Monetary Fund loan conditions and U.N. development programmes."[50] The fact of transnationalism has always been central in international relationships, but the problem, as is the case so often in discourse, was not the recognition of a new departure but finding a name to carry it forward.

A pause here enables us to reflect on a familiar tension between theory and methodology. Although the power of new ideas is cumulative, the contest to name them is often the greatest stumbling block, primarily because of the holding power of accepted method and the dominant lexicon that sustains it. Moving beyond these not only challenges the orthodoxy but also unsettles the power of accepted academic ritual—because it challenges the hold of gatekeepers. Small wonder, then, that change calls forth innovation, imagination, and, above all else, intellectual courage. Its importance for social theory is really quite obvious: What drives change—a series of events or the naming of a new name?[51] It was this power of residual understanding—especially security understanding—that ironically protected minority rule in South Africa, even during the worst excesses of apartheid. This explains why demands for change rested on the principle of popular sovereignty and why the tokenism that was presented by many constitutional reforms was so roundly rejected. The questioning of the minority's legitimacy was especially intense in the aftermath of the civil rights movement in the United States because the accepted practices of state sovereignty were increasingly sublimated to an ascending understanding that equated racial discrimination with the idea of illegitimacy.[52] To understand the effect of this development on South Africa we must again examine the idea of sovereignty, only this time from an instrumentalist point of view. Ali Mazrui offers a helpful litmus test as to what constitutes sovereignty: control over territory, supervision of the nation's natural resources, effective and rational revenue extraction, maintenance of adequate national infrastructure, capacity to render basic services; the maintenance of law and order.[53] By every measure, South Africa's minority enjoyed these in abundance; indeed, the state's understanding of its own sovereignty was constructed to service their needs in these areas. For the minority, therefore, state sovereignty was an instrument of giving to those within the chosen circle—*their* South Africa was the quintessential developmental state. By the mid-1980s, however, *their* claims upon, and their capacity to sustain, *their* rights to *their* state and *their* sovereignty were under siege.

Those who contested South Africa's status quo were informed by the same quite settled understandings. Their long-term hope was that South Africa, which was for them a gobbling state, could become a giving state: that instead of deliberately underdeveloping the majority it could be used to develop them. These ideas found expression in the Freedom Charter of

1955, which, as some would have it, is a socialist document in the tradition of the Communist Manifesto.[54] But an equally correct reading of the document suggests that it was a product of its times: firmly positioned within the stream of post–World War II social reconstruction associated with the ideas of John Maynard Keynes.

Using an approach first offered by Immanuel Wallerstein, I want, as promised, to bring capitalism into the argument. In southern Africa, as we have already seen, capitalism never allowed its aspirations to be determined by national boundaries. This was the transnationalism to which we have already referred: In this setting sovereignty is no longer—or not strictly—a spatial-cum-political notion; it can be understood to lie in, say, the global economy or the environment itself.[55] These new forces of international relations were less preoccupied with the traditional spatially. located understandings of sovereignty and more with the idea of global sovereignty that was constructed out of supply-side economics.

The emergence of the new South Africa is explained by the country's rational, commonsense response to the inevitability of market solutions to political problems and the resulting link to the totalizing power of economics as public discourse unleashed by discussions around the idea of the market as a means to international policy. For economists, the notion of sovereignty is associated with the dismantling of national barriers in all areas except security that are said to be the preserve of particular circumstances and particular expertise. This point is set down by John Kenneth Galbraith. "The basic decision in economic life," he wrote in 1992, "is what is to be produced." "In the case of military production, the effective decision lies *with* the military. It is there that the basic decisions as to force and weaponry are made. These are not matters on which civilians are presumed to have knowledge; they can comment and even criticize, but they cannot effectively intervene."[56]

The idea that the market had an important role to play in the "solution" to South Africa's problems was not new. In the late 1960s and early 1970s, an intense debate on the future of the country focused on the "relationship between capitalism and apartheid."[57] At the center of this exchange was the so-called O'Dowd thesis, which held that "apartheid would eventually be brought down by the simple functional logic of the market—as the contradiction between the free market and the racist limitations on this market grew, the former would replace the latter."[58] Although this was embraced as a counter to the idea of national liberation and socialism, O'Dowd's position was less thesis than heuristic device: general and vague and ethnocentric.[59] It paid little attention to the situation on the ground but was powerfully instructive. O'Dowd's perspective was a South African version of Walt Rostow's classic anticommunist manifesto, *Stages of Economic Growth*—especially the famous "take-off" phase with its removal of structural constraints and emergence of an entrepreneurial class.[60] Old-style nationalist politicians, still wedded to the national social origins of their party, viewed the O'Dowd position with some suspicion. But by the early 1980s, an alliance had developed between the business community and the government. The public intellectual and economist Jan Lombard caught the mood by this comment:

> We all know that the crucial battle for the minds of the South African people has begun in earnest. . . . In the leading cultural institution of the Afrikaner people, the *Federasie van Afrikaanse Kultuurvereningings*, the idea of the free market economy as a political philosophy was thoroughly thrashed out as a principal theme of the annual congress less than a year ago . . . the battle lines will be drawn between the political philosophy of the free market economy, on the one hand, and the political philosophy of social collectivism on the other.[61]

Given this, it is no surprise that the apartheid government and the business community sought to "reform" the country by the introduction of limited changes to the constitution.

Concerted efforts to routinize the solution offered by economic growth and political change took the idea of the market even deeper into public consciousness. To great acclaim to the business community, one of the icons of the Chicago School, Milton Friedman, visited South Africa in the mid-1970s. Then sponsored by the business community, organizations like the Free Market Foundation flooded conversations in both the public and policy communities with the "reasonableness" of the solutions that the market was said to offer.[62] Like similar developments elsewhere—the founding of the Heritage Foundation in the United States is an excellent example, as is the Adam Smith Institute in the United Kingdom—the message highlighted the naturalness of the market as a tool for both understanding and managing political conflict. Its solutions were appealing when set against the obduracy of two competing forms of politics: first, apartheid's efforts to reform itself—not to mention its levels of taxation to maintain its security!—and second, the violence that, according to state propaganda, the liberation movement, with its public commitment to both Marx and socialism, was held to represent. As the 1980s ripened, the "solutions" to be offered by the market became more attractive to elites, and the ruling National Party appeared willing to jettison its national social baggage almost in direct proportion to the ANC's continuing embrace of communism—or, rather, its unwillingness to immediately embrace the common sense offered by market solutions.

It was a short step from here for South Africa's elites to accept the embryonic idea of globalization as a means to interpret a world and as a ready solution embedded in the neutrality represented by the market to all public policy issues. This path was smoothed in the late 1980s by a rash of scenario-building in the country, underpinned by the promise of rational choice theory.[63] The inability of reconciling the sovereignty approach to the country's politics with the sovereignty requirements of economic growth and participation in the global economy was a recurrent theme. The message was as deceptively simple as the scenario-building method itself: the economic cost of maintaining the state's sovereignty for the privilege of a minority only was far too high to achieve effective rates of growth needed not only to feed the country's majority but also, when the chips were down, to prevent a revolution by those who were excluded. In effect, traditional obsession with narrow sovereignty was not reconcilable with minority rule; it was best, therefore, to shift the frame, open the political process, and draw all South Africans into the warmth promised by South African sovereignty. So, South Africa's counterintuitive response to its mounting security dilemmas was based on sovereignty, security, and the promise of continued privilege to be delivered by a "free" market.

This was the moment that was described by Francis Fukayama as "the end of history": Western economic and political liberalism would bring an end to all conflict, including South Africa's! Because it offers light to the relations between South Africa and the region, one further word is in order: one of the scenario-building exercises was explicit about the country turning its back on southern Africa.[64] A few years later, in 1994, the African Development Bank echoed the call: "What is clear is that for South Africa national interests are paramount, while regional issues are secondary and likely to remain so."[65]

But the search for solutions—even those presented by a globalizing world—can be momentarily held captive by history. In South Africa, none was stronger than the legacy bequeathed by South Africa's security concerns. Here, conveniently for globalization, apartheid's military-industrial establishment provided a bridge between past and present; the discourses over the communist onslaught and the urgency to defend civilized values in Africa masked a series of state subsidies. The most obvious was employment: in apartheid's final years, South Africa's security forces (the police and the defense force) were the country's largest employer of white labor. A parallel set of subsidies could be found within South Africa's armaments industry, which had developed a strong and competitive international reputation.

So security concerns became enmeshed with the idea of a globalizing market. Arms sales, as a means to foreign currency, were presented as a plausible and profitable means to economic growth.[66] In South Africa's case, this innovative end of the country's technology was tied to the arms industry—an echo of Jürgen Habermas's notion that "economic growth is kept going by innovations that . . . are *intentionally* tied to an armaments spiral that has gone out of control."[67] Even in a world dominated by the market, defense subsidies are acceptable.

On the other side of the great apartheid divide, South Africa's liberation movements faced the same "end of history," but their search for solutions was harder. The ideological straitjacketing of structural Marxism framed an idea that control of the state was, as we have seen, the path to both power and development. Thinking on future economic policy was, quite frankly, weak and mired in the rhetoric of national liberation. Within and without the country, a multiplicity of simple, simplistic, and even simple-minded slogans reinforced the notion that the struggle for South Africa was a struggle for the sovereignty of a state that would forever be giving and that could, with a legitimate government, satisfy the needs of all its people.[68] As the end-of-history thesis took hold, however, these particular explanations became less and less plausible: the ANC in particular was vulnerable to buffeting by the power of new economic forces. A broad alliance, the ANC had always been susceptible to the diversity of impulses that lay beneath a veneer of unity. This veneer was certainly extended— even overextended—by its bifurcation: an external exiled wing that required ideological conformity as it fought both the war of national liberation and the diplomatic campaign to isolate a sovereign state, and the internally based United Democratic Front. For all its lip service to the rituals of struggle, the latter was more catholic than the ANC and more easily incorporated new and divergent impulses into an ever-broadening agenda that aimed, above all else, to end apartheid. But what is perhaps more crucial from the perspective offered in this book is that the ANC was never intent on overthrowing the order in South Africa. It was, however, very interested in trading places.

Faced with positions over which they had less and less control, the protagonists in the struggle for South Africa were attracted by the prospects for negotiations that would move them from an unhappy past to a future that promised to be more manageable. This analysis suggests that without the compelling discourses offered by globalization, South

Africa's transition—the "miracle"—could not have been achieved. Closer scrutiny, however, reveals that things were less miraculous than deal-driven.[69] Central to the exercise was an intentional ambiguity around the rationality of a free market and the control dimensions offered by the idea of state sovereignty. The latter were carried by Robert Thornton's "administrative practices," whereas South Africa's new government adopted neoliberal economic policies that have become the envy of many (as the financial press likes to say). Put differently, the reasonableness of the market solution and the continuity offered by administration and security have permitted more continuities than change in South Africa, notwithstanding that the deep transformation rhetoric upon which apartheid's ending was premised promised far, far more.

Security Tales

This closes one moment of metanarrative, but some important footnotes need to be added. Upon coming to power, South Africa's new government announced the Reconstruction and Development Programme. This boldly proclaimed itself as "an integrated, coherent socio-economic policy framework [seeking] to mobilise all our people and our country's resources toward the final eradication of apartheid and the building of a democratic, non-racial, non-sexist future."[70] Less than eighteen months later, this neo-Keynesian project had been replaced by a program called GEAR (named for the Growth, Employment, and Redistribution strategy). GEAR aimed to cut government expenditures within the Maastricht targets to promote growth to 6 percent per annum, thereby setting the stage for international investment that in turn requires a more malleable labor market.[71] The program was endorsed by the highest voices in the land and carried forward by Thabo Mbeki, the man designated by Nelson Mandela as the country's next president.[72] The financial press was scarcely able to contain its joy at this appointment in a party that less than a decade earlier was committed—certainly rhetorically—to socialist policies as the answer to bridging South Africa's racial divide and creating economic justice.[73] But more sober analysis reveals that this neoliberal economic solution does little more than juggle the single idea of redistribution through growth in an economy that continues to display a perennial southern African problem, that is, white wealth and black poverty. What the policy offered South Africa's people was trickle-down economics and trickle-down security.

Very little is settled in South Africa: repeating this emphasizes an old, but also a very new, idea in politics: change is the only constant. So, it is no surprise that more often than not the ANC government seems closer to business than it is to its formal allies in the South African Communist Party; at other times, quite naturally, it is not.[74]

What does this all mean for security? South Africa's turn to the politics of the region has been fraught with Byzantine ambiguity and plain common sense, both manufactured and other. How is one to understand the security policy of a place that at one and the same time commits itself to the international fight against habit-forming drugs but in which many of its poorest people live exclusively from cash generated by them; that is committed to controlling arms but whose only internationally competitive industry—so its people are told—is the weapons industry? And how is one to explain its regional security policy, which relied on its neighbors to deliver it from political oppression but periodically turns on an electric fence to keep those very neighbors out?

One response offered by mainstream security studies is easy: like any state, South Africa must defend its national interest and protect its sovereignty. Any response must therefore be purposeful, directed, and preferably swift, because to play with a state's security is to play with fire. But as Jim George once pointedly noted, this approach suggests that interstate relations can only be viewed as conflict—one within a universalized, historic truth associated with violence.[75]

On closer examination, however, each moment in the regional relations is complex and value-laden. As a result, there are no quick answers, no ready ways to unpack the multilayers that underlie these interpretations of what constitutes truths. This explains why there are no guarantees that the celebratory hopes in the region engendered by the ending of apartheid can refoster, without initiating further deep-seated change, the reality of community in southern Africa. Small wonder, then, that translating the experience of struggle and resistance against apartheid into policies that are accommodating of the fears and aspirations of near-neighbors is a frustrating experience.

South Africa's experience suggests that transitionary politics involves an exchange between the fear represented by security discourse and the "solution" offered by the market. This is a transaction moment, one that is ceaselessly (and therefore ambiguously) written in the present as both history and future but one that can be easily resolved. As Rob Walker has caught this process, "grand visions of the future have been linked to promises made by particular groups to effect change after gaining power, promises that have been broken either by the nature of the struggle for power itself or by the nature of the power that is attained. Too many revolutions have been swallowed by all powerful states."[76] Continuities of policy in the name of political change have marked South Africa's efforts to re/insert itself into the life of the region.

As South Africa moved toward a multiracial democratic form of government, many observers felt that the most hopeful and tangible outcome of the demise of apartheid would be the much-heralded peace dividend in the region. And South Africa's role as a regional (and perhaps continental) peacemaker was the subject of much discussion throughout the subcontinent. At workshops in Cape Town (June 1994) and in Windhoek (July 1994), the clearly changing definitions of both threat and security were articulated.[77]

These suggested that in a region where myriad, growing, and intractable threats derive from regionwide conditions of chronic underdevelopment and domestic instability, a continuing emphasis on traditional notions of national security based on secure borders patrolled by strong militaries was out of place. In the absence of apartheid southern Africa, the region faced no defined external security threat. Insecurity in post-apartheid southern Africa seemed so obviously rooted in economics—uneven development, inequalities of resource access and allocation, unemployment, and poverty. Problems—later to be securitized—such as drugs, arms, and illegal migrant labor flows were named as symptoms of structural inequalities. In these circumstances, therefore, security in southern Africa could obviously not be ensured through arms acquisitions and traditional forms of interstate military cooperation. Instead, it was forcefully argued, security should be promoted by a concerted attempt to address the region's and continent's subordinate place within the global economy.

But the hope that peace could deliver security through sustained integration and surrendered sovereignty was short-lived as South Africa's new government fell back on old national habits. Historically developed forms of political organization and resulting state-centered struggles for majority rule helped entrench and add weight to traditional approaches to security. South Africa's decade-long policy of Total Strategy, with its emphasis on securing its international borders from the Soviet threat and strengthening its domestic security, facilitated the deepening of inside-outside conceptions of interstate relations. Security, therefore, continued to be pursued via military strategies of deterrence and force for national ends, an epistemological process that was speeded by the rise and flourishing of new sites of security knowledge.

Their path was smoothed by a confluence of perception and problem-solving. As postapartheid South Africa searched out a position on regional security in its first years in office, it sought legitimacy for the process of military integration within the country, and only standing outside history could do this. The integration and reconciliation of previously sworn enemies into a reformed, representative South African National Defence Force brought the technical and managerial issues of system and project management close to the debate on security—drawing ideas of rational choice and opportunity-cost into a realm that would, perhaps, have been better served by understandings of history and philosophy. Defense economists, lawyers, political scientists, international relations expertise, and management skills were all drawn to the quickly unfolding discourse around military reform as security studies. In this conflation of purpose as problem-solving, the ideas that regional security was best solved through the opportunities presented by the state as actor were readily at hand. More progressive ideas of turning swords into ploughshares—through the creation of military "brigades" involved in developmental work—were quickly rejected as uneconomic, inefficient, and beneath the esteem of trained fighters. And efforts to develop a regional institute to monitor issues of peace and security across the region were simply dismissed as utopian.[78] By suspending questions, old ways of knowing security were given a rite of passage into the new situation.

As they had done for more than a century, South Africans—now with a new and legitimate government—quickly opted to live up against their neighbors rather than among them.[79] As a result, people in South Africa and in the region have turned to other sources for their security—from enhanced security systems in the white suburbs, whose surveillance is enhanced by the power of market rationality, to the emergence of gangs and "big men" in the townships, where access to money offers the best form of protection. As much as military power set the course for the management of regional relations, so too internal forms of surveillance were drawn into the rationality and efficiency offered by the market.

By engaging with the multilateral processes of regional security, South Africa's new government found instruments of engagement that were well established elsewhere, but these same instruments would not shift the structural deficits that faced the region's people. The so-called Frontline States framework presented a positive instrument, especially in terms of securing short-term stability, but the institutionalization of a framework to settle regional conflicts was long in coming. Interim efforts, like peacekeeping, that were borrowed from abroad were popularized by state-makers and took on a sinister hue when set against the determination by the region's states not to share sovereignty. Hurried choices made early and under pressure from state-makers, therefore, wrecked the hopes of millions of southern Africans for a better, more secure future.

For a few brief sentences, I want to insert an idea from the respected Zimbabwean sociologist Marshall Murphree. In a valedictory speech to the University of Zimbabwe, Murphree used the Shona proverb *Ganda rinopetwa richirinyoro* (A hide is best folded when it is raw and wet) to make this point. "Some things should have changed earlier, and because they haven't yet it is now more difficult to change them."[80] This captures the horror represented by continuities in moments of transition. The threat—for that is what this has become—is that the choices authorized by South Africa's new legitimacy in the region may endure for generations. Named as the routine politics of regionalism and incorporated by the region's policy process as security, these routines will not free the region's people but will continue to repeat the past as future.

However triumphantly acclaimed by the international community, the region's new ways will not serve to consummate the single purpose to which all southern Africa's people devoted their lives as they struggled successively to end colonialism and apartheid. So, the very newness of the new South Africa and the awakening of a southern African code of security behavior may not, as many hoped, dim the region's prospects for violence. Indeed, at the time of this writing, the region was aflame with conflicts both ignited and reignited by the persistent failure of the region's new routine of making peace to deliver more than proverbial talk, as we shall now see.

4

Writing Migration as Neoapartheid

I couldn't help laughing
It was cruel, I know. But it was also stupid.
Because I now realise that Oskar was
Giving me an object lesson in philosophy.
He was showing me that about that of which we
Know nothing, we should remain silent.
—Oskar Wolberheim

N o moment in the life of the new South Africa has been so busy with the techniques of social control, the traps of security, and the tropes that construct states than the debate around the movement of people. This suggests the direction of a chapter that follows the tributaries of a series of discourses on migration in postapartheid South Africa in order to show how the new state has been authored by the security-making techniques of the old. My purpose is to demonstrate how the violent unfoldings of this discourse have constructed the idea that migration to South Africa is a threat. These continuities and the violence that attends them suggest that received understandings of the state and its security have not changed; indeed, they have been reinforced notwithstanding the celebration, the fresh beginning, the new start that was said to accompany the ending of apartheid.

If anything, South Africa's new encounter with migration—and the ensuing xenophobia this issue has generated—have sundered the theoretical assumptions that once anchored ideas around the country's exceptionalism.[1] This has driven discussion on possible futures for the region toward more sophisticated forms of social theory than was previously thought possible or even necessary. So, because migration has opened "an opportunity to examine how boundaries that separate inside from outside get constructed," this chapter uses, as we will soon see, a range of approaches drawn from critical literature.[2] To follow this trajectory, however, will require an informed sociohistorical narrative that interrogates the continuing domination of realist theory in the affairs of the region.

Because orthodox security debates in southern Africa and elsewhere insist on the holding power of boundary lines, the issue of migration can be addressed only in a specific predetermined way: migrants are always and forever aliens, outsiders, unwashed. Put in a language more familiar to international relations, traditional security studies insists that boundary lines grant sovereign privilege in order to draw a structural distinction between migrant and resident. Critical literature sees a different triangle between citizen and border and migrant. The issue of whether migration should be, or indeed is, a security question is set by the intensity of a policing process; in theory this means the structure of language or the routines of security discourse, but in practice this means placing armies and erecting electric fences along, essentially, the same boundaries.[3] The critical project sees efforts to control and police both national boundaries and intellectual discourses as serving particular interests and seeks to uncover these practices by simply asking, Who benefits?

A close reading of this chapter will reveal a progression of ancillary goals and some methodological innovations. The first highlights the violence of the discourse in order to recall the far too many instances of sheer cruelty against migrants to South Africa.[4] Much of this brutality is reminiscent of the worst excesses of apartheid, as the following story relates:

> In September 1998, three migrants to South Africa were savaged by a mob on a train: one, a Mozambican, was thrown out while the other two, both Senegalese citizens, were electrocuted as they climbed on the roof trying to escape the crowd. This violence was visited by members of a crowd who were returning from a rally in the country's administrative capital, Pretoria, who had gathered to protest under the banner of an organisation called "Unemployed Masses of South Africa" who claimed to represent 32 000 jobless people.[5]

But there are others, too. In October 1998, eighteen people suffocated to death in an unventilated transport container that was smuggling them across the border between Zimbabwe and Botswana. Their destination? South Africa. The cost of the fare? about U.S.$20.[6] But these risks are not all they face. In the same month, the South African press reported that "another Mozambican immigrant" had been killed and eaten by wild animals while crossing the border between Mozambique and South Africa.[7]

To the second of the ancillary goals: it was the increasingly revered Hannah Arendt who raised the possibility that banality and evil are twins—that the most horrendous crimes can be located in a "deficit of thought," "a specific quality of mind and character."[8] For the purposes of this chapter consider this simple question: Why have South Africa's rainbow people fashioned a xenophobic nation? As we seek an answer, it will be plain that names have been named. Let me be clear about the purpose of this technique: my objective is not to point fingers at individuals or, indeed, at institutions but rather to point out how—again, on the level of the banal—migration toward South Africa's miracle has come to be seen as both threatening and hostile and why the policy responses are so redolent with the discourse of control.[9]

The third ancillary goal is interested in the relationship between migration and the construction of national identity. The place we continuously call "South Africa" is the product of an endless process of migration. Viewed reciprocally, the simple truth is this: without the movement of people to the space known as South Africa, there would, quite simply, be no state, no South Africa, and, to raise a paradox to which we will often return, no place to which migrants migrated.

The discursive direction of this critical argument suggests that migration is ceaselessly used to stabilize national identity and settle contestations around state security.[10] This contrasts, markedly, with mainstream international relations, which teaches that borders are fixed, durable, and inflexible. In southern Africa, critical scholarship shows that the search for security can be innovative and pregnant with the possibilities provided by human agency by suggesting that national boundaries are unstable, transient, and flexible—or, quite frankly, that they don't matter at all![11] To achieve this I will frequently cross established disciplinary boundaries using different optics to look at the region's history. As a result of this repertoire of approaches, readers who are informed about southern Africa will discover that a familiar world is kneaded in an entirely different fashion, whereas critical readers might discover familiar themes and techniques applied to what is, perhaps, an unfamiliar condition.

But the business of this book is also with the business of policymaking, and we must say something on this subject. We have already noted that the question of migration has been a difficult one for the new South Africa. Notwithstanding the promise of new beginnings, this issue, more than many others, confirms the holding power of one particular rendition of history—national history—especially in troubled times. As Walter Benjamin suggested: "To articulate the past historically does not mean to recognize it 'the way it really was'. It means to seize hold of memory as it flashes up in a moment of danger"[12] This power—the force of national memory and privileged recollections of political events—limits rather than opens the range for policymaking. Exploring this enables us to identify the many silences that exist between the seeming bustle of policy and social theory.

Picking up Bad Habits

The notion that South Africa lives up against, rather than with, its neighbors is a recurring theme in this book.[13] This was located within the discourses that lead to state-formation in southern Africa that set South Africa apart and above its neighbors. The debates over migration in South Africa, if anything, have reinforced this routine patterning of interstate relations in southern Africa. On the issue of migration, however, there is much more. Seen from the neighborhood, South Africa is an aggressive state—particularly to migrants. The derogatory term *amaKwerekwere*, used to describe migrants to the country, is interpreted as a signal of danger, a deep threat to personal and community security.[14] To understand how this has happened, we must turn to the power of discourse.

In the early 1990s, the movement of peoples generated renewed interest in international relations. Much of this work focused on policy, specifically the immediate task of managing the movement of people across international borders, especially in Europe following the Kurdish crisis. The ascendancy of policy discourses in the North reopened a near-dormant engagement with migration as an issue elsewhere—including the rediscovery of localized migration as an interstate issue in both Asia and Africa.[15] Then, the horrendous events in the Great Lakes in 1994, drawing on another round of Afro-pessimism and feeding on the growing literature on state failure, focused international attention on possible configurations that the mass movement of people could take on the continent.

This was itself a migration of the issue, from local issue to international item to security threat. This is exemplified in the following quotation from Myron Weiner: "Migration and refugee issues, no longer the sole concern of ministries of labour or of migration, are now matters of high international politics, engaging the attention of heads of states, cabinets, and key ministries involved in defense, internal security, and external relations."[16] By using the license offered by realism, cross-border migration was drawn away from the domestic to the international, resettling it as an issue of what foreign policy analysts sometimes call "high politics." This formulation was to travel well. In South Africa, Myron Weiner's work—both the article quoted above and the book that followed—were quickly drawn into reinforcing a series of foundational assumptions about the movement of people toward the country.[17]

The hegemony of this position was amplified by the support it received from other quarters. So, the perspective of migration as a security threat was echoed by the Harvard political scientist Samuel P. Huntington, who in the establishment journal, *Foreign Affairs*, argued that the failure to control U.S. borders was the single greatest item in the security of the United States.[18] I have singled out Huntington because he has a loyal following in South Africa. In 1981, for instance, he delivered a talk to the country's political scientists suggesting ways in which apartheid might be reformed: before the end of apartheid, his paper was often used to justify efforts at reform by the white minority government.[19] And in 1997, following the publication of the book *The Clash of Civilizations and the Remaking of World Order*, he received an honorary degree from Rand Afrikaans University.[20]

Huntington's ideas are drawn from the multicultural debate in the United States—a debate that was urged on by the establishment liberal historian Arthur Schlesinger in his 1992 polemic, *The Disuniting of America*.[21] And the epochal end-of-era writing of the Yale historian Paul Kennedy essentially drew from the same intellectual well, both to explain areas of global change and to sound warnings over the cross-border movement of people.[22] In the United States, fears over multiculturalism were translated into strong policy initiatives; most dramatically, these were reflected in 1994's so-called war on immigrants, which was an integral part of the House Republicans' Contract with America initiative.[23] In Europe, a parallel response to this disciplining of diasporas, to coin a phrase, came to be known by the metaphor of a fortress Europe.

As South African responses to the intensity of the debate deepened, local academics were also drawn to a parallel argument that was being advanced by the Third World School of security studies. This suggested that the primary security concern of third-world polities was threats to the legitimacy of states.[24] Policy responses to this literature followed, with choices predetermined by realism rather than embracing the more nuanced subaltern realism advanced by more reflexive third-world security theorists like Mohammed Ayoob, on two pivotal issues.[25]

First, the government early invoked the idea of the national interest to promote its new policies, and this assertion of government-directed control was far stronger than similar claims had been under apartheid when, indeed, the legitimacy of the state was continually under threat.[26] Like other states, the argument ran, South Africa would exercise its policy options when it was in the national interest, and migration to South Africa was not to be exempt. Second, policy responses were said to derive from an international system that was forged on power considerations alone.[27] South Africa was, relatively speaking, developed and powerful, especially in southern Africa; therefore, it was positioned to stake out an assertive position on cross-border movement in the region.[28] Importantly for what will follow, both positions were openly contemptuous of morality and history: the former was seen as "misdirected," and the latter dismissed for having no limitations and no ending.[29] These theoretical assumptions became the commanding perspective of South Africa's government, especially the Ministry of Home Affairs, and its coterie of policy advisers; many, but not all, of these advisers were drawn from the ranks of South Africa's past.[30]

This elevation of migration to high politics drew South Africa's new government far closer to the boundedness of realist interpretations of the social than they had signaled while in exile or while in electoral opposition immediately prior to the first democratic election.[31]

Our immediate interest is not with these policy outcomes but with the discourse that informed them. Certainly South Africa's policymakers drew their power from the deepening public disquiet, especially in the press, over the influx of foreign blacks into the country, but their organic power, as Antonio Gramsci might have put it, rested on the hegemonic authority of constructions of danger and the link between them and the search for national identity.[32] Not a little anger and fury were added to the public perception of the migration issue, as well as the determination of policymakers to do the proverbial something, by the fact that those involved in policy debates were "prone to hyperbole and exaggeration."[33] Taken as both theory and method, however, it is difficult to disagree with the verdict of the geographer Jonathan Crush that the academic approach to the issue amounted to "pseudo-science."[34]

In this framing, surveillance and control—rather than the understandings that might be offered by alternative explanations of migration as a social condition—became the overriding policy consideration.[35] Given this, the solutions initially offered to the problem of cross-border movement of people to postapartheid South Africa were settled within the disciplining boundaries affirmed by the principle of state sovereignty, notwithstanding a rhetorical understanding (to use a striking phrase from the economist Francis Wilson) that migration had made the region. South Africa's government, through the responsible minister, asserted that both refugees and migrants were considered to be a "problem."[36] There was a muted concession to this position from the then–deputy president, Thabo Mbeki, destined to become South Africa's second democratically elected president. Speaking at a meeting of church leaders, he reminded South Africans of the hospitality that had been shown them by other countries during their own years in exile and urged a regional solution to the problem.[37]

Pretoria's Hobbesians

The policy analyst Maxine Reitzes (in collaboration with Chris Landsberg) had the early insight to call these practitioners of pseudoscience "South Africa's Hobbesians"—a good term considering that no new policy options were forthcoming from a government that continued to rely on dated relics from apartheid's gory days to police migrants. Long considered the most vicious of apartheid legislation, the legislation was concerned with keeping races separated, in keeping especially blacks out of white areas, and in policing the movement and whereabouts of blacks. In short, these were policies "designed to control the movement, settlement and location of Black people throughout the South African space economy."[38]

But nothing had prepared the country for the public response to the cross-border movement of people. The sheer emotion, not to mention the powerful role of the press in making migration a public issue, became inexorably linked to the processes of change. If anything, the juxtaposition of change and fear was a constitutive relationship between the idea of common nationality and the constructed threat of migration to the country. This conjuncture was caught in a banner headline that appeared on the front page of *The Argus*, a Cape Town–based afternoon newspaper.[39] Under a screaming 108-point headline—"ALIEN 'INVASION'"—the paper reported that South Africa had recently deported 132,000 "illegals," 80,000 of them "back to Mozambique." But placed immediately above the headline were these eight words: "YOUR NEW SOUTH AFRICA MAP IS INSIDE TODAY." The sensationalized threat of the alien was the price that South Africa was seemingly paying for its new cartography—and its new nationhood.

As this sense of crisis deepened, the policy community seemed to act against the backdrop of panic—more properly called xenophobia—among many, if not all, of South Africa's publics. In addition, this othering of migrants was linked to feelings of superiority derived from the sense of economic development that had been built on apartheid and inflated by the success of South Africa's transition; ironically, however, these constructed another underclass around the same conceptual primitives upon which apartheid had once rested.

Again in retrospect, this was not surprising. At the time, a narrative of nationhood was directed toward consolidation of a common South Africanness under the signifier provided by the idea of the rainbow nation, the trope first articulated by the Nobel laureate Desmond Tutu. In its very essence, therefore, the new South African position on migration was, unlike the U.S. experience, accepting of the desirability of multiculturalism but was, like the U.S. experience, deeply antagonistic of migration. Perhaps unexpectedly, the debate quickly took on a vituperative form that—all too often for coincidence—was riddled with connotations of race and reminiscent of the country's unhappy past.[40] Presently we will uncover the roots of these racial codes, but first I turn to constructions of the security threat posed by migration to South Africa.

The first of these was linked to neoliberal economics. Population movements from poor to rich countries constitute an economic threat by squeezing the middle class in more prosperous societies; this, it is argued, is not conducive to the success of market-driven democracies.[41] So, migration to South Africa was constructed as an economic threat to the prosperity of the country's people along this causal chain: by diluting the human capital stock, migration would weaken the country's economic potential and, in so doing, lay further burdens on a country already struggling to overcome the inequalities of apartheid.[42] If this economic argument was rooted in particular understandings of the power of economics, other debates were more banal.

In a second construction, politicians and the available pool of security state-makers pointed toward threats that seemed to exist or could easily be manufactured. So, for instance, the proliferation of habit-forming drugs in the subcontinent was linked to the cross-border movement of people.[43] All too quickly, other links were drawn between population flows and concerns in other fields of public policy, like health—the linkage between migration and the HIV/AIDS pandemic readily suggested itself and indicates how easily health discourses are recruited into the security field.[44] The poet Ingrid de Kok caught this when she remarked how "elements of the hygiene discourse underpinned by arguments for stability and law and order persist in planning documents, newspaper commentaries and local debates even" in the new South Africa.[45]

The naturalization of these discourses and constructed threats was easily accomplished through the power of public discourse on nationalism, on the imperative of neoliberal economics, and on the strengthening borders (to mention only three of many) and of the recourse to the totalizing appeal of population movement as an issue of high politics. Building on the idea of the rainbow nation, the new South Africa signifies a cleansed beginning for the country's people. But the celebration shows, as we have already seen, a darker side: the constructed face of national identity, the harbinger of a nationalism used for the purpose of privileging.

The power of these constructions and the threat they came to pose suggest how effortlessly the debate was drawn toward policy as a form of social closure. Once again, however, we reach ahead of ourselves, running the familiar path much loved by those who have so easily made migration into a "massive problem," as a leading policy pundit was quick to describe the migration after attending, apparently, a single roundtable on "order [and] security."[46] To appreciate the complexities of the issue, we must turn where few of South Africa's Hobbesians have dared to venture. We must look to history.

History, Migration, and the New South Africa

The possibility that the end of apartheid would lead to a significant movement of people from the continent to South Africa was predicted before that system's formal ending. In the late 1980s, as activists and intellectuals worked to weaken and divide the apartheid government, the migration issue entered the discourse of political change and transformation at the margins.[47] However, following F. W. De Klerk's speech on February 2, 1990, which set the course for South Africa's move toward democracy, possible migration to the country was increasingly drawn to the forefront of public debate.

So, for instance, a keynote address delivered to the biennial conference of the then Development Society of South Africa noted:

> All the evidence suggests that the ending of apartheid will deepen, not weaken, South Africa's attractiveness to the people of the region. This means that when southern Africa's own Berlin Wall—apartheid—finally comes down, a tide of humanity will cross over into this country. To avoid the resulting long-term social dislocation, planning for these migrants needs to commence as soon as possible.[48]

But the innocence, not to mention naïveté, of these early signals, as well as pleas for both sensible and humane policy and its planning, was swept away in the desperate pattern of politics and, later, violence that attended South Africa's transition.

The academic community offered early, crude explanations and provided tentative mappings of the initial course of migration and its effect on interstate relations in southern Africa.[49] These were largely in vain; the power of realism swept away not only the best of intentions but also hopes for more socially conscious policymaking. Like most things in the world of the social, however, setbacks are seldom simple binaries. Security-minded policymakers have had to face a painful truth: their efforts both to restrict the cross-border flow of people and to more deeply securitize migration have reinforced "one of the greatest paradoxes about the contemporary practice of sovereignty: even as states are increasing their efforts to control their borders, they [lose] ground."[50]

Aletta Norval has demonstrated the constructions of identity, as well as the link between identity and nationality, that were central to the socio-historical narrative that first created and later secured the apartheid state.[51] Appreciating this work takes us closer to viewing migration through a political-historical lens.[52] Her approach momentarily places the movement of people as the dominant narrative in the construction of the old South Africa—a white-ruled European state in southern Africa, a state successively aligned to Holland and Britain (but later to other European countries) in a series of "long and special historical relationships."[53] No small part of this link was the role of signifiers: Britain as "home" for South Africa's English speakers, the Netherlands as "*die stamland*" (tribal land) for Afrikaners.

We must pause here to lay down, in a hurried paragraph, an ontological marker that was initially raised in Chapter 1. The political shape of southern Africa—its division into states as means to a community dominated by one of their number, South Africa—is, for our immediate purposes, the central focus. There are, of course, many other southern Africas; a regional ontology sketched by the notion of a southern Africa of people, for instance, is centrally juxtaposed against the region of states in this book. For now, however, identifying and naming these *other southern Africas*, these alternative futures, is the business of Chapter 6. Appreciating this helps explain the special relationship to which we have just referred—and to which we now return.

The "special" aspects of the relationships between South Africa and Holland and European states were, of course, the power of naming, the discourse of racial exclusivity, and the role of money. Let us be clear about these: the political form of southern Africa—its division into states—was the product of Western imaginings supported by agents of the local. The power to name and carve out South Africa as a distinctive space was, as black scholars have ceaselessly mentioned, an act of great violence and force.[54] The making of the South African state was patently linked to understandings of racial superiority and spurred forward by the irresistible arguments of the purse that the discovery of diamonds and gold promised to deliver to "home" and then, later, a construction called "empire" that served to secure that same home.

Taken together, the power of naming, notions of racial superiority, and concentrations of power set both the theory and practice of the debate on security in South Africa for close to three centuries. The old South Africa enjoyed far more potent links—political, cultural, and economic—with these northern places than it did with the state structures that came to surround it and that were drawn to become Larry Bowman's "subordinate state sub-system of Southern Africa," a construct of place we have already encountered.[55] The energy spent on these "special" relationships was also geared toward drawing migrants to the country to reinforce a particular form of national identity and to allay the security fears of the settler minority.

In the construction of the South African state, then, migration has always been a source of security, not a cause for insecurity. The great mass of this migration occurred during the nineteenth-century export of Europeans all over the globe and at the same historical moment when notions of military strategy, upon which the discipline of security studies was to build, were first codified.[56] This, as well as decisionmaking about technical development especially in the military field, was centralized and then guarded from public scrutiny and debate.[57] Given the link to security, migration to South Africa was always carefully controlled by empire and successive minority governments to service narrow ideological ends.[58]

Because the debate on migration to the new South Africa has played out in such fundamental—indeed, brutal—terms, and because the discourse on race has hovered close by, it is necessary to insert another factual point: the migration of whites to South Africa continued until the very ending of the apartheid system, although under a scrics of changing incentives. Consider, for instance, this report on immigration to the country set out in *The Official Yearbook of the Union of South Africa:* "From 1924 onwards, immigrants from countries situated in eastern, central and southern Europe arrive in increasing numbers each year."[59]

My purpose in inserting a neglected historical-political story line in the contemporary migration issue is remedial, not palliative. The proliferation of policy advice proffered on the movement of people to the new South Africa—particularly the determined efforts of security epistemes to reinforce the link between migration and security—has strongly paralleled right-wing thinking on this issue, especially in the United States and

Europe as we have seen. Anthony Messina has noted that this latter work has given little attention to uncovering the historical roots of immigration policy; neither, for that matter, has it been paid to the role played by migration in the making of states.[60] Recognizing this draws the narrative forward to the link between migration and the early making of the South African state.

Deep within the founding myths of white power in South Africa stands the huddled image of some 180 French Huguenots who settled in the Cape Colony in the late 1680s and early 1690s. The celebration of their role as a distinctive force in the early sedimentation of the place that was to be called South Africa, as well as their contribution to the development of Calvinism in the region, was central in the construction of Afrikaner (and later white) identity in the nineteenth and twentieth centuries. In more recent times, the role of the Huguenots as the genius behind South Africa's internationally competitive viticulture continues the celebration of their position in the making of South Africa in this, the globalizing world of the twenty-first century. Stripped of this mythmaking, however, the Huguenots were little more than outsiders seeking a new inside.

The importance of the Huguenots to the current discussion, however, lies beyond the largely symbolic role they played in the building of the white state and the European sophistication that they were said to have brought to distant South Africa. It lies in the findings of recent scholarship. Confirming George Orwell's dictum that those who control the past control the future, this work shows that the French Huguenots present a distinct moment in the unfolding story of state formation in Europe. In a compelling study on refugees and the displacement practices of statecraft, Nevzat Soguk argues that the flight of Protestants from France under Louis XIV was "something that happened in the course of statecraft." The revocation of the Edict of Nantes was initiated by the French state in formation, and the flight of the Huguenots "manifested the difficulties of statecraft [because these events effectively] escaped the control of statecraft." But the resulting homogenization of the country, through religion, set the scene for French "proto-nationalism." "In all, the Huguenot displacement was part and parcel of a larger shift in practices of government by which the absolute state would begin to acquire the characteristics of a modern centralizing state."[61]

This difficult situation was seemingly well appreciated by the Dutch East India Company that at the time controlled the Cape, to which South Africa's Huguenots were carried. Rodney Davenport notes how quickly and purposefully they were encouraged to integrate into mainstream agrarian life—at a place called Franschoek near the current university town of Stellenbosch—of the Cape.[62] It was this very construct of the Cape that would eventually be drawn forward in order to make the South African state. This event was "one of the earlier in a series of events that, from the seventeenth century to the twentieth century, firmly established both in imagination and in practice, the notion of statist territoriality, in the territorial boundedness of life as the single most significant defining property in the existence of communities."[63]

The French Huguenots became the icon that represented the migration of Europeans to South Africa, a bridge to Europe signifying the country's modernity or, as its white leaders used to say, its development. During the Cold War, both were powerful arguments in assessments of South Africa's strategic importance to the West. The link to Europe appeared as the central discourse in the country's formal politics for close to three centuries. So, the once vociferous exchange between South Africa's two white communities—Afrikaans-speakers and English-speakers—was almost entirely grounded in the political conversations, both domestic and international, of nineteenth-century Europe. Using Foucault to inform her gaze, Kate Manzo confirms, "Major struggles during the colonial era [i.e., prior to 1945] in South Africa involved Dutch settlers in their relations with colonial administrators [both Dutch and British], with European capitalists, and with missionary and antislavery societies."[64]

Indeed, within a series of sequential political tussles between South Africa's two white communities, as well as in conflicts between black and white, the issue of population movement was often pivotal in tipping the balance, strategic and other. In the early 1820s, for example, special immigration schemes brought some 4,000 settlers from various parts of Britain, mainly from England, to the eastern Cape. Their influence on the life of the country has been profound; it was they who helped to consolidate the language of administration—of empire—into the language of the new South Africa. Between 1860 and 1911, Indian indentured laborers arrived in South Africa; estimates suggest that there were more than 150,000 of them. Their presence greatly enriched almost every aspect of South African life, including its current politics. Numbered among those who came to the country to help defend their rights was Mohandas Gandhi, who lived in Natal between 1893 and 1914.[65] The Chinese also came to South Africa as indentured labor (some 63,000 of them on three-year contracts to work in the gold mines). Although most returned home, a few remained to be joined, in more recent years, by numbers of Chinese from Taiwan, in particular.[66]

Perhaps the most significant moment in which the movement of people has directly inserted itself into the politics of the country is also the most overresearched—and the least understood. This was the sharp deterioration in the relationship between South Africa's two white communities over the appellation "Uitlander" (literally "belonging to the outer lands" but more commonly translated as "foreigner"), which was applied to non-Afrikaner whites who had settled on the Witwatersrand ore reef following the discovery of gold in 1886. Their political recalcitrance, their greed, and their undoubted duplicity—essentially an unwillingness to countenance Afrikaner understandings of sovereignty—led to the infamous Jameson Raid of January 1896 that led to the South African War of 1899–1902.[67]

Significant? Why?

By drawing forward the Cape Colony and joining it to a fledgling state called the Transvaal Republic, the peace that ended that war provided the founding act of the state we know as South Africa. The boundaries of the South African state were drawn at the same moment, and it was upon these borders and understandings of sovereignty that other states in the region came to be formed. This political structure has endured longer than any others in the history of modern southern Africa.

The catalyst for this event was the right of migrants to participate in formal politics, in particular voting rights for Uitlanders in the Transvaal Republic. On this interpretation—and if the longevity of political institutions is a test of strength—the policy responses to migration offer great lessons to be drawn from South Africa's history.

Because this is so, and because the narrative on migration to the new South Africa is so manifestly emptied of history, it seems opportune to briefly recall the more common reasons for the movement of people during the nineteenth century. Consider these: overpopulation and destitution in certain parts of Europe—especially Ireland, Scotland, and southern Italy; the disorganization of traditionally accepted economies and the widening of a capitalist base following the Industrial Revolution and the flourishing of, particularly, British imperialism; and, of course, political and religious fallout, especially for minorities, both ethnic and religious.[68] Suitably adjusted for the considerations of time and space, each of these might apply to the question of migration to postapartheid South Africa.

A further lesson from the same rendition of history is instructive. In the simple-minded application of Myron Weiner's ideas to local conditions, South African pundits incessantly draw attention to two linked ideas: first, "to anti-foreigner sentiments [that] can have an adverse impact on domestic political stability";[69] and second, to the role that migrants could play in fostering the political interests of foreign powers within

South African sovereignty.[70] If we again adjust for time and space, President Paul Kruger of the Transvaal Republic must surely have been exposed to the same enclosing arguments that link sovereignty, threat, and state survival in the late Victorian era. If, as some are wont to suggest, migrants to South Africa are symptoms of the phenomenon that contemporary conversations call "globalization," then Kruger's security advisers may well have warned him that the Uitlanders (who, as he is once said to have famously proclaimed, "have come for our country") were symptoms of an earlier form of globalization, that is, imperialism.

Countless writers have shown that the presence of the Uitlanders reinforced Afrikaner identity, strengthening their affinity for the soil and national sovereignty and reinforcing the ideas that led to Afrikaner nationalism and eventually to apartheid.[71] As conditioning factors to group behavior, these myths certainly made it difficult to dislodge successive white leaders.

Interesting though it unquestionably would be, my objective here is not to set out further archaeology on this dimension of migration to South Africa; neither do I want to further pursue the issue of the relationship between South Africa's two white minorities. My purpose in using this methodology has been to establish that migration to the country and the contestations between two white groups—one loosely described as Dutch and the other as British—were central in the discourse that constructed the white state and its understandings of security. The wider point suggests the contingency of the idea of sovereignty in southern Africa, an idea, as this chapter aims to suggest, that constructed a state based on migration.

Migrancy in the Making of South African Power

We must finally turn to the movement of people and economic growth in southern Africa. This commenced with the discovery of minerals. And prosperity in South Africa and the region would not have followed had it not been for cheap migrant labor.

The central economic debate in the making of modern southern Africa (as we learned in Chapter 3) has been between two contesting schools: free markets and revisionist.[72] In the 1970s and 1980s, this contest proved to be the battle for the ideological soul of South Africa. Obviously, the Cold War setting in which this contestation took place accentuated the differences between the two positions and much inflated the claims of the protagonists. But divided and antagonistic though the two positions were, the one issue on which both could agree was that the South African economy was primarily built on cheap labor, most of which was migrant and much of it sourced from beyond South Africa's borders.

We have also learned that migration of people in the region is not new. According to Jonathan Crush, "Migration to South Africa from the region dates back more than 150 years. Indeed, long-distance migration for employment pre-dates the drawing of international borders by the colonial powers in the latter half of the nineteenth century."[73] And we have seen how the economic historian Francis Wilson reinforces the argument by pointing to the constitutive role of labor migration in the formation of a southern Africa of states: "One definition of the fourteen-country membership of the Southern African Development Community is that, apart from Mauritius, the Seychelles and the Democratic Republic of Congo, all the countries at one time or another provided labour to the [South African] gold mines."[74] This, the catalytic role of migration, especially labor migration, in the generation of wealth reveals that "great fiction of world politics, which has guided the actions of poets, priests, peasants and patriots since the nineteenth century, namely, that nations have the right, if not the destiny, to rule themselves, in their own nation-state, on their own territory."[75]

In southern Africa, but elsewhere on the continent, too, this fiction is largely explained by what some call a "regional economy." A range of instruments that facilitated the cross-border movement of people, however, speeded the building of a transregional economy in which South Africa is both beneficiary and facilitator. So, South African mining houses established a centralized recruiting agency (the Witwatersrand Native Labour Agency) to regulate the flow of migrant workers into the country's mines. This arrangement has enjoyed a special place in the affairs of southern Africa, a place beyond the normal trappings of sovereignty. Operating through a series of bilateral labor agreements between South Africa and select states, South Africa's mines have pursued what Crush helpfully calls their own "foreign policy."[76] The object of this policy was to ensure that migrant labor remained a commodity—easily managed, contained, and always at hand. Under this arrangement, migrant workers had to leave South Africa every year after eleven months and reapply for employment from their home countries. Moreover, their accommodation at the mines was provided by the mining industry, minimizing the responsibility of South Africa's government for their welfare as well as reducing the possibility of them filtering into the country's growing townships and thereby remaining permanently in the country. The migrant labor system built up South Africa's economy and helped the apartheid government maintain its racial exclusion policy. So, ironically, even though the migrant labor system seemed to violate orthodox interpretations of South Africa's sovereignty, it was in practice an important component of it.[77]

These migrant labor flows, with few and very particular exceptions, have continued throughout the course of political quarrels and constitutional change.[78] And notwithstanding the fury that has accompanied the flow of other migrants to the new South Africa, this dimension has not been subjected to public scrutiny or the machinations of a new generation of security state-makers. As a result, the new South Africa, like the old, has operated two migration gates—one on labor migration, which has been open, and another for other forms of migration, which has remained officially closed.

Continuous violations of sovereignty have been permitted in the pursuit of economic growth. These dispensations—for they are dispensed by power and ultimately serve wealth alone—are not unique to southern Africa. As Michael Shapiro has pointed out, states "have kept 'foreign populations' at a distance conceptually, [but] other practices of industrially and economically advanced states have produced flows of such people across state boundaries."[79]

The centrality of migrant labor in the making of southern Africa has been a focus of the revisionist school of regional historiography.[80] As a result, core discussions about processes of political change and, understandably, wealth distribution in both South and southern Africa have been driven by theoretically informed understandings.[81] These have sought to emphasize the mutually supportive, almost clientelistic, relations between organized business interests, especially mining, and state power in South Africa, explaining the region's state system through the optic offered by political economy.

The compulsion of labor to migrate, as we might call it, in southern Africa remains located in the folds of the historical bargain that has thwarted, in the pursuit of growth and accumulation, the border processes routinely required by the region's geopolitics. Its effect has been profound: southern Africa's people have continuously serviced South Africa's growing wealth and its assertion of political and strategic hegemony over the states that have been constructed around it.

Writing Migration as Neoapartheid

To mark migrant labor as a social category is to use the two migration gates, which we have already noted, as a basis for policy. If the region's mining economy required low-paid workers, they were recruited from the rural areas of both South and southern Africa. But the process of recruiting from the regional periphery—to use a trope from international political economy—to work at the region's core was not restricted to the mining sector alone.

As South Africa's wealth grew, more and more migrants were drawn into a moneyed economy. This quest for modernity in the region greatly ruptured traditional life patterns, as Ruth First noted. Indeed, most peasant households throughout southern Africa were wholly dependent on remittances from migrant labor; as a result, the system has fashioned every economic sector in southern Africa for more than a century.[82] Within apartheid South Africa, this process was eventually known by the spatial euphemism "urbanization"; in policy terms, particularly in South Africa itself, urbanization was witness, through the policy instrument known as influx control, to some of the bitterest forms of minority violence. As this chapter draws to a close, we must spend some time considering both the language and the long-term fruit of these policies.

Let me say again why it is that we are revisiting this manifestation of the unhappy past: my technique throughout this chapter—indeed, the entire book—has been to insert into the current debates a sense of a different past than those too readily celebrated by mainstream narratives. The argument suggests that amnesia—or rather remembering a certain, often distorted version of the past—has been an essential tool in the making of the new South Africa. But the practice of an amnesia that celebrates the ever-present opens, as Jürgen Habermas has warned, the space for corrosion of social purpose, for a failure to accept moral responsibility for the past. This has happened in South Africa on many occasions, and it continues with the issue of migration.

As policymakers and the policy community have searched for mechanisms to control the flow of migrants to the country, they have, as both Reitzes and Crush have suggested, looked backward to influx control—a mechanism of surveillance that stood at the core of apartheid. Caught in a maze of complex legislation, the policy aimed to keep blacks from entering the privileged world of white South Africa, except in particular circumstances. It rested on a series of utilitarian arguments caught in the words of a government commission, in 1922, which recommended that "natives should only be allowed to enter the urban areas to minister to the needs of the White man and should depart there from when he ceases so to minister."[83]

If (after violence) complex legislation was the core of social control in apartheid South Africa, then influx control was the true measure of the success or failure of the ideology. Its most notorious legal manifestation was the Section 10 legislation (1952) that denied the right to live in an urban area to any African who was not born there unless he or she had lived in the area for fourteen years or had worked for the same employer for ten years. The Section 10 legislation reduced to seventy-two hours (from fourteen days) the time allowed for blacks to find employment in urban areas.

At the root of these policies—cased in legal niceties—was a series of institutional concerns little different from those that today have securitized the issue of migration both in the new South Africa and in other parts of the world: fears of the spread of infection (especially HIV/AIDS), the possibility of depressed wages, fear of undercapitalized competition in the marketplace, and the prospect of declining property values.[84] These were at the core of the social concerns that first prompted, and then justified, influx control.

It was, however, in the everyday discourses of policymakers and politicians who analyzed the social world to be policed that the mechanisms of control were rooted and in which they remain located. The same disturbing language, the same knots of argument, are found in efforts of the press, policy analysts, and politicians to approach the issue of population flow into the new South Africa. Because this is a discussion on migration to South Africa and the role it has played in the making of the state, this analysis will be incomplete without hearing the distant voices that in the 1920s and 1930s drove South Africa's policy planners to initiate control over the influx of blacks to urban areas. Listening in to conversations on the "problem of native urbanization" seventy years later, Gary Minkley, in the South African port city of East London, writes of the inscription of "blots on [the] landscape" of white South Africa. "Social scientists, planners and administrators," he writes,

> Variously identified what was lived and perceived with what was conceived. In the very language of [these] investigations and reports, the "advance of irregular urbanization" and the "fungus of haphazard planning, insanitary housing, disease and crime" were associated with the increasingly dominant urban form of "pondokkie slum." Defined in these representations of space, in fact the congested point around which they all cohered, was a body and an identity "intimately acquainted with his wilderness," this "evil," this shapeless "fungal growth": "The chief offenders are Natives."[85]

With deliberate intent, I have traversed the literature that has, for roughly three decades, mapped and spoken to the issue of migration—

labor and other—to South Africa. The purpose has been not to reinforce the point made by Jonathan Crush that "the history of migration in Southern Africa is one of the most researched and well-documented academic fields in the region."[86] Rather, it has been to link this work, this insight, to contemporary readings of threat analysis in order to historicize it, so to speak.

The fusion of migration and security in postapartheid South Africa was inherent in the processes that drew South Africans toward a postapartheid identity and a policy repertoire that built on forms of social control associated with the country's apartheid past. But these mechanisms of command also carved out privileged space for South Africa, setting the country apart from its neighbors as a distinctive and privileged spatial and political entity.

Mainstream writing in international relations and in security studies has failed to map this—notwithstanding that the resulting sedimentation has determined the course of regional relations, including the ceaseless movement of people for more than a century. This approach to knowing has simply failed to recognize that "how things develop depends in part on *where* they develop, on what has been historically sedimented there, on the social and spatial structures that are already in place."[87]

So, notwithstanding its obvious relevance to an understanding of southern African affairs, orthodox international relations and security studies in South Africa have paid scant attention to the question of labor migration to South Africa.[88] Why? For one thing, these were considered a natural part of the regional intercourse, and when they were not they were explained by the special status of labor migration to South Africa's mines or by the idea of a regional economy.

The dominant picture of the region is a world of states, organized through an optic that has purported to provide the order described by Auguste Comte and the hierarchies offered by Charles Darwin. In this, South Africa was both anchor and guarantor of regional security. Certainly successive Western governments, as evidenced in Henry Kissinger's infamous National Security Study Memorandum 39 study, took the view that what mattered in southern Africa was the future of state security and South Africa, a compliant, preferably white-ruled, pro-Western capitalist country.[89] Mainstream security analysts in South Africa certainly followed this lead by northern epistemes. But as we have suggested here, there was another southern Africa: a region of people. Migration is a manifestation of this world. This was the world, historically speaking, of "low" politics, or the world of "no state" politics in southern Africa. It did not involve fundamental or key policy issues because, as an infamous paper on migration to South Africa once suggested, migrants were "ours for the taking."[90]

Understanding the deepening intensity of the social relations between South Africa and its neighbors was, mercifully, left to the work of others: musicologists, sociologists, anthropologists, and, in South Africa's case, social historians. Their labor mapped the region's rich texture and traced many of its hidden pathways, its hidden faces, and its hidden lifeworld. They have shown benefits aplenty, benefits that have escaped statist eyes. The centuries-long ebb and flow of migration to South Africa is deeply embedded in regional lore—its cultural networks in music, art, and litera-ture are integral to the vibrant social texture of southern Africa.[91]

Very little, I fear, was transmitted from this toward orthodox security studies, partly because the intellectual register of most of this other work was revisionist and therefore inherently critical of a regional subsystem that was dominated by a racist and capitalist state. In the world of security studies, capitalism in the region was a progressive force rather than a vio-lating and penetrating one, a force that brought in its wake development, stability, and security. But the other view saw things differently: as Patrick Harries notes in his fine study of Mozambican migration to South Africa's mines, this revisionist mode of inquiry believed that migrant labor, far from being a force for good, led to "exploitation and cognitive disloca-tion."[92]

This discussion would be incomplete without a return to Hannah Arendt, who knew life as refugee, as exile, and as a citizen of a new coun-try. In her essays in *The Origins of Totalitarianism,* in which she drew in part from the story of southern Africa that we have just traversed, she argued that the loss of political community, more than any other adminis-trative act, deprived individuals of their security, their humankind.[93] Fol-lowing her participation in the Zionist cause during and after World War II, the foreclosing processes of Zionist nationalism, upon which the state of Israel was founded, dashed her own hopes for humanity. In southern Africa, the reassertion of South Africanism appears to have rediscovered techniques of administration and control that, although used in the name of security, are witness to Arendt's catastrophic influence of the national-state system. But because this state system is built on violence, the horrific treat-ment of migrants to the new South Africa suggests that any other approach to the issue will be resisted with the same.

5

Ordering Southern Africa

A politician is a bird
A laugh is a water drop
And crying is believing
—Oskar Wolberheim

It appears perverse—no, mischievous—to generate critical questions on the multilayered processes that appear to be moving southern Africa toward peace.[1] After all, the subcontinent has been marked by violence for most of its recorded history. This being so, simple logic suggests that any (and every) impulse in the opposite direction should be encouraged. But as the endings of both the Cold War and apartheid have painfully taught, movement and remaking are not the same things.

This conjuncture provides the introduction to a chapter that demonstrates why the road to a lasting peace, let alone order, in southern Africa through the mechanisms offered by intervention—humanitarian, peacemaking, peacekeeping, peace enforcement, or any other—will prove difficult, if not impossible. My purpose is to interrogate the wider processes, and the discourses that underlie them, that have suggested that liberal internationalism, especially the new interventionism (to use the term captured in a title edited by James Mayall), offers southern Africa the means to peace through democratic ordering.[2]

Given that purpose generates much anxiety in this book, we must be clear about what it is that I am suggesting here. South Africa retains a capacity to visit great violence on southern Africa—this is obvious. Nevertheless, things are now patently different from apartheid's silent genocide of innocent people that was done in a backward region in the name of civilization and Christianity under cover of a military strategy called "forward." So to compare that wanton destruction, euphemistically called "destabilization," with the newness of the new situation appears to be grossly unfair. But much remains the same; this includes, as we will come to see, the new words that are read from old security scripts. These scripts continuously open both wounds and worry for South Africa's neighbors; add to this South Africa's propensity for war—and it has waged far more war than any other state in Africa—and the fears of southern Africans are plain. So let us be plain about my purpose in writing this chapter: supremacy and peace are not the same things in southern Africa, particularly because a propensity to violence has offered South Africa legitimacy in its own eyes and in the eyes of others.[3]

This reads like prejudgment. Thus it seems necessary to recall the purpose of the critical project. What is it that we are doing in this book? Why do we constantly overturn what seems logical? Why do we make mischief when we should be affirming policy masterstrokes? Why do we incessantly seek to insert the past in conditions that are patently new?

In an important essay, Craig Calhoun reminds us that critical theory demands critique in four senses:[4] (1) an engagement with the contemporary condition that is rooted in a belief that the existing state of affairs does not exhaust all possibilities; (2) an account of the conditions, historical and cultural, on which the theorist's own intellectual activity turns; (3) a continuous reexamination of categories and frameworks, including, of course, their historical construction (this is particularly important in this chapter); and (4) critical theory provides a confrontation with other forms of social explanation, showing up points, good and bad, and building toward stronger foundations for understanding and emancipation.

Affirming this teleology sets the scene for innovation. Unlike the others, this chapter is the site of a country study; accordingly, the argument builds toward a thick description (to summon an analytical construct from Clifford Geertz) of South Africa's armed 1998 intervention in Lesotho. This event was a decisive moment in the history of the region, but it was also an event symptomatic of the violence that is endemic in a social community built on sovereign states alone. Why?

Global change has had a profound effect on South Africa, as we have seen, but external perception of this change may well represent the true danger to the region's people. South Africa's residual strength, its technological highways and byways, its developed economy, its skilled people—all are often said to offer the proverbial beacon of hope to an otherwise doomed continent. This particular interpretation of the facts both of the region and of change has generated the following reductionist logic: southern Africa must anchor the entire African continent; the anchor's anchor—as it were—is South Africa, with the reflected glory of its successful transition, its freed-up, market-friendly economy, and, from a global security point of view, its strategic location. We have seen these features before, of course: once it was called the Nixon Doctrine—a ritual chaining of political capital generated anywhere in the South to the policy goals of the North—especially in security studies, where geopolitics counts for all.

The impulse to link northern security concerns to southern political capital was at the heart of two strategic doctrines: collective security and containment. The first had its roots in Immanuel Kant and Jeremy Bentham, but its emotional hold for the world of policy lies in its all-for-one and one-for-all appearance and the mythology of its first codification in the League of Nations. But the twist in the tail of this new (but very old) collective intent is to be found in its link to containment—a baseline Cold War policy, the fruit of George Kennan's labor on the thoughts of Clausewitz. Notwithstanding—no, because of—these impeccable credentials, any hope that these approaches to security could deliver emancipatory progress to the weak, the impoverished, and the South ends right here. Persuasive and pervasive, containment inflicts acquiescence on a case-by-case basis. And collective security turns today, as it has in the past, on the appeal offered by the status quo. Because the new interventionism is a derivative of both containment and collective security, we will soon see why they have come to have a profound effect on thinking on contemporary international affairs, even in distant southern Africa.

Dream, Diatribe, and Discourse

South Africa did not apply to join in the building of a new international order; more properly, it was catapulted into accepting a role. How? Suggestions that a postapartheid South Africa would inevitably be drawn into then–UN Secretary-General Boutros Boutros-Ghali's Agenda for Peace program were the subject of mooted discussion early in its transition, but like many issues, this one remained hanging during the welter of postnegotiation politics.[5] Among the many unanswered questions was this: Given its influence under the old regime, could South Africa's military accept a role under rule by the majority? Hidden behind this conditioning question are two others that will much interest us here: How professional was South Africa's military? And how would South Africa's military be called to account for its long years of destabilizing southern Africa?

This fate of South Africa's military may have been left to the longer process determined by legislation, bureaucracy, and reconciliation had the postapartheid government not been harassed into making a statement on the issue of its role in the new interventionism. How it happened can only be described as bizarre. Immediately upon the inauguration of Nelson

Mandela as South Africa's first democratically elected president in May 1995, Al Gore, the U.S. vice president representing the United States at the event, raised the issue of South African military support for multilateral efforts to restore order in Rwanda. Little might have been known of the request except that it took place during a photo shoot between Mandela and Gore—and that the request was played and replayed on national television!

Five paragraphs of background on the idea of intervention and the role of order in South Africa itself will help to situate Gore's audacious invitation. As violence deepened during the 1992 talks-about-talks stage of the transition, South Africa's future president, Mandela, called for the deployment of an international peacekeeping force to establish order in the country. Speaking after a tour of Alexandra Township, in northeastern Johannesburg, where more than thirty people had been killed and 2,600 rendered homeless in the preceding weeks, the ANC president said that he would be placing this demand urgently before the minority-ruled government. He also made it clear that the ANC would be approaching the UN Secretary-General and the secretary-general of the Organization of African Unity with a view to dispatching monitors to the nerve centers of violence (as he called them) in the provinces then called Transvaal and Natal.

Echoing Mandela's call a few weeks later, other antiapartheid leaders agreed to appoint a committee to facilitate international monitoring of violence in the country.[6] These concerns were the subject of a UN Security Council debate a few months later. On this occasion, Mandela stepped back from his earlier position and called instead for the appointment of a special representative to investigate violence and assist the United Nations in deciding the most appropriate measures to overcome it; he added that this could include monitoring of the situation on the ground. In a response to this speech, South Africa's foreign minister at the time, Pik Botha, signaled that the South African government was prepared to accept some monitoring role for the United Nations but stated that the Security Council could not take over the role of the government. Correctly, observers believed this to be a significant shift on the part of the minority regime, which until that point had wholly rejected external interference in the country's internal affairs. During the same month (July 1992), apartheid's security forces were exposed as being inadequate. The report of a commission headed by a respected judge, Richard Goldstone, suggested that the security forces had been responsible for rape and other assaults during domestic security operations.

In January 1994, the link between peacekeeping and order again entered the national discourse when the country's Transitional Executive Council sanctioned the formation of the 10,000-strong National Peace-keeping Force (NPKF), which would comprise members of the ANC's armed wing (Umkonto we Sizwe), members of the national security forces, and soldiers of the Bantustan militaries. Its task was to bring order to the troubled East Rand. To the considerable embarrassment of the sponsoring bodies (and, it has to be said, many of the country's citizens), the NPKF exercise dismally failed, and the efforts at domestic peacekeeping were discontinued; the NPKF forces were subsumed instead into a new defense force.[7] Nevertheless, debates around peacekeeping—its role in South Africa and in building a new international order—were firmly on the South African policy agenda.

To understand the significance of the issue, we must look more closely at postmodernity in the form of Michel Foucault. Distrustful of anyone who sees progress in social arrangements, Foucault prefers to see history as a series of dominations that discipline specific moments and ways of knowing.[8] It is to this latter point that we must now direct our attention.

At the moment of South Africa's transition, a relatively untested new think tank, the Institute for Defence Politics (IDP, as it was then called) openly propagated a role for the military beyond the one it had enjoyed during the apartheid years.[9] By successfully sustaining military culture beyond the end of apartheid, this group was set to become the country's postapartheid defense intellectuals. Staffed entirely by former officers of the apartheid defense force, with university degrees in military science, the IDP both constructed and controlled the meaning of security within the national discourse both during, and way beyond, the transition. Over time, and in the absence of a competing voice, the Institute for Security Studies (ISS), successor to the IDP, established a nearly exclusive right to speak about security in the name of South Africans.

In its earliest days as the IDP, it collaborated with other security state-makers like the South African Institute for International Affairs (SAIIA), the country's oldest institutionalized network of foreign policy expertise, which enjoyed financial support from South Africa's business community. In the new South Africa, the SAIIA had crossed the divide between a traditional preoccupation with diplomatic issues to assertively focus on security issues, regional and other. Through the public interventions of both the IDP and the SAIIA, the location of the national security was regularized as common sense—the methodology of both bodies was alarmingly simple: threats were posed by any deviation from the norm that linked scientistic geography and realist theory to the imperative of market economics.[10]

The role played by these knowledge-based networks in the making of southern African security issues has been largely neglected, but some new work promises to change this.[11] However, epistemic communities have been well theorized in other settings, particularly in the United States.[12] Such work suggests that these groupings, through a rarefaction of their own knowledge and its incessant technical reworking, can become distanced from other forms of knowing, especially alternative lifeworlds.[13] Nevertheless, their impact on the world of policy is significant. Calhoun notes that their interventions remove social decisions from the rational-critical discourse of "citizens in the political public sphere," and make them the "province of negotiation among bureaucrats, credential experts, and interest group elites."[14] When we briefly consider South Africa's decision to purchase sophisticated armaments, this very phrase will cross our paths again. For now, our concern is with tracing continuity of policy purpose in South Africa's security epistemes.

The work of the ISS has patently influenced policymaking and public opinion in defense as well as security matters. An evaluation of a training for peace project in southern Africa reports that an "interlocutor in [the country's] defence ministry confirmed that the ISS contributed tremendously to the rationalisation of thinking in the . . . defence establishment through providing them with a better appreciation of South Africa's role in the African region."[15] In contrast to this official applause, alternative and critical interpretations of the same issues were increasingly starved of the foreign funding that they then had enjoyed during, and prior to, the country's transition.[16] In addition, the sheer output of work on intervention, in particular, suggests how security in the South all too often is driven by the fashions of policymakers and by northern funding. The lesson is clear: in times of flux, security agendas easily fall into the hands of those with credentialed expertise and those willing to secure the status quo.[17]

There is a thread to the making of South Africa's security past here. We must briefly follow it in order to make another point about method. If academic work on terrorism was a growth industry in the 1970s, then work on forms of liberal interventionism became the growth area in the 1990s.[18] And if the South African work on terrorism was mired in a problem-solving mode (to use Robert Cox's term again), then South African work on intervention has again seen the same. This method quickly fixes the limits of a problem bringing technology and the techniques of management to mediate between a limited number of variables. Its social purpose is plain, as is its ideological intent: suspend any possible negotiation of the structural constraints to change in order to ensure continuity.[19] Like all status quo work, it fails to look beyond the immediate categories or, in Hegel's vocabulary, its preoccupation is with the immediate, thereby demonstrating no understanding of the issues at hand.

This approach to securing international order was bolstered by the staged reality (to use Jürgen Habermas's term) of interventionist wars, like the Gulf War and the conflict in Bosnia. These suggested that order in the new world was both imperative and necessary, even if that meant exercising violence to establish it. Given this, the issue of the new South Africa's compliance—no, its duty—to the emerging global priorities flowed without a pause to reflect on the lessons that might be drawn from its own past in the region. But if duty represented one side of this prosthetic understanding of global politics, the other was the reassertion of the old realist idea of threat.

Let me repeat a refrain here, one that is to be found in many other parts of this book: South Africa's transition must be judged as a lost opportunity to recast the region and its security in fundamental ways—a failure to seek a new future for the region beyond the geopolitical framings provided by Westphalia in southern Africa. At the very moment when intellectual energy should have been devoted toward rethinking long-held ideas on peace—on the very idea of region—policy discourse fell back on old security habits, on constructing southern Africa and its people as an eschatological threat.[20] Old ideas were resuscitated by the continuities offered by amnesia, at home and in the region, and old forms of security policy were recycled by the reductionism of rational choice theory. Those who made the new South Africa's regional security policy were not encouraged to reach outside a repertoire of old choices for the new times that international politics seemed to be enjoying. There was, as a result, little chance or even the inclination to reassess the utility of the conceptual equipment, or the strategic logic, that had driven South Africa's interventionist policies in the region for more than two decades. In Raymond Williams's terms, then, there was no effort to contextualize the language of intervention in the history of the region and the history of intervention in the language of the region. As a result, South Africa's postapartheid approach to the region was grounded in three fatal certainties: clarity, surveillance, and discipline—a panoptical mythologized by Bentham, theorized by Foucault, and perfected by apartheid, a system of certainty that allows domination and order to produce and reproduce themselves without having to constantly fight to maintain their hegemonic status.[21]

This approach to securing southern Africa froze, rather than liberated, the region within the policy routines imposed by sovereignty, including the notion that ordering it (to use part of a phrase from Bill Maynes) was compellent.[22] Therefore, it was entirely appropriate to use force to fashion the internal behavior of recalcitrant neighbors, especially—no, because—they were weak. This is an important idea for the remainder of this chapter, as we shall see, but inserted here it helps to draw the particular of the regional toward the general of the global.

The link between violations of sovereignty and the norms of the new world order was first proclaimed and delivered by the United States, whose violation of sovereign others was based on expediency and justified by one consideration only: national interest. Although sanctioned by the Monroe Doctrine of 1823, the motives for individual U.S. interventions during the Ronald Reagan years came to differ—there were almost as many motives as there were interventions! But it was the U.S. experience during the Gulf War that narrowed a gap between its own interests and those of the United Nations on the issue of intervention. And it was in this closing that the managerialist politics of the new interventionism was distilled from the ideas of collective security: here, too, the idea of collective action was drawn toward a new form of containment. As Jürgen Habermas noted at the time:

> The politically decisive distinction exists between all those who take the UN's jurisdiction seriously and, therefore, want to permit participation only in operations under UN command, as opposed to those who want to procure a broader political and military room for action for individual nations or union of nations.[23]

Under his doctrine of a new world order, President George H.W. Bush provided differing renditions of the same clash to justify interventions: Operation Provide Comfort was ostensibly launched to restore the sovereignty of oil-rich Kuwait, Operation Restore Hope to reconstitute the sovereignty of distant, dusty Somalia. So both the theory and practice of violating sovereignty, as well as the sense of confusion experienced at the end of the Cold War, dragged a perilously weak United Nations into domestic politics in various corners of the world. But as many had once warned early seafarers, here be dragons. As the new interventionism was being applauded across the globe, many forgot an old adage: "ideas will prostrate themselves before interests every time."[24]

The idea of contributing to a new order for the world resonated well with South Africa's postapartheid government, a government that was coming to occupy a strong position, certainly symbolically, in the affairs of what was increasingly called "global affairs" (as opposed to international affairs). Given the alternatives witnessed in places like Rwanda and the former Yugoslavia, the political capital from South Africa's "miracle" transition and its residual strength in its region made the drift toward global engagement appear almost natural—a call to global duty, even.

By October 1994, six months after South Africa's new government was in power, the moment had arrived: Foreign Minister Alfred Nzo stated that South Africa's role in invention was (as he put it) "inevitable."[25] This idea was not uncontested in the country, however.[26] The cabinet of South Africa's Government of National Unity was divided on the issue.[27] Both the National Party and the Inkatha Freedom Party—both with a traditionally hard-line record on security—opposed sending South Africans to join UN blue helmets in Angola, for instance. South Africa's ruling African National Congress took a different position. The defense minister and his deputy favored intervention, arguing that South Africa—through apartheid's policy of destabilization—had contributed to the appalling conditions in Angola. The press noted, however, that both the minister and his deputy felt a moral debt to assist a country that had hosted their own forces during the struggle for liberation.

We shall presently appreciate the policy importance of this development within the country and in the region, but I must first reach toward external perceptions of southern Africa that confirmed South Africa as its leader. Why was this?

Both the insertion and the assertion of South African power in the region had guaranteed more continuity than change. The ending of apartheid confirmed the region's geopolitical structure—a structure that relied on a hierarchical framing to give it form and, indeed, purpose. This view of South Africa's international position resonated with another, more operable response to the post–Cold War condition: the pivotal states theory, first advocated in the establishment journal *Foreign Affairs*.[28] There is a hidden link here between the idea of pivotal states and the theory of hegemonic stability, conceived first by political economists in their efforts to assert the power of the dollar in the early and mid-1970s, by drawing closer to security studies and regime construction by realists like Steven Krasner and Robert Keohane. The hypothesis is worth repeating because it adds credence to the role that South Africa (it was hoped) would play. Stable international regimes (especially in the regional setting) depend on a hegemon setting rules and norms and then superintending their operation by using its capability to encourage other members to work under its hegemonic power.[29]

This particular rendition of global affairs confirmed the notion that South Africa alone was the region's hope and, by extension, that southern Africa was Africa's hope.[30] Notwithstanding the terror that South Africa had inflicted on the region's people through the long years of destabilization, this reassertion of social Darwinism meant that its armed power would not be formally truncated, as had the power of both Germany and Japan, in circumstances not dissimilar, following World War II. This preserved South Africa as the region's unipolar moment (as the neorealist Michael Mastanduno might have suggested following his ideas of the United States after the Cold War) or its "great power in the heart of a region" (as Habermas insisted on describing the post–Cold War position of Germany).[31] This reinscription of southern Africa's traditional hierarchy of states was to have major implications for the conduct of South Africa's policy in the region. Finally, the international community confirmed the military's role in the region's political future (as we witnessed in U.S. vice president Gore's request that South Africa assist in the intervention in Rwanda). But the force of defense and security epistemes undoubtedly smoothed the force of this acceptance. As a result, South Africa's military was drawn ever closer into the arc of policymaking that was setting an agenda based on the premises of intervention.

In the region, however, this drift in events was read not as a moment of celebration but against the high cost of experience. As a result, the ease of South Africa's international acceptance compounded, rather than decomposed, the sense of urgency offered by South Africa's power over the local and certainly reinforced, rather than relaxed, the idea that South Africa would exercise its old dominion over the region. The metaphors of war used by South Africa to describe its new engagement with the region certainly perpetuated these residual fears. As David Simon has shown, South Africa's postapartheid business community drew more upon military images than marketing ones to explain their expansion into the region.[32]

What had enabled the region's unhappy past to return in this way? In a moment of intense political change, South African policymaking readily embraced the hegemonic policy ideas represented by the idea of a new world order. On numerous occasions, Nelson Mandela's speechwriters cued the phrase—"the new world order"—in for him. In obvious ways, of course, these policy ideas would represent a departure from the country's unhappy, violent relationship with the region, but as had happened far too often in the region, another had replaced one conceptual tyranny. The new order in southern Africa was a reassertion of South Africa's hegemony in regional affairs, particularly as they related to security. The brutality associated with apartheid's regional strategy of destabilization had been replaced by a South Africa that offered the region the seemingly endless opportunities articulated under the emerging idea of globalization. If the new interventionism was aimed at compliance and appropriate domestic behavior, the new South Africa was well positioned to play its role—indeed, to do its duty.[33]

South Africa's freedom of action in the region seemed inevitable in other areas, too. In the age of neoliberal economics, responsibilities as well as advantages were quickly passed to pivots in the poorer corners of the globe. If constitutional change had shifted South Africa from international pariah to participant (to use the title of a book published by the SAIIA), then belonging to the emerging global economy was an essential ingredient of responsible international behavior.[34] In applauding the country's constitutional change and South Africa's swift reinsertion into international relations, Conrad Strauss, a leading South African banker and then national chair of a security episteme in the making, the South African Institute for International Affairs, put things this way:

> After the long isolation of the sanction years, South Africa can now as a full democracy, rejoin the community of nations with pride. This . . . challenge . . . must also be seen as an opportunity for South Africa's business community to play its full part, alongside the Government of National Unity, in *conceiving new policies for this new age*. These policies will have to *synchronise our realities* with those of the world in which trade and global competitiveness are as important as the political dimensions of diplomacy.[35] (Emphasis added)

With its strong commitment to the opportunities purportedly offered by the marketplace, this view captures the tenor of much South African writing and thinking on diplomacy in the early and mid-1990s. The argument quickly moved between the celebration associated with endings—Cold War, apartheid—and the triumphs associated with new beginnings—an order of "realities" in which peace, order, market prosperity, and democracy were seamlessly linked. What secured these discourses, of course, were the unquestioned assumptions associated with the idea of new forms of freedom, on the one hand, and the subterranean message of military power on the other.

In the policies of the new, as in the old, the language of opportunity, of freedom, of emancipation invariably hid an iron fist. But where was the license—the legitimacy—for South Africa to discover the region it had so wantonly destroyed to be found? In the idea of intervention. It is to this issue that we now turn.

Intervention: The Pathway from Pariahhood

First to the compulsory genuflection that has run the course of this writing: the region's transformation from war to peace seems astounding. In the not-too-distant past—when apartheid scuttled the Commonwealth Eminent Persons' Mission to South Africa—it appeared that southern Africa was programmed for destruction. Today, things seem very different. But what does this tell us? Echoing a phrase we already used, this may say more about the failure of international relations to explain the region than it says about southern Africa itself. Set in any comparative framing, for example, the region's turnabout appears quite commonplace, ranking no higher than the democratic transformation of Latin America in the 1980s or the end to the divide in Europe after the Cold War.

A more critical reflection shows, however, that any lasting achievement in the region's struggle for peace is less certain. As the twenty-first century opened, a three-line setback for the proverbial whips of democracy occurred in Namibia, in Zambia, and in Zimbabwe. In each, the organic crisis of state legitimacy—not to mention the economic deprivation of citizens and the horror of the HIV/AIDS pandemic and the specter of starvation—suggests how the region's state system is wanting notwithstanding the panacea promised by liberal democracy and access to markets. In each country, the day-to-day lives of people appear captive to the immediate power of mafioso militaries or mobster corporations, and political parties have turned to Nic Wheeler's idea of state gangsterism.[36] It is certainly true that valiant efforts—in the press, in the courts, among nongovernmental organizations—continue to keep the idea of freedom, self-determination, even emancipation alive, but the region's recent report card is, shall we say, poor. This is in sharp contrast to the optimism of the early and mid-1990s, when the prospects for a new kind of regionalism seemed to spur—and be spurred by—the idea that the new world order could deliver boundless opportunities to southern Africa.

For instance the ending of decades of conflict over Namibia in 1989 was considered the beginning of a quick march to democratic polls in southern Africa under the closing stages of Samuel P. Huntington's idea of a Third Wave, a reworking by U.S. political and constitutional science of neo-Kantianism.[37] The Namibian settlement involved the United Nations, through the UN Transition Assistance Group (UNTAG), in a supervisory role, even though power, exercised by an administrator, remained vested in the authority of the apartheid state. Although much lauded, the UN role in Namibia was weak and fragmentary; for example, even before the all-important cease-fire, UNTAG's participation was cut back due to budgetary constraints.[38] Elsewhere in the region, a similar pattern of democracy by negotiation and external intervention seemed to promise success. Accords signed in Rome involved the United Nations both in a demobilization process in Mozambique and, immediately thereafter, in supervising both parliamentary and presidential elections. This UN effort was known as the UN Operation in Mozambique and involved some 7,500 UN troops and 350-odd military observers.[39] In a third regional conflict, Angola, the United Nations by the end of the 1990s had thrice been involved: twice UN troops were deployed on the ground. In the end peace, when it came, did so with the death of apartheid's longtime ally, Jonas Savimbi.

This conjuncture between the promise—indeed, the reality—of peace, order, and external intervention powerfully influenced the search for security throughout the 1990s. Multilateralism, as we have seen from our brief reference to the Gulf War, seemed the only secure pathway toward a new way for the world. This moment promised, as Francis Fukayama pointed out, endless economic opportunities and world order through liberal democracy.

The task of carrying the message to the region was left to what Gramsci famously called "organic intellectuals," whose responsibility was to secure the status quo in the midst of political change. Encouraged by the funding offered by foreign donors, especially from the well-disposed Nordics, South Africa's security and defense epistemes turned their considerable energy, their organizational skills, and their focused attention to the business of authoring a strategic mission for postapartheid South Africa.[40] But it was a mission with two ancillary goals: first, within its unfolding in southern Africa it offered the means to mediate the multiple tensions involved in the amalgamation of previously warring militaries; second, it ensured that the military remained a force to help build the South African nation. The former was firmly rooted in the now familiar frame provided by Robert Cox's problem-solving theory, and the latter was derivative of a strain of modernization theory that insisted that strong militaries were integral to the making of third-world nations.

However, many questions remained unanswered. But how could intervention in the region operate? Who would make the decisions? What role would there be for the recently refurbished regional community, now operating as the SADC? What role for the residual lever for regional security—the Frontline States? We now turn to answer these questions, and as we do so we are initially briefed on our country study.

At a meeting of the Frontline States organization in Harare in June 1994, South Africa's new president, Nelson Mandela, declared that the country would play a role in helping to solve the region's problems. This was the first public signal that postapartheid South Africa could actively intervene in southern Africa. The meeting decided to send a small committee to review the deteriorating constitutional crisis in the enclave state of Lesotho.[41] Anticipating this move, in January that same year the countries of the region had taken provisional steps toward the formation of a regional task force that could be used in regional peacekeeping.

The catalyst for this decision had been the smoldering crisis in Lesotho.[42] Using preventative diplomacy, rather than peacekeeping, as the point of intervention, this early initiative registered some success.[43] In concert, three presidents—South Africa's Nelson Mandela, Botswana's Quett Masire, and Zimbabwe's Robert Mugabe (some analytical accounts insist on calling them "the Troika")—agreed on a course of action that helped to return the elected government to power in Lesotho the following month.[44] The path to the Harare decision and the agreement to act was, however, strewn with rumor.[45] But—more importantly, perhaps—it witnessed the use of intimidation by South Africa.[46] The country's crack paratroopers, who are stationed in the neighboring Free State Province, were dropped in full sight of the citizens of Lesotho's capital, Maseru, on the South African side of the border; this was a rerun of an old apartheid ruse. In retrospect, however, it was the nature of the intervention that effectively sowed the seeds of further conflict because it reinstated the Basutoland Congress Party as the country's government, a move that made the three intervening powers—South Africa, Zimbabwe, and Botswana—the guarantors of the country's democracy and its orderly behavior in the region and, indeed, in the global community.[47]

Although highlighting the contradiction between preventative diplomacy and the theory of a democratic peace, the move certainly mirrored forms of intervention that were emerging elsewhere in the international community. This was to be confirmed weeks later by the direct U.S. intervention in Haiti to restore the government of the ousted Jean-Bertrand Aristide (an action in which South Africa was also invited to participate). Southern Africa's newly found confidence to effectively deal with regional issues, however, was a function of South Africa's presence. But something more was at work: international legitimacy, not to mention credence, was delivered to the intervention by the active role played by Nelson Mandela. This personalization of regional multilateralism was, however, largely missed by those who hailed the Troika's intervention as an important development in the making of regional order.

But intervention by hegemons, the record shows, is seldom without a price. The question that was not asked at the time was this: Where would all this end? If truth were told, the intervention relied upon an accord among partners with quite disparate goals and ambitions. Nevertheless, so encouraged were the Troika by their early success, and by the applause their action received at home and abroad, that in February 1996, when the region faced a deteriorating political situation in Swaziland, they discussed the possibility of launching a Lesotho-type initiative for dealing with the political conflict in that country. The message was abundant and clear: the leaders of southern Africa's strongest states, led by South Africa, believed that intervention offered a wholly appropriate means to promote democracy, stability, and regional community. As Nelson Mandela noted at the time, "Southern Africa cannot sit back and allow the subversion of democracy in any of our countries."[48]

But the position was stalked by paradox. There is very little real sense of community between southern Africa's states. This may again sound mischievous: after all, the region's states claim to be joined in the Southern African Development *Community*, and a treaty, protocols, a sense of renewal, and even a few buildings attest to their commitment. So, how are we to understand this? Constructivist theory suggests that what binds community is not structures—treaties, protocols, and buildings or even renewal—but the subjective idea of feeling part of a community. Sadly, this, above all else, seems absent within the regional community organizations in southern Africa. Using Ferdinand Tönnies's 1887 binary of gesellschaft and gemeinschaft as taxonomy, the SADC is not located where social relations are intimate, enduring, or multistranded but near the former, gesellschaft, where social relations are impersonal, anonymous, and contractual.

Appreciating this reinforces a hard truth about southern Africa: notwithstanding postapartheid undertakings to cooperate, SADC is a creature of Westphalia—a system

> of sovereign states which [settles its] differences privately and often by force (or threat of force) which [engages] diplomatic relations but otherwise [pursues] minimal cooperation; which [seeks] to place their own national interest above all others; and which [accepts] the logic of the principle of effectiveness, that is, the principle that might eventually makes right in the international world—that appropriation becomes legitimation.[49]

This absence of intimacy explains why the region's interstate politics, its sense of regional security, its search for order have relied on conflict and preparing for it as its raison d'être. Does this sound mischievous, or misdirected, or misinformed—even, perhaps, trite?

Yes, if the discourses of interstate community building in the region are taken at face value. Let me explain. While the events in both Lesotho and Swaziland were unfolding, the renamed and redirected SADC was experiencing its golden age. Discussions around its future, in particular, flourished, and it seemed as if South Africa's transition would resuscitate the region and stabilize the SADC's identity as southern Africa's hope for Africa's future. As a result, the long-anticipated social Darwinist moment in southern Africa seemed to be at hand. In 1995, foreign ministers from the European Union and SADC met, for example, in Berlin, where a hundred years earlier the convention that sanctioned the division of Africa had taken place. At this gathering, ministerial groupings agreed to promote closer trade and political, regional, and economic contacts.[50] SADC was also active in a range of new projects—economic and other—and was also looking toward deepening its role in the security sector, even establishing its own army.[51] It was commonplace at the time to situate SADC in a world of networked regionalisms that seemed—effortlessly, almost—to be building toward globalization by regional multilateralism.[52] But Tönnies's binary ceaselessly cursed SADC's hope for a sure identity, a strong region, and a golden future.

The failure to recognize that the SADC was less than it pretended to be eventually corroded the media hype and propaganda that were frantically being used to build its image—and South Africa's averred pivotal role in it. As the SADC's limitations became increasingly obvious, another tack was adopted to build the region. Frantic efforts were made to argue, by analogy, that SADC was a primitive form of European integration.[53] Few who suggested this, however, paused to remember that comparing regional experiences is fraught with methodological problems.[54] The hard truth we have already seen is that beyond the rhetorical gestures at bonding, southern African states are not prepared to share sovereignty, to become a community, even a security community. Why? The history of the SADC suggests that the organization was conceived as a collective attempt to defend the sovereignty of individual states from apartheid's destabilization. In this spirit, it is sobering to recall that the first binding agreement that SADC reached to share sovereignty was the 1995 agreement on water that was entered in the midst of a devastating drought. This accomplishment was, however, only possible after Nelson Mandela, South Africa's new president, had warned the meeting about undue speed toward full integration; this, he put it, might encourage "negative migration trends in capital skills and labour."[55] We return to this issue in Chapter 6 when we turn to the role of water in the making of a new region.

This unfolding of events seemed to support an old notion: the region's hegemon was unwilling to share sovereignty, although it might be willing, if necessary, to incorporate weaker states in order to protect its interests.[56] The triumphalist face of southern Africa suddenly seemed to show all the region's old characteristic—rank displays of power from the most powerful! For all the talk of change, as it has been from the onset of the region's recorded history, the affairs of southern Africa continued to pivot around the strongest player. This was, and remains, South Africa—the first in a community of unequals.

The notion of ordering southern Africa, of achieving regional peace, of restoring democracy, of freeing markets—or a host of other new images and clichés—is fatally wedded to a long-established hierarchy of power that continues to dog the region and its affairs. This explains why, more than a decade after change was ignited in South Africa, significant corners of the region are still at war. Decades of strife have left a legacy of deep mistrust and crippling misunderstanding: as economic circumstances deteriorate and small arms are readily at hand, prolonged—indeed, renewed—conflict appears inevitable throughout the subcontinent.[57]

Why conflict persists is a core question for policymakers. But answering the question is impossible without standing outside the Westphalian framings that policymakers use to construct, describe, and prescribe the region and its ways. As a result, policy prescriptions constructed around intervention are not easy—no, they are simply impossible.

The Unstated Problem of Memory

The idea that South Africa should be interventionist in southern Africa has two roots. First, the end of the Cold War had delivered a moment to reconstruct the world around a series of liberal principles, especially democracy and the opportunities of the marketplace. If these were necessary principles for the establishment of a new order in the world, intervention in the cause of peace, democracy, and humanity was the ready means to do this. The second root believed that South Africa had a pivotal role to play in ordering "its" region. Both were regularized within public debate and embedded in policy priorities of the new South Africa—a process that was smoothed with the assistance of externally funded projects that supported defense and security epistemes. These formed the background to the acceptance by South Africa's cabinet, in October 1998, of a white paper on South African participation in international peace missions.[58] I want to use Habermas's words on the same policy moment in Europe to make this point about South Africa. The postapartheid government was "under pressure from the military, which has lost sight of the enemy and the image of the enemy, and which wants to compensate for the military's loss of purpose by acquiring new international theatres of operation."[59] We have, however, again reached ahead of ourselves, and we must return to the unfolding of wider events.

The deepening international debates on peacekeeping in Somalia and in the Balkans, especially the legal justification and technical appeal of those operations, flooded professional and popular literature in South Africa, just as it did elsewhere. This regularization of state violence was nervously watched by South Africa's neighbors. Would the region's hegemon be benign or assertive? Would it be drawn backward to its traditional pattern of regional aggression in the cause of new world ordering? These questions could never be answered to the satisfaction of southern Africans, of course, because who could say how much transformation of South Africa's military was sufficient to purge it of its dark past?

For its part, South Africa's military, encouraged—indeed, assisted— by the defense intellectuals, was at pains to stress that the declared goal in peacekeeping, both in the region and elsewhere, was professional. In testimony before South Africa's Truth and Reconciliation Commission, military leaders suggested that even under apartheid they were a professional military. But these claims invariably ignored a fundamental point: South Africa's military singularly failed to anticipate the collapse of Soviet communism and entirely misread the nature of the changes within their primary domestic and international adversary—the exiled ANC. So questions of their professionalism should have prompted Jean Baudrillard's question: "If their culture was so mistaken about others, it must also be mistaken about itself?"[60] Issues of military culture and professionalism need to be called into deeper question by academic commentators as well as the press. As the tragic lesson of experienced peacekeepers—the Canadians, for example—in both Cambodia and Somalia shows, even the most experienced professionals can commit gross violations of human rights.

Cast within the unfolding discourse around intervention, South Africa's future role in its desire to anchor southern Africa seemed perfectly reasonable. But what was to be done with the historical record?

Like the U.S. experience in Vietnam, South Africa's decades-long frontier war, especially its most recent phase (destabilization) in southern Africa, was increasingly lost to public consciousness.[61] As questions were raised over South Africa's military past in the region, policy discourse drew upon the comfort and assurance of the idea of professionalism. The sense of continuity and the promise of progress this offered crowded out the space that political change offered for new understandings of the region and examining the reasons for a violent past. Postapartheid policy on the ordering of southern Africa, therefore, is located in set-piece understandings of the region's history. Located in a frame that privileges geopolitics, states, and the system they construct are the only—indeed, the natural—means to explain community in the region. In this framing, order in the region can only be an order that supports the interests of the hegemon, and structures that sustain the hegemon's regional position must enjoy precedence above all others.

One is South Africa's armaments industry: its potential to create jobs, garner foreign exchange, and secure South Africa's technological superiority not only in southern Africa but also throughout the continent.[62] There is no place within the immediate discussion to rehearse arguments around the holding power of this industry, but we must note that South African arms have helped fuel conflicts in South Africa's near abroad.[63] But the irony is this: the same industry has been said to set South Africa's national interests in southern Africa.[64]

This historicizing of events yields an alternative rendition of South Africa, the region, and, indeed, the world. South Africa's involvement in southern Africa, especially if it required intervention to secure order, reinforced the security discourses, and the economic power, of the very state that created the conditions for the construction of national borders in southern Africa. So, however welcome and celebrated South Africa's transition might have been, it is not the end of southern Africa's history. The triumphalism of change in South Africa, and the idea of a new beginning, have made it difficult to see that embedded deep within the same state "is a strategic culture which has not changed [and as] the state reaches into its collective memory it [is discovering] that routine responses to challenges are more . . . attractive . . . than even the acknowledgement of the necessity to think long and hard about creative responses."[65]

Nevertheless, South Africa's peace warriors, to coin a phrase suitable, perhaps, only for this moment, increasingly drew from recent international experience to establish their interventionist credentials. More than anything else, their approach championed the technical aspects of the "mission"—casting intervention in narrow nonpolitical terms—a process that sanitizes its true purpose. This approach, quite obviously, avoids the necessity of asking the important political and moral questions that are at the base of the new interventionism, as they are in other types of international politics. So, in a twist of logic, the political change enabled South

Africa's warriors to reinforce the self-same Clausewitzian logic that served the country so well, so efficiently, in the past.[66] Intervention is old regional politics by a different name!

This chapter has run nearly three-quarters of its path, and, as promised, we must turn to the country study. We have already opened the box that is marked "Lesotho," but in two sentences let us remind ourselves of the surrounding circumstances. A troika of regional presidents intervened in August 1995 to reestablish democracy to the country; their approach relied on restoring the embattled Basutoland Congress Party to government. But I promised then that the intervention would not end the long-simmering conflict in that country, and I want to complete the immediate story before drawing some lessons from the country study.

So Far from God

In August 1988, three years after the constitutional intervention, violent protests broke out in the capital of Maseru.[67] These were sparked by allegations over electoral fraud in the general election that had taken place in May.[68] On September 11, the commander of the Lesotho Defence Force (LDF), the national army, announced his resignation. This followed his detention earlier in the same day, together with a number of other senior officers, by a group of juniors acting in support of the demands of the protesters. This mutiny deepened the confusion in the country; by September 16 civil servants had joined the protesters, and all government offices had been closed. This turmoil was aggravated by the delayed publication of the report of an investigative team, the Langa Commission, headed by a South African judge, which had been established to examine the claims of fraud in the troubled May election. The commission's report was eventually released on September 17. In important ways, however, the findings of the report had been discredited way before its release. South African media, for example, suggested that SADC heads of state had interfered with the contents of the report.[69] Upon its release, the Langa Report (as it was called) confirmed these suspicions by acknowledging that the election had been marred by serious "irregularities and discrepancies" but ambiguously declared that there were "insufficient grounds" to annul the poll. It must be said that not a little of the symbolism in the relationship between South Africa and Lesotho is located in the fact that South Africa's minister of safety and security, not foreign affairs, led the delegation that delivered the Langa Report to Lesotho's government and the country's people.[70] If there had been a hope that it would quell the anger of the protesters, let alone restore order, this was mistaken. Inconclusive and vague, the report fueled anger and led to further unrest. Additional discussions followed over possible solutions to halt a deeper deterioration of the situation; South Africa's minister of safety and security was again the messenger declaring that a military intervention in the country would be the last, least desirable solution to the crisis.[71] This was September 21.

What happened next might have been drawn from Europe in the late 1930s. Lesotho's prime minister requested military intervention from the four SADC states—Botswana, Mozambique, South Africa, and Zimbabwe—which had sponsored the Langa inquiry. Its purpose? To stabilize the situation in the country.[72] Reflecting on the event, Khabele Matlosa notes that the prime minister's letter "graphically [painted] a picture of impending civil war in Lesotho and a covert military coup in the making."[73] The request was not without its own constitutional dilemma, however: it was made without the knowledge of the country's king, Letsie III, who was described by the prime minister in his request to the foreign government's as "part of the problem."[74]

Early on the morning of September 22, some 600 South African troops entered Lesotho. Poorly briefed, they met an unexpected resistance from dissident members of the defense force as well as from civilians outraged by their presence. Not until September 24 did the South African National Defence Force secure the LDF barracks, the royal palace—the main site of the demonstrations—and, some tens of kilometers away, the Katse Dam, located on the Lesotho Highlands Water Scheme, which supplies water to South Africa. It remains unclear, at this writing, whether the attack on the latter facility was part of the original mission. Strong rumor suggests that the decision to target the dam was made on the spur of the moment. In an email exchange on this point in April 2002, my friend and sometime collaborator, Khabele Matlosa—citizen of Lesotho and scholar of southern African affairs—pointed out:

> I, personally, would not go along with the rumour that the decision to attack the military garrison on the Lesotho Highlands Water project was made on the spur of the moment. It was part of the grand scheme and probably at the heart of the entire SANDF intervention for South Africa had to first and foremost guard its economic and strategic interest around the joint water project even before being concerned about political stability in Lesotho. This observation reinforces the argument by many conflict resolution scholars that major conflicts in the world at large and Southern Africa in particular since the collapse of Apartheid and Cold War are primarily resource-based conflicts. From this angle, I would argue strongly that the South African military intervention in Lesotho

was driven by its interest in the Lesotho Highlands Water Project first and foremost. If this is the case then, the attack on the military personnel guarding the dam could not have come by accident; and the fact that the project was the very first target of the entire military operation makes perfect sense in terms of the hierarchy of South African interests in Lesotho.[75]

Nine South African soldiers and fifty-eight members of the LDF died in the fighting, as did some forty-seven civilians. The intervention was justified by the South African home affairs minister, Chief Mangosuthu Buthelezi, and the acting state president, who had made the decision, as necessary to restore order in Lesotho following the alleged army mutiny.[76] (South Africa's president, Nelson Mandela, was in Canada on an official visit, and Deputy President Thabo Mbeki was in Malaysia attending the Commonwealth Games.) On September 24, South Africa's cabinet endorsed the decision, calling it "principled and correct," and congratulated the South African troops for the "firm manner in which they have conducted themselves."[77] The arrival in Lesotho of some 300 Botswanan soldiers late on September 22 gave credence to the claim that the action constituted an intervention not by South Africa but by the SADC to prevent the overthrow of a democratically elected government. Others, however, believed that "Botswana's intervention only served to legitimise what would otherwise have been dubbed a South African invasion of Lesotho, to pass as a SADC intervention."[78] But whatever claims to multilateralism were made, it is impossible not to see the intervention as a wholly South Africa–driven affair. Khabele Matlosa notes that all the initiatives to resolve the conflict were led by South Africans; South African High Court Judge Pius Langa led the eponymous commission; a South African minister led the negotiations; and a South African officer led the military intervention.[79] Given this, it is impossible not to see South Africa as the rule-writer: concomitant with its immediate and compelling power, South Africa was "dean, administrator, regulator and [immediate] geographer" of the decision and its consequences.[80]

On September 23, South Africa's oldest daily newspaper, *The Cape Times*, carried a banner headline (under one that stated "LESOTHO INVASION BACKFIRES") announcing that "EVERYTHING SOUTH AFRICAN IS BURNING." If this suggested the wanton destruction that followed upon the intervention, it was the full-color picture that covered a quarter page that caught the eye. A bloodied, bandaged, and dead South African soldier, one of nine, lay face-down on the back of a military truck, his face caressing a large military boot; next to him lay a light machine gun. The invocation of this brutal image is deliberate. South Africa's intervention in Lesotho was not a glorious moment for the region's state system—or, indeed, what the new world order had promised the region.

Given this, it is not surprising that a cacophony of voices, including (ironically) the military epistemes, roundly condemned the incursion. Defense intellectuals pointed fingers at the failure of politicians to understand the situation on the ground, a failure of intelligence, lack of a clear doctrine, and the illegality of the intervention, but were equally quick to point out that the losses, even the setbacks, suffered by the South Africans had helped to meld together disparate forces.[81] In other words, despite the disastrous outcome the incursion was "great for the army's integration process."[82] Notwithstanding the widespread condemnation of the action from elsewhere in the region, defense commentators insisted that the crisis had highlighted the need for a "clear intervention policy" in southern Africa.[83] South Africa's deputy minister of defense went a step farther, invoking the necessity to shed blood for South Africa's new nationalism, for its place in the region. In an article distributed by the Department of Defense, he claimed that

> the Lesotho invasion proved that the transformation of our armed forces has worked, in spite of all doubts whether it was truly possible, the historic importance should not be lost. A watershed has occurred in which the unity of the SANDF has been forged in the heat of battle and sealed by the blood of the fallen.[84]

South Africa's leaders defended the decision and rebuffed the strong criticism with a mix of scorn, threats, and self-justification.[85] More thoughtful commentators, fortunately, set these responses in an appropriate and comparative context by recalling similar moments in military history, including the institutionalized U.S. pacification of Vietnam's people, where Orwellian-speakers frequently used words "with their meanings virtually opposite to their usual senses."[86] Opposition parties, groupings, nongovernmental organizations, and the churches condemned the move, and the unions, who were (and remain) partners of South Africa's government, started a fund to help rebuild Lesotho's essential services.[87] Official justifications were difficult to sustain given the orgy of destruction and chaos in Maseru and smaller centers, with total damage being estimated at some U.S.$10 million.[88] The target of this was, as we have already noted, South Africa's economic interests.

On September 25, three days after the onset of the operation, the Afrikaans-medium newspaper *Beeld* carried this headline: "SA STEL

LESOTHO 'IN BEHEER'" (South Africa in control in Lesotho).[89] In the report, the South African force commander declared that Lesotho's government was finally in control of the country. A further 450 South African soldiers arrived on September 27, however, in an attempt to quell ongoing disorder. Although many dissident LDF soldiers were said to have fled with their weapons into the country's mountainous terrain, some 1,000 of the estimated 1,800 rebels had surrendered by September 28. More than 4,000 refugees sought safety in South Africa in late September, along with the majority of the country's expatriate population.

So why did South Africa intervene in Lesotho?

In her analysis of the U.S. intervention in Haiti, Karin von Hippel isolates seven justifications why "force was necessary in a small country that in no way threatened international peace and security."[90] They are: "Haiti is in the US sphere of influence"; "democracy was denied to another country in the western hemisphere"; "the refugee problem was threatening to overwhelm the United States"; "the US administration had suffered continual humiliation by the ruling juntas since the 1991 coup"; "human rights abuses were severe"; and the situation in Haiti caused "the total fracturing of the ability of the world community to conduct business in the post–Cold War era."[91] With suitably changed words for time and place, the same can be found in South African justifications for the decision to invade Lesotho.

The continuous and increasingly confident discourses over order in the post–Cold War world helped to establish in the official South African mind the idea that it was imperative to do something in Lesotho, especially because keywords—democracy, peace, order, regional stability— were continuously associated with both the intervention and its aftermath. Then, drawing on the anarchy problematique that underpins realism, the policy community had located Lesotho's constitutional crisis as part of a world of threat—a world to bring to order. As Jim George notes in reference to Guatemala, what precise danger could a small state like Lesotho possibly pose for South Africa? The answer is inherent in the question, of course: "All . . . actors in the discursive system will be located somewhere [on the] threat agenda."[92]

In the days before the decision to invade, the linkages between order in the region, democracy in Lesotho, and the possibility of South African intervention were never far from the thoughts of South African columnists and the suite of credentialed expertise upon which they drew for supporting commentary.[93] The same links were reflected in the reported thoughts of both bureaucrats and politicians.[94] What is also clear is that the ongoing preparations—training exercises, secondments of military personnel to peacekeeping operations elsewhere, academic and policy conferences, public debates, and the like—over the idea of interventionism had naturalized the military intervention to restore democracy within the country's policy discourse. If this is obvious, the direction of this conversation is revealed by critical theory; the invasion was preferable to addressing the deep-seated processes of disaffection within Lesotho or the regional circumstances that had almost entirely disempowered the country's capacity to exercise its sovereignty.

Using the taxonomy developed by Oliver Richmond, South Africa's first foray in Lesotho should be considered "first-generation"; by using the procedures of diplomatic practice and conflict management, South Africa sought to restore order, to restore democracy, within a framework that privileged state sovereignty.[95] But seldom is this sufficient. The very next step, the use of force—"while the rest of the international community look in the other direction"—to reestablish the status quo is not unknown.[96] Abusively using article 51 of the United Nations Charter as a fig leaf (to borrow yet again from Jürgen Habermas), the Soviets had invaded Afghanistan, Thatcher the Falklands, and the United States Panama, Grenada, and Haiti. In the post–Cold War years, interventions in the name of order, or democracy, or the ubiquitous idea of governance are commonplace. The pattern is the same; this *democracy by force* (to use the title of Karin von Hippel's book) has witnessed powerful neighbors intervening in the conflicts of the weak.[97] In a comparative sense, then, South Africa was not operating out of the ordinary for the times, but the act itself raised questions about other motives, its other interests in the region, especially because the intervention so closely approximated apartheid's policy of destabilization.

The question remains: Why?

Drawing on the idea of an expanded security agenda, Khabele Matlosa answers the question this way:

> The prospects of the [Lesotho] conflict for the Highlands Water Project; possibilities of the conflict's degenerating into outright civil war and spilling over into [South Africa's] own borders, especially in the context of the impending general election of 1999; the ominous prospect of massive overflow of illegal migrants and political refugees through its own borders; and the intensification of cross-border trafficking of small arms and narcotics.[98]

But if these material considerations suggested possible motives beyond the force of the immediate discourses, the question of what made the past was soon drawn to the fore—memory, perhaps, of South Africa's long and very violent history in the region, but memory, too, of the socialization, both individual and national, that had made things possible. It took the press to point out that the force commander, Colonel Robbie Hartslief, had led an apartheid incursion into Angola in the 1980s.[99] And the Afrikaans press, traditionally hawkish but more contrite in the new South Africa, took the point even farther. In a sympathetic profile of the colonel, it pointed out that his love of shooting had been developed in his schooldays. The same story recorded, however, that he had received training in "peacekeeping" in Canada, in Ghana, and in Germany and had been posted to Bosnia.[100] But if this portrait was intended to help reinforce the heroism and myths associated with commanding men in battle, and so bypass South Africa's destructive record in the region, it was the idea of memorials that draw another, far more somber picture of what had happened during those fateful September days.

Writing in South Africa's leading business weekly, the *Financial Mail*, Patrick Laurence, a scholar of Lesotho politics and a journalist, caught the horror of relations past and the uncertainty of the moment future with this paragraph: "A plaque near the Maseru gate commemorates the 42 people killed by SA commandoes in 1982. The epitaph of the intervention by post-apartheid SA may well be the memories of the plundered and burnt-out shops of Maseru."[101] At the time of the Lesotho intervention, and even at this writing, the history of destabilization in southern Africa remains wholly unreflected upon, even wholly unaccounted for— scarcely touched upon by South Africa's Truth and Reconciliation Commission. There has been—to use an apposite metaphor given the wanton destruction and death delivered by destabilization—no closure on this issue. As a result, South Africa and its neighbors share a past but no memory beyond the tropes conditioned by modernity. In short, they have no way, beyond the routinized and formalistic multilateralism represented by the SADC, upon which to build a future.[102]

If anything, however, multilateral efforts to further integrate the region were diminished by the attempt to portray the action in Lesotho as an SADC affair; as the *Sowetan*, the region's largest-circulation black daily, pointed out in the second day of the fighting, the SADC was "running chaotic" in Lesotho.[103] The intervention in Lesotho reinforced and reaffirmed South Africa as the first among a region of unequals. In this setting, then, the SADC is the formalization of the region's hierarchical structure, a form of multilateralism constructed around South Africa's power, which is underwritten by the United States and the European Union and is theorized by Nordic conceptions of "new regionalism."[104] If this is so, then the events in Lesotho in the spring of 1998 may well have determined who has the right to formulate what is to count as the region's memory, "as well as what should be taken as the relevant materials for [its] formulation."[105]

Any judgment suggests that South Africa's decision on Lesotho was rash—a rashness born, perhaps, of the power of mimicry and sanctioned by the new world order discourses, a call to policy action encouraged by an ensemble of new controlling values. But hopes of building a new South African nation by paying close attention to international duty also, surely, played a role. This seems to have been important in South Africa, where the long years of regional destabilization remain (as I have stressed) largely ignored notwithstanding the pious undertaking that the country's rebirth was founded on the hope that amnesty could be traded for truth. But status quo intervention (to again appropriate Oliver Richmond's taxonomy) is wholly misplaced in southern Africa because it reinforces, imbalances, and reasserts the maldistribution of wealth, of power, of life itself; this is because, quite simply, the country that dominates the region writes the rules—always has, always will, to use Robert Rotberg's idiom.

A case can be made (and Oliver Richmond does so) for intervention in southern Africa and elsewhere, but this moment lies way beyond the intervention envisaged by the discourses of order. Emancipatory interventions nest close to, but are not identical with, the spirit of Boutros Boutros-Ghali's Agenda for Peace program, with its need to address the "deepest causes of social injustice and political oppressions." These narratives have not been developed, however; neither have they been encouraged in the unfolding discourses around order and peace in southern Africa. Instead, the rushes to surveillance and discipline have only helped to create the unhappy past as the new southern Africa, a past characterized by the domination by the powerful and the insecurity by the weak.

As suggested in the opening lines of this chapter, it is plainly disingenuous to question the idea of peace and order in a region that for a century and more has known only war and conflict. Quite obviously, too, Churchill's "jaw jaw" alternative is preferable to "war, war," but it is too simple to equate this process with peace or order or security. In the search for quick policy responses to the unfolding regional challenges, the idea of peace—its making, its keeping, its ordering—was delinked from the many layers of complexity that underpin social relations—international, intercommunity, interpersonal. Throughout the subcontinent, however, hidden forms of association and hitherto missed lifeworlds have been drawn to the surface.[106] Many—no, most—of these live counter to the order demanded by states. Social identity is not preordained nor, indeed, is the idea of what constitutes order preordained in southern Africa. Like life itself, order is a community process lived through distinctive and often quite incomprehensible social exchanges.

In these pages, much attention has been given to issues of method and purpose. The power of critique has been used to show how security cultures defy particular forms of historical change because policy requires hierarchical constructions of southern Africa. But great care has been paid to the analytical potential to be yielded from microhistories (in this case, South Africa's intervention in Lesotho). All too often, critical theorists are accused of being removed from the realm of the empirical. My purpose, especially in the excavation of a country study, has been to disprove this claim. In so doing, however, my hope has been to open up new understandings of the possible—of what *could* have happened—both for South Africa and southern Africa.

In southern Africa, peace and order are not simply the absence of war in the aftermath of the victory over race, the dawn of democracy, and the imposition of markets. To succeed, security should reflect the possibility of what Andrew Linklater has called "new forms of community in which individuals and groups can achieve higher levels of freedom."[107] Given its history and the undoubted accomplishments of its struggles, southern Africa should be ideally geared for new explorations. The only question is: Will its peoples be allowed to try? And turning the page will bring us to the search for an answer to this question, a search that begins now with the thoughts of another greatly mourned soul, the social theorist Pierre Bourdieu, who near the end of his life suggested that the vision of the engineer must be abandoned in favor of the vision of the gardener.[108]

6

Continuity and Community

WHO are we?
Who ARE we?
Who are WE?
What are we? Is that simpler?
It is a function of man to ask questions.
Every question presupposes the form or shape
Of its answer, otherwise it wouldn't be
A question. It would be a noise like this: WAAAH.
So, "Who are we" is not a question, it is a noise. Am I, then,
fulfilling my function as a man by
Making noises?
—Oskar Wolberheim

This chapter pursues an idea—advanced earlier—that southern Africans believe that the state system no longer offers solutions to their everyday problems: it neither delivers security nor satisfies a desire for community. As a result, they are driven to find fresh terrains of regional intercourse, like cross-border trading, and to explore old ones, like cross-border migration.[1] These searchings, I have suggested, plainly lie beyond colonialism, apartheid, and nationalism—the framings that have authored contemporary southern Africa. My analytical concern is, therefore, with exploring the idea of community in southern Africa, its making and remaking, but my political energy is directed toward ideas of taking and retaking community in southern Africa.

We must begin with the now familiar engagement with critical theory: first, how we theorize community in southern Africa, and second, how we are to understand the conundrum of state as community in southern Africa. The focus then falls on alternative forms of community in southern Africa. These forms are collected together in two distinct diagnostic moments. The first, sovereign compromise, considers the possible futures offered to the region by interstate cooperation in the field of water.

My sympathy lies, however, with a second moment of collected ideas: sovereignty, saints, and sinners. The juxtaposition of the latter two words with the first suggests an incongruity, but a careful reading will show that this is only an illusion dictated by the holding power that the term "sovereignty" has on the affairs of the region. The other terms, "saints and sinners," together stand for many other forms of social inter-action that I seek to excavate. All too often, these are given short shrift in homage paid to sovereignty. My purpose is to challenge this authority by showing that beyond the constructions offered by states and their making, other forms of community in southern Africa enjoy a rich life. By exca-vating these, my hope is that new understandings of both community and security in the region will be given voice in its affairs. But before all this, however, we must engage the idea of community.

Theorizing Community

"Vague," "illusive," and "slippery": these are just three terms used to exculpate the word "community" from the role it plays in contemporary social science. But accused it stands, accused of what Zygmunt Bauman has recently called the "warm circle"—"a cosy and comfortable place"—well remembered, of course, but, sadly, seldom experienced.[2] Or as Charles Tilly approaches the same idea, "the peaceful, hierarchical little communities . . . their grandparents inhabited" for which people long.[3] Not an auspicious beginning these, neither for the theorist nor the policy-maker. Small wonder, then, that in the roughly thirty years since the pub-lication of Raymond Williams's classic work *Keywords*, there seems every historical reason to search beyond his jostling for conceptual space. Com-munity, he said, was a "warmly persuasive word to describe an existing set of relationships, or the warmly persuasive word to describe an alternative set of relationships."[4] Searching, yes, but is there space to be found? No. So, where to now?

We might begin somewhere else, perhaps by raising a core question in southern Africa's search for community (core it may well be, but it is seldom asked in the real world of policymakers). How is it possible that gated communities—those "heavily guarded, electronically surveyed," rich ghettos that mark every city in the region—are preserved as the epit-ome of sophistication, development, and achievement?[5] What kind of community is to be born from this new form of apartheid in which the razor wire divides the wealthy from the "'messy intimacy' of ordinary city life"?[6] Given this, how can community be known and understood beyond a world created by the security industry, the region's fastest growing sector and, purportedly, the creator of more jobs than any other? At one end of these questions lies the social engineering of modernity in which the spontaneous emergence and reproduction of order, critical theorists believe, is not to be trusted. With the self-regenerating institutions of pre-modern society gone forever, order was designed by the power of reason and maintained by day-to-day monitoring and management.[7] But does this recognition clear away the conceptual confusion and move us toward a clearer understanding of what constitutes community—especially for the purposes we seek in this book? No, seems to be the answer. So, again, where to now?

As they reach this point, most writers turn to where we have all been, Ferdinand Tönnies's binary—gemeinschaft and gesellschaft—the former standing for the local, the intimate; the latter standing for impersonal, contractual, anonymous forms of community. In order to draw the argument forward, I will presently employ a binary that parallels this famous form. More immediately, I want to dwell on the relationship between memory and communities yet to be built—to pursue, in other words, the path to community favored by Charles Tilly. Social scientists all too often construct community around stable hierarchies, established traditions, and the routines of discipline.[8] The gated communities of southern Africa's late modernity represent the ending of the certainties and solidarities of the past, the collapse of an older order. They cannot, therefore, achieve immediate community. So, to gain peace of mind, immediate threats are manipulated, managed, modified, but this extracts a heavy price in freedom of movement. In contrast, critical theory looks beyond these moves and sees gated communities as evidence of existing inequities, a world of deep-seated injustice. The goal is to expose these in the certain belief that a more equitable, more just, more democratic world is possible by seeking community within structures whose goals are equity, inclusion, and an ideal speech situation. How does this apply to the idea of community in southern Africa?

Before the ending of the Cold War and apartheid, the search for community in southern Africa seemed to be remarkably straightforward. Now, however, the region has yielded astonishing complexity. Although the South African state has been deracialized (to use Mahmood Mamdani's word), the patterns of discrimination continue—especially within South Africa, the region's strongest state. But in the affairs of the region, South Africa continues to dominate, notwithstanding the appearance that it is weak and ambivalent. In this reading, not much has changed in southern Africa since the ending of apartheid. As in the past, structural violence threatens prospects for community. But things have changed, which is why multiple sites of social conflict have emerged: race, class, identity, resources, land, ecology—six in a listing that might well be endless. The evidence of these is to be found throughout the region.

To explain this contradiction, we must turn to the work of Clifford Geertz, who insists that anthropology is not a science in search of laws.[9] Instead, he believes that "culture [is] a distinctive configuration of meanings that must be understood on its own terms."[10] The purpose of his social inquiry, therefore, is not to deify the "Continent of Meaning and map out its bodiless landscape."[11] It is, or should be, guessing at meanings, assessing the validity of these guesses within cultural framings, and then drawing explanatory conclusions from those that are most applicable. Using this technique, the goal of theory is not to produce a unified body of universally valid and predictive knowledge; rather, it is to fashion a vocabulary that is both contextualized and interpretative and that makes description possible.[12] For the pedagogic purposes intended by this book, it is important to contrast Geertz's approach with the mechanical routines of orthodox security studies and international relations. In the guise of knowing, the latter do little more than classify, describe, and—far too often for any good—offer policy advice on matters of life and death. This may seem an unnecessarily blunt attack, but let me substantiate it by again recalling the words of the first book on national security to be published in southern Africa: "analysis has [to] become policy oriented: it has to provide, through the development of a variety of options, a concrete input into the decision-making process and at the highest level."[13]

Highlighting the relationship between knowledge and its production serves two immediate purposes. First, it reinforces the divide between contemporary understandings of southern Africa and ideas of what it was that the region once promised. Second, it reintroduces the Foucauldian idea that power has an extensive hold on social science. For a brief moment, we must stay with the latter. We have already noted that positivist routines permit policy-oriented framings, like realism, to explain community and security by ignoring their social complexity. Nevertheless, this same compression has forced successive forms of organization upon southern Africa—empire, white nationalism, decolonization, black nationalism, and, most recently, regional multilateralism—all these have been the fruit of grand historical narratives.

Each moment in its respective unfolding has not produced community but has given, instead, an ideological and geopolitical shape to regional affairs. This shape has made a fetish of the borders that are drawn on the maps that hang in classrooms, conference centers, and cabinet halls throughout southern Africa. This explains how it is that the baton of state security easily passes from colonial governor and last racial overlord to the hero of the liberation struggle. By reaching into the heart of the nation through schools, the places of moneymaking, and the decisionmaking chambers, the order-as-security idea fixes state borders as the true guide to community. In contrast to these official accountings of the region, the interpretative approach to social science—making strange of what is assumed to be commonsensical—has never been applied to the idea of community in southern Africa.[14] By drawing on Clifford Geertz's discussion of new nationalisms (as he called them), we are able to see both the universal and the immediate.

In an essay first published in 1971, Geertz focused on the search by the independence-seeking countries of the South (he called them "new states") for both identity and community in the wake of "the great revolution against Western governance of Third World peoples."[15] To guide his empirical inquiry, Geertz distilled two impulses from the energy that fired the search for nationhood: one was driven by the narrative of grand history (he calls this "epochalism"); the other clings to patterns of behavior drawn from more immediate narratives (this he calls "essentialism"). The astute reader will see that I have employed a technique, the binary, which elsewhere in this book is derided.[16] So, I must offer a few words of explanation. The power of binaries lies in their facility to draw, define, and contrast extremes; this is often helpful in holding options to the light. But beyond this illustrative utility, there are, quite obviously, severe limitations to the use of binaries. As a result, they dare not dominate analytical frames: when the contrasting poles are clarified and analyzed, binaries must be collapsed before any lasting conclusions are drawn. This, too, is Geertz's approach. He is not interested in keeping epochalism and essentialism separate for any length of time.[17] Rarely, he notes, "is [a nationalist] ideology anywhere purely Essentialist or purely Epochalist."[18] The example of India enables Geertz to establish this point. So, "Nehru's image of 'India' was doubtless heavily Epochalist and Gandhi's doubtless heavily Essentialist; but the fact that the first was a disciple of the second and the second patron of the first, demonstrates that the relationship between these two routes to self-discovery is a subtle, even paradoxical one."[19]

As with all binaries, the illustrative distinction between the two poles is the key to much of what follows. Because this is so, and especially because one term—"essentialist"—is so loaded with many hidden meanings, I want to dwell on it for several explanatory sentences. The notion of essentialism is well established in social science, where its meaning—

regretfully, in my view—has taken a pejorative turn. In what follows, however, I employ the term in benign form—a form close to, but not coincidental with, "primordial" as used by Anthony Smith.[20] As I use it here, "essentialism" is rooted in experiences that are close at hand, within a web of immediate social relations; for these purposes, then, the notion is driven by narratives of the local, suggesting sites of intimate social engagement or immediate networks of social sympathy.[21] In order to further mute the deprecatory power that the term "essentialist" has come to represent in contemporary times, I have used a number of other words to capture the sense I wish it to hold for the duration of this particular argument. Cast in this fashion, the term enables us to see another side of community: the social world beyond the homogenization of the grand narrative and the codes that mechanically couple community in southern Africa to states. It is certainly not my intention to use this binary to smuggle in a local version of Samuel P. Huntington's discredited clash-of-civilizations theory, and any effort to do so would be a total misrepresentation of the local, the immediate, the social network that I use in the chapter.

It is obvious that the technique on offer here contrasts sharply with the routine way in which the idea of community has come to be constructed in southern Africa. We have already noted how this happens, but it may be helpful to reinforce the point. For too long, the hand-me-down ideas of security have unquestioningly accepted that sovereign states clustered around South Africa offer the certain path to regional community. The result has been a clouding of the collective imagination on the region's future because it offers the opportunity for only the selective exercise of memory.

The development of the region's state system, and the community its state-makers have constructed, separate southern Africans from a shared history. In contrast, the discovery of a common regional purpose, so necessary for (and I choose this phrase carefully) sustainable security in southern Africa, is through the theoretical and political openings offered by the local, the immediate, even the personal—not, I insist, the statist. Such communities of the local (to coin another phrase) are not cast by anodyne considerations of the external; rather, they are forged by shared concerns: they are not preset by geopolitics but charted by the ordinary, the everyday. The power of the local as a means to understand community has been well developed in literary circles in South Africa as we shall come to see.[22] In order to flourish, these everyday sites require reflexive modes of understanding about the social—understandings that state politics dares not sanction because they promise to recover what colonialism, apartheid, and nationalism have erased. The conclusion is clear: the local threatens the global. Ernesto Laclau's particular threatens his universal; Geertz's essential threatens his epochal.[23]

In urging a reinterpretation of southern Africa—a new ontology, if the reader prefers—I suggest that the dominant portrayals of political community in southern Africa are increasingly at odds with events on the ground. To understand this, we must make another theoretical move. If, as Geertz does, we confine the notion of essentialism to culture alone, its analytical power is dimmed. If, however, it is extended (or, as I prefer, updated) to include a range of new items like the environment and health and water and, indeed, faith—which are *essential* to life's being—its analytical power is strengthened.

Let me briefly summarize my concerns to this point. This chapter seeks to understand and suggest alternative routes to community in southern Africa; these are to be found in places other than those established by the grand historical narratives. As a technique, I have turned to a distinction offered by the anthropologist Clifford Geertz—a distinction between the discourse of the local and the discourse of the global. All modern efforts to construct community in southern Africa have been driven by the power of the latter, a top-down approach that insists that the only route to community in southern Africa is afforded by so-called (often only self-styled) *nation*-states. But this approach, as I will show in what immediately follows, offers no understanding of the disparate, often random impulses that have made for, and made, the states in southern Africa.

As the discourse of liberation unfolded in southern Africa, the idea of the universal was preferred over the local: while the pull of the traditional was strong in the struggles for liberation in a dozen countries in the region (including South Africa), the dominant discourse was rooted in the struggle for state power—an idea rooted in epochalist accounts of history. Because freedom (and the exercise of power under the ritual associated with self-determination) and modernization (with its disciplining routines of states and their boundaries) were two sides of the same philosophical coin, there could be no other understanding of political liberation other than that offered by the concept of statehood.

Strictly speaking, this is not true. To illustrate the exception, let me point to two South African cases—one near at hand, the other at some historical distance. The pan-Africanist idea has been resilient in South Africa notwithstanding successive statist efforts to destroy it.[24] The identification of South Africa's struggle for freedom, for instance, with the struggle of blacks for liberation throughout the continent was—indeed, remains—a powerful force. The other example involves the region's Afrikaners who were scattered across the face of the subcontinent until the clarion call of nation-building associated first with Paul Kruger's Transvaal Republic and fifty years later with Hendrik Verwoerd's South African Republic.[25] These exceptions, however, do not detract from the core argument. The way to community was possible only through the sole permissible method of international accounting: the state. So it was the region's path to liberation turned on imported rituals that made states by excluding outsiders and including insiders as a matter of political course.[26]

This approach to the idea of region, its security, its community, is rooted in what the literary theorist Rob Nixon calls "the great tradition of colonial historiography"—an interpretation of events through which historians ride roughshod over the local.[27] This same tradition chartered nationalist stories in which, for all the talk of liberation, the hope for community in southern Africa was imprisoned by the great ideas of nationalism. Understanding this suggests why any (and all) efforts at building solidarity beyond colonial maps—say, by unifying the struggle for liberation in four separate states like South Africa, Namibia, Mozambique, and Zimbabwe—were thwarted by the exclusionary powers of boundary-making. The position was, of course, anchored by the Organization of African Unity's determination to honor, above all else, the sanctity of colonial boundaries. But the supplementary arguments that supported this position were manifold: in South Africa, the idea of exceptionalism, of industrialization, and later of apartheid;[28] in Namibia, the complicated arguments over the country's status in international law; in Mozambique, the mix of sheer rigidity and cruelty that was said to attach to Portuguese colonialism; and in Zimbabwe, the myopia first of British-style federalism and then of London's betrayal of the majority that led to the unilateral declaration of minority rule in 1965. These four explain the rationalizations of history and the appropriations that were made to support and sustain the grand narrative of state-making when, instead, calls for solidarity were required.

However, national approaches to emancipation have proved self-limiting: confining the ontological focus to the state system, they have failed, as I have been at pains to stress, to reach beyond routine understandings of state power and its twin, national interest. They have blunted, rather than sharpened, the possibilities of reaching toward a regional community that is more responsive to the needs and the desires of southern Africans. The hesitation to move beyond the comfort zone (to use a powerful modern idiom from psychology) represented by the state is located in the idea that to be secure a political community must be fortified by material wealth.

This explains the failure of the immediate beneficiaries of liberation—the region's elites—to confront the power exercised by state-makers. For the former, with rare and marked exceptions, the immediate accomplishment of emancipation seems to be primitive economic accumulation. Small wonder, then, that the impact of emancipatory discourse on public policy, particularly any suggestion that sets people above possessions, is nowhere to be heard in the discussion of community in southern Africa. As a result, the search for regional community is caught in international legalisms that fail to address power relations, in calls for financial accountability that hide the failure of democratic governments to account to voters, in protocols, summitry, flags—all the catastrophic techniques (a phrase that I have carefully chosen) of modern multilateralism.

But the high-flown nature of these rituals fails to highlight innumerable arguments—especially theoretical ones—for communities from below. And so the idea that capital intrusion in the region first drew southern Africans into a single economy has been forgotten in the determination to settle the question of national economic growth within the discourse of markets. The lessons for community that flow from this are entirely ignored. Although the region's single economy is corralled within South Africa, all the region's people have contributed to its common wealth. Concentrated in South Africa, however, its bounty has not generated an equal distribution of its riches. This, more than any other factor, represents an obstacle to the creation of a genuine security in southern Africa. Here, again, paradox stalks the argument. Appreciation of the potential for everyday community in the region is also not possible without understanding the social sites that have been born from the mingling of cross-regional contact. But accepting this highlights the duplicity of South Africa's position in the region: the country is a potent symbol of community through statism but simultaneously is situated at the crossroads of a vibrant, bottom-up regional community.

Is there a way out? Can localization deliver a more comfortable, more secure community? Will Geertz's essentialism yield a new region? I believe a positive answer can be given to these questions. To seek out this alternative path is to move from the quiet death represented by the region's violent past, its unsatisfactory present, and the unequal future it promises. It means searching for a cosmopolitan community, a region of no hierarchies, a life beyond the states. In order to see this future, we must move away from the theoretical rumination that has detained us to alternative expressions of the region's lifeworld.

Sovereign Compromise

Preoccupied with defending the narrow interests of privileged minorities in selected states at specific moments, community in southern Africa has been for the powerful, rarely ever for its people. However, political change in the region, especially the ending of apartheid, has opened the way toward alternative forms of interstate exchange. Because much recent celebration has attached itself to a rediscovery of the region, we must map this particular interaction.

This is an important moment in the discussion. Let me explain why. Sites that offer an exchange of sovereignty are much in vogue in southern Africa: peace parks, spatial development projects, and the sharing of power grids are forcefully advanced as a rational way to resolve regional tensions, to dissolve ecological worries, to create jobs, and to grow the region's economy.[29] All these, it is often asserted, will deepen the prospects for regional peace and community. My impatience with this discussion is not with the idea of assuaging sovereignty (it should be clear from the foregoing chapters that I have a residual, rather than rational, sympathy with this idea). My concern is with the purpose to which these new departures are being put. To be plain: they seek to empower the already empowered and further weaken the already weakened.

Does this necessarily have to be so? The common management of water by states is a good point of entry into an alternative understanding of the same issues. The region's states have come to understand that drought, which has dogged development for so long, does not recognize political boundaries. To write this is not to engage in some postmodern speculation on the nature of southern African society in a new century; rather, it addresses that real world much celebrated by policy pundits, thereby challenging, once again, realism's claims that critical theory needs to be, well, realistic! Until ways can be found to manage the consequences of drought and flooding in the region, southern Africa will remain—as it has been for decades—vulnerable to crop failures and food shortages.[30]

For some time, the question of water has been part of the region's security discourse.[31] Much of the orthodox defense establishment's thinking about water security turns on claims that by 2025 several of southern Africa's states—Mozambique, Tanzania, and Zimbabwe—will face water stress while several others—Lesotho (considered by many to be the region's water-rich country), South Africa (the region's economic hub, its anchor, its pivot, to use words that have already crossed our paths), Botswana (its most stable democracy), and Malawi—will suffer what is termed "absolute water scarcity." Recently, these claims have come to be contested, with critics pointing out that the measures used to make these predictions do not factor in the region's abundant groundwater resources or water available from lakes.[32] Neither do they consider that a great deal of the region's per capita daily water requirements is met not by blue water (surface water) but by green water, which is through the consumption of rain-fed agriculture.[33]

Estimates like these can only be what the term implies—a judgment, an approximation. Moreover, there is no denying the fact that millions of southern Africans in all of the region's states already face water stress *and* absolute water scarcity. My purpose is not to criticize the methodology or to question the science, however; rather, it is to point out how readily realism translates state-centric, aggregated approximations into alarmist policy perspectives. So, the projected water scarcity in the region has been translated by the use of metaphor—the view that population growth and changing climate will lead to interstate conflict over "white gold."[34] Rather than blindly accept this claim, we need, instead, to ask a question: Whose interests are served by this thesis? Clearly, the language and the state-centric, aggregate framing of water scarcity serve the status quo. In southern Africa, the formalized use of water has overwhelmingly served irrigation, mining, industry, and settler households. It has taken from everyone else. Management of water, therefore, seeks to ensure continued supply to those who have already been privileged. In so doing, it deliberately sidesteps any questions pertaining to preexisting conditions of scarcity born of unequal access.

Expectedly, critical theory follows a different trajectory by suggesting that the long-term implications of southern Africa's coming water shortage represent both a conceptual and a real-world challenge to policymakers. This necessitates a need to reconcile national borders, with real issues like access to fresh water. Here, counter-facts play an informative role. Consider this: if the region's political geography has turned on colonial boundaries, its economic geography has turned on access to minerals. As a result, the symbols of its modernization—industries, urban sprawl, developed mines—are all located far from adequate supplies of water. Satisfying their demand, then, has required the power of the state to harness the existing water supply. Elaborate transfer schemes exist throughout the region. As populations in urban areas grow and demands for diminishing resources of water increase, state-makers continue to turn to supply-oriented solutions. Faced with potential political opposition in their capital cities, leaders see supply as a powerful assertion of the fact of the state and, of course, its political power. This fact not only buys votes; it also makes for influential coalitions—international capital, local industry, and, of course, the state. Moreover, this conceptualization of so-called water security as equal to increased supply sits nicely within the zero-sum calculations associated with orthodox security studies: the state and its means of production—mines, industries, plantations—need securing. Hence, the policy option that is generated is instinctively drawn toward the colonial command: might makes right. So, economically poor and landlocked Lesotho's single strategic asset—water—is mechanically set against the shortage of water in rich and developed South Africa. Thus the following dismal conclusion can be drawn: conflict is inevitable, and, given its power, South Africa's will—born of national interest and strategic calculations—will surely triumph. This averred certainty is buttressed by sets of arguments that point to South Africa's scientific and technical know-how, an approach that reduces complex social lifeworlds to narrow technicist and managerial reality. This construction reinforces the idea that what is good for the powerful is good for the region. What is most certain, however, is that this construction historically and currently reinforces sovereign claims in all southern African states.

With these thoughts as background, I will now report on interstate efforts to manage water resources in southern Africa. In 1995, the SADC heads of state adopted the Protocol on Shared Water Course Systems, which aimed to develop close cooperation for judicious and coordinated utilization of regional watercourses. Based on the Helsinki Rules (on the use of international rivers) and the Convention on Non-Navigable Rivers, the SADC protocol on watercourses encourages regional conventions regulating the common utilization and management of the water resources of shared rivers. Viewed within a comparative frame, then, there is nothing new or revolutionary in southern Africa's approach to this issue and, following international experience, it suggests that time and effort will be required before the benefits of the protocol can be realized. This means that a range of political and legal adjustments, as well as new policy directions, needs to be crafted in each southern African country. Additionally, connections between sustainable water resource management and agriculture, power generation, wildlife, protection of the environment, food security, and the priorities of economic development must also follow before the full benefits of the protocol will be realized. As in other areas of policymaking, water resource management needs to be integrated and coordinated with plans for economic growth, development, and the environment. This drift in the argument suggests how national policies will have to be lined up before the region's people can enjoy the overall benefits of sharing joint watercourses and also suggests how, by locating sovereignty at some distance from water itself, the implementation and development of sound community policy are encumbered.

Clifford Geertz's categorization helps us clearly understand the impossibility and contradictions inherent in this situation. Because states will determine their interests in this, as in other fields, their relations are cast in what we might call a "holding bind." The successful implementation of the SADC protocol on watercourses is possible only by a lineup of national interests—a condition that, strictly speaking, is a contradiction in terms. The epochalist nature of the holding bind—states determine their own national interests—entirely misses the deep sets of shared cross-border interests not only in water but also in a multiplicity of lifeforces that stand at the base of the idea of community, that is, networks of the local. The relationship is paradoxical: the impulses of immediate community draw together through a myriad of shared interests around water and its conservation and multiple networks of the local; but the powerful practice of the global—resting on the idea of a sometimes distant nationalism—draws them apart. The very language of interstate conflict and the tiered hierarchies among states erase understanding of the multiple dependencies and interdependencies experienced by individuals and local communities across the region. For all the promise of progress, therefore, recent approaches to the management of water in southern Africa appear to reinforce, not dismantle, the borders separating the states that share a single water resource.

The prudent path to both security and community lies, I suggest, in the opposite direction than that programmed by states and their protocols: if southern Africa wants lasting security and community, then water must enjoy no sovereign value. But even this is wrong, for water must enjoy a pansovereign value: it must become the region's sole security referent, its only boundary. Putting water at the center of the security discourse will emphasize the communality of interests between the region's peoples and reinforce the interests of the states in preserving their most vulnerable resource. This will anchor lasting community from which other forms of security will grow.

A central stumbling block in implementing these alternative policy options is the hold that modernist ways of thinking have on the region's politics. As we have already noted, these might well acknowledge the centrality of water in the affairs of the region but immediately draw the issue toward closed security thinking: the resulting discourse turns water into an object of security; as we shall see in Chapter 7, it "securitizes" water by means of the Speech Act.[35] This move emphasizes interstate conflict above interstate cooperation irrespective of the circumstances on the ground, and it is here that the lingering suspicion continues that water wars in southern Africa are inevitable.[36] The implication of this way of thinking about water in the region has already been experienced. Because it offers an insight into the life-and-death implications of ways of knowing southern Africa, let us follow a case of conflict for a few short sentences before drawing a wider lesson.

Two sister states, Botswana and Namibia, have forcefully contested the ownership of a small uninhabited island in the Chobe River, known as Kasikili in Namibia and Sedudu in Botswana. The dispute was settled before the International Court of Justice in The Hague, but not without considerable anguish in the region.[37] Certainly, the island's nominal land-mass was the subject of the difference of opinion, with the waters of the Chobe River being a secondary issue. However, a closer inspection reveals that the conflict was over a wetland; it seems, therefore, to be a classic interstate conflict over an ecological issue.[38] Now to the lesson: such tension illustrates the way in which the haphazard construction of colonial boundaries—if used as security referents—draws out the darker side of regional life. Recasting security in southern Africa within the simple-minded binaries so loved by realist theory returns the search for community back to the treacherous apartheid years and ignores the hopeful breakthroughs that have been made in the development of a common approach to water and its management.

The tension between the statist route to joint management of water resources and the alternative is most markedly illustrated in the relationship between South Africa and Lesotho. We have already noted that the destinies of the two countries are inseparable: lack of jobs in Lesotho will impact South Africa, and economic decline in South Africa will corrode Lesotho's already spare economic base. The policy challenge is to nurture transnational development on both sides of the divide that nominally separates states—but this cannot only be driven by states alone, especially when one, South Africa, is said to be strong and the other, Lesotho, is axiomatically assumed to be weak. To succeed over the longer term, the management of water between these two states needs to be rooted in a shared sense of community. There are many instances of cooperation in the relations between Lesotho and South Africa, from interfamilial to informal-sector linkages (in effect, social sites or multiple networks that recognize no border).[39] In addition, as we have seen, there is cross-border cooperation between the states on drought relief and river basin management. But how the two can be drawn together remains caught in our paradox. Indeed, as shown in Chapter 5, South Africa's 1998 incursion into

Lesotho, paradoxically, demonstrated the weakness of the Lesotho state, in reasserting its claims to sovereignty.

Spontaneous border-crossings like those between South Africa and Lesotho suggest that quotidian communities of the local, below the state level, in pursuance of common societal goals, are common forms of association in southern Africa. We are midway through this chapter and will now ask its most important question: Why are issues, like access to water, the issues of life and death, removed from essentialist associations and placed within epochalist ones?

The recognition of interdependencies and multiple sites of social interaction has important implications for the study of security in the region and elsewhere. Because this is so, I want to be clear about what it is that I am suggesting in this argument. My intention is not simply to broaden, as Barry Buzan might, the concept of security to include water while retaining the state as the primary security referent. To do this would be to securitize water, which would deepen regional conflict and make the region further captive of the state that can best secure access to water and is in a position to husband its distribution. As the work of the Copenhagen School has pointed out, efforts to broaden the security agenda are often nothing more than efforts to sustain military expenditure; in southern Africa, this move would merely foster the unidirectional discourse on security that inflicted such deep pain during the apartheid years. But neither is it my intention to simply switch the debate from military security to human security. The latter is an important issue, to be sure. The pioneering work done by the United Nations Development Programme in stressing the idea of human security has helped to break the stranglehold that the military enjoyed over the security discourse in southern Africa and elsewhere. But perversely it empowered the military, for the expansion of the security discourse enabled the military to redefine its role in multiple new ways. Nevertheless, the power of the debate on human security has set the routine practices of strategic accounting into sharp focus: when set against, say, the Human Development Index, military expenditure seems expensive and wasteful and, as countless studies suggest, goes no way toward the eradication of poverty. For these reasons, critical approaches (as Ken Booth and I suggested in 1995) must be strongly supportive of the efforts to propel the idea of human security to the forefront of the development agenda.[40] However, to intentionally draw a strict and pedantic distinction, the debate on human security is a debate around development, not around security or community.

My interest, in contrast, is to shift the notion of regional security through community away from states and toward new appreciations of community in which water (among other issues) will play the central organizing role. To do this means that the region's scarce water resources will have to be drawn even closer to the lives of southern Africans. How is this to be done? Helpful breakthroughs have been made in the region—these, too, lie beyond the long-term framings associated with state power; for now, however, it seems that they must be initiated by states. Changes in the governance of water in South Africa, in particular, have revealed a willingness to overturn preconceived ideas of community (and the importance of water as a community resource) in favor of a discourse of sharing. Because, as I will presently suggest, the state will not simply vanish in southern Africa, I first want to report on this development.

Historically, the right to use water in South Africa was bestowed (an important adjective in this context) by the private and near-absolute ownership of land in accordance with the riparian principle rooted in European law. This notion of ownership—itself embedded in contract theory—coincided with the racial politics that characterized the country's apartheid system. However, the advent of democracy enshrined a bill of rights that guarantees sufficient access to water to each citizen of the country (which South Africa's Department of Water Affairs and Forestry has set at a minimum of twenty-five liters per day within 200 meters of a person's home). The desirability of spreading limited resources of water more equitably while protecting its ecological base has compelled all South Africans to recognize that long-established approaches to the management of water must change. A suite of policy initiatives has been introduced; these have been underpinned by three principal concerns: participatory governance, social equity, and environmental justice. Of particular importance has been the move toward a much greater focus on demand management and integrated water resource management on a catchment basis. These both have important implications for the idea of community. Without community involvement, either locally or regionally, it will not be possible to manage and protect water resources. South Africa's National Water Act of 1998 obliges the responsible government minister, in allocating water under the new system, to take account of the water needs of the country's neighbors—a world first. This suggests the sense in which water can become a means to community.

The purpose of this critical reportage has been to suggest that natural systems respond to a different set of borders from those offered by statemakers, be they colonial or other. Watercourses are the focal point at which states can recognize their joint dependency on natural resources in achieving human security. This is an epistemological question, however. What practitioners privilege—and what theoreticians ignore—when they think about the issue will profoundly affect the region and its people. However compelling this insight, it will not be easy to effect change in this direction; like the proverbial generals planning for the next war, states are creatures of habit, and their plans more readily reflect past rather than present needs and seldom anticipate future needs. Experience suggests, however, that supposedly ingrained approaches to security issues can be altered if education and public discourse can be brought to bear first on the world of ideas and then on policymakers. Indeed, southern Africa's recent history teaches powerful lessons of change. Were this not so, how can we account for the fact that apartheid ended and that this particular discussion on security in southern Africa could be framed in ways so patently different from those so frequently suggested by neorealist thinkers? And how can we explain the astonishing complexity of the region's social science that was once thought so simple? Whatever mainstream theory may suggest, agency can triumph over structure. So, it is possible to change security priorities in southern Africa by thinking differently about what is to be secured. With the sure knowledge that this can happen, I turn toward a different kind of southern Africa: a region without states at the base of community.

Sovereignty, Saints, and Sinners

To look beyond the present moment is to look in several directions at once—to recover forgotten stories, to relocate hidden pathways toward self-discovery, and to search for community impulses far below the heights represented by Geertz's epochal thinking. It is not to be arrested by one conception of time but to appreciate that there is not one, but many, timelines—each of which must come to enjoy equal weight if community is to begin anew and if it is to flourish.

For all its sense of state-directed coherence, contemporary southern Africa is the product of accident. Rather than an organically evolved framework of civilization, by state and capital penetration, the region sustains itself with and between what Clifford Geertz calls "bundles of competing traditions [which] have [been] gathered accidentally into concocted [national] frameworks."[41] The evidence of this is everywhere to be seen. So, for instance, the exercise of sovereignty by South Africa and its close neighbors has always been far less than it has pretended to be. This is witnessed on the streets of South African cities, where pavements are stacked with curios made not in South Africa but in its neighborhood; it is to be found in the number of citizens from South Africa's near-abroad who occupy key positions in the government of the new South Africa and the sectors—commercial, financial, and academic—that support it.

To recognize this is to again move the argument onto the tricky conceptual ground that we have traversed before. Let us quickly retrace the typography. Colonial history and colonizing cartographers have given the notion of southern Africa a form of sorts. This history and this cartography, however, live under the continual threat of subversion by efforts to uncover the precolonial past by Africanist historiographers and by postcolonial experience. Inevitably, the ontology of southern Africa is rendered unstable by that which threatens to liberate the region from the grip of our current understanding of it. Quite clearly, then, any alternative southern Africa contrasts with the colonially determined ontology that the region can only be a community of nation-states that have been secured by colonial borders. Why has it taken so long to see this?

The search for this other southern Africa was temporarily hidden beneath the necessity to frame the discourse of emancipation around the issue of race. Let us be clear about this: sequencing has been central to emancipation. For instance, there could be no ending to apartheid without the international campaign for self-determination that arose at the end of World War II. This campaign was itself contingent on the ending of slavery. Understanding the importance of sequencing leads to an appreciation of the task of emancipation that lies immediately ahead in southern Africa, a task that involves the identification of local narratives that will first anchor and then drive an integrative revolution—a more radical form of community than that which has thus far been thought possible. By "radical form," I mean community that lies outside the frame presented and represented by states: the creation of "a truly just and democratic community."[42]

I wish to offer three renditions of local community at work in the region: these are located in archaeology, in church history, and in musicology. By providing real alternatives around which another southern Africa is forged, these examples illustrate the limits of grand narratives.

Before presenting the first, however, a cautionary tale: in southern Africa, there was a momentary and very violent congruence between anthropology and international relations around the issue of race. Its central preoccupation was to draw their disparate understandings of community together in the service of ideology.[43] This took place in South Africa and became the basis of the country's apartheid policy. It proceeded from eugenics to a predisposition of Afrikaner nationalist academe with the epistemological routines of *"volkekunde"*—the Afrikaans word that means the study of both races and nations—and culminated in the circling of intellectual wagons around the racial privilege.[44] The end of this road was grand apartheid: the creation of separate and independent "national communities," each with its own protocols of diplomacy, national flags, and security routines derived from apartheid. The ease with which the creation of these so-called independent national states took place was, admittedly, a function of apartheid's firepower, but it was also the result of what then seemed to be the power of common sense. It was also preconditioned by the easy, unquestioning routines through which social scientists and politicians both created and uncreated borders in southern Africa throughout the closing years of the nineteenth century and into the twentieth century. This experience offers both lesson and caution: it confirms that the idea of states as community in southern Africa was more constructed than predestined, but as apartheid so tragically showed, it also signals the dangers attending the manipulation of ethnicity in the cause of grand constructions.

Nevertheless, an appreciation of the idea of ethnicity in southern Africa does draw "alternative bundles" of community to the region's surface.[45] Archaeological research recognizes that across the face of southern Africa community identities exist that predate and, perforce, defy the fragmentation represented by colonial borders. There are countless examples, but one good example will have to stand for many. William F. Lye and Colin Murray suggest that the Sotho-Tswana people of southern Africa are scattered across several international borders and, at the time of their writing, were subjected to the "administrations of six governments": those of Lesotho, Botswana, and South Africa; of the newly "independent" Transkei and BophuthatsTswana; and of QwaQwa, the Southern Sotho "homeland."[46] This mapping highlights the arbitrariness of boundary-making and suggests how established communities are torn apart by the colonial orderings that gave southern Africa its current form. The strength of the example additionally lies in the way it highlights apartheid South Africa's arbitrary use of borders to randomly create a series of political communities—statelets and other remnants with limited degrees of sovereignty—to support its racial ideology.

Any hopes that the ending of apartheid would hift the idea of community in the region away from states seem dim. Consider this example: in May 1995, Matthews Phosa, once the premier of South Africa's Eastern Transvaal Province, suggested that he would seek to create an "economic bloc" with both Swaziland and the southern provinces of Mozambique. For centuries, the indigenous people of this fertile triangle of African *lowveld* have considered themselves united by the bonds of blood, barter, and the search for a better life. They speak a common language; the area engages in a rich exchange of goods, labor, and contraband; and—as has happened so often in Africa—the border between the states stifled community life. In essence, Phosa had reasserted a series of truths that were previously erased by colonialism, apartheid, and the search for nationhood. By offering solutions to people on the ground, he challenged the founding myths—the epistemological faiths—that created the region's current maps; he probed alternative forms of community.[47] Although his initiative was greeted with equanimity, we must judge it for what it was: an attempt to author new norms of community.

To the second example: a recently edited book on the history of Christianity in South Africa draws from an alternative narrative to explain the making of modern southern Africa. Its purpose is plain: grand narrative of the region is increasingly in "danger of assuming that [South/southern Africa] turns entirely on the twin pivots of obsessional slogans [of nationalism] and economic greed [both associated with modernist discourses]."[48] Chapters on both Pentecostal and Ethiopian-based, African-indigenous churches (AICs) reveal extensive cross-regional bondings and highlight the potential for further growth of communities across the subcontinent. The AICs are the "largest and potentially the single most important religious group [in South/southern Africa], and, in spite of weaknesses and divisions, their vitality, their rootedness in the African traditions, their capacity for innovation will most likely have a decisive influence on the history of the church and society in the changing [South/southern Africa]."[49]

The South Africa–based Zionist Christian Church, with its extensive following across the entire region, presents a compelling example of both developing identity and community-in-formation beyond national borders. The lasting impact of this cross-border evangelism is, of course, wholly uncertain, but a comparative frame opens an interesting suggestion for community-making in southern Africa.[50] In contrast to the grand historical accounts of the uniting of the American colonies in the early eighteenth century, revisionist church history suggests that it may have been mainly the work of the Methodist-Calvinist evangelist George Whitefield who, by virtue of his energy and the power of his preaching, drew colonists as far apart as Georgia and Massachusetts together in a community.[51] This community would, with time, grow to be political—in the constitutional sense of the word.

The third example draws together a series of associations that are at once local, progressive, and cultural. Music plays "an important role in defining Southern Africa" because it reinforces old, and forges new, identities.[52] Musicologists suggest a distinctive patterning of communities in the region. Groups located south of the Zambezi sing with harmonies in octaves and/or fifths, but groups farther north sing in thirds; the harmonic patterns in some areas of the region are distinct from music farther north and from other styles located in South Africa proper. However, a wider grouping also exists. The lower Zambezi Valley uses harmonic cycles and a yodel style that musicologists believe are suggestive of a larger community—wide in its geographical spread—ranging from the pygmies in central Africa to the San in the south. These musical clusters exist where similar life elements, based largely on localized influences, create a distinctive musical culture.

Music in southern Africa, as in the rest of the continent, has an important political power because it is linked to life's rituals and crosses the traditional and the modern sectors.[53] The region's music has become truly mixed and mingled as a result of the to-and-fro movement from, particularly, the region's economic core, South Africa. The musicologist Gerhard Kubik, for example, has highlighted the influence of returning mineworkers on music in Malawi.[54] The process of developing a regional music has been deepened by the growth of a recording industry that, although located in both South Africa and Zimbabwe, is cross-regional (and international) in its sweep. As a result, there is a nascent southern African popular music culture that, because it unites people across national boundaries, has significant long-term social implications—and emancipatory potential—for the region. Importantly, this popular music represents a threat to accepted understandings of regional life. Kwaito music and South Africa's "township jazz" are strongly antistatist; they are a melting pot of world music, protest music, and speak the language of the underbelly, the other lifeworld. Interesting, too, this music is one of South Africa's only nonimperial exports to the region and to Africa; urban-dwellers from Lagos to Nairobi to Blantyre know this music of Abdullah Ibrahim, Miriam Makeba, Brenda Fassie, and T. K. Zee.

These three examples suggest that the route to another southern Africa—a community still to be imagined, to twist Benedict Anderson's famous phrase—lies beyond the discourses of state power, beyond the present multilateral techniques with their emphasis on hierarchies of power, and beyond the holding power of borders with their rituals of exclusion.[55] To raise the idea of alternative pathways to regional community, however, runs the risk of counterpressure (even counterforce) from the disciplining legitimacy of state policy upon which orthodox security studies feeds. There is nothing new in this potential for violence, of course: state security-making during the apartheid years was used to protect the narrow sectional interests of the region's perceived realities that put white minority power at the center of every security calculation. South Africa's vicious policy of destabilization stands as testimony to the failure of the region's state system. New forms of cross-border patterning, both old and new, communities of the local, and the emergence of powerful new social networks for which these three examples stand are, I suggest, unstoppable, certainly on this reading. Counterpressure may slow them down, but the time for a regional community of the local will come.

It is not surprising that southern Africans are searching for understandings of community that lie beyond struggles that until now have centered on the unfolding discourses of colonialism, statist power, and, more recently, economic liberalism. In a globalizing world, it is also not surprising that the purpose of governments and the hopes of the region's people are drawn in different directions. States in southern Africa continue to be captured by epochal accounts of history, which invariably bring them into conflict with essentialist understandings of the social. Let me draw close an example to illustrate the horror of those caught in the middle of the paradox that has stalked this entire argument.

A tragic (but all too typical) example of statism is offered in the seeming determination of the government of Namibia to push purposefully ahead with the construction of a dam on the Kunene River on the border between Namibia and Angola in the face of opposition from the Himba people.[56] When the authorities in the distant capital, Windhoek, appealed to the power of nationalism, they draw on the grand themes associated with the epochal discourses—here in the guise of modernization, development, and independence—and so clash with the local perspectives of the Himbas.[57] One government minister, Hidopo Hamutenya, graphically expressed the binary divide when he said that the Himbas should be "in ties and suits, rather than being naked and half dressed."[58] This "ethnic cleansing by dam-building" is, of course, not unique to southern Africa.[59]

As they arm themselves for endless conflict in southern Africa, orthodox security analysts have shown themselves incapable of reaching beyond the routines of violence. This has been forcefully illustrated in South Africa: as the country has engaged the region since the ending of apartheid, it has reverted to the statist type. The thinking that fashions its options in the region appears captured by the same impulses that encouraged apartheid to nearly destroy southern Africa in the 1980s. True, as the 1990s progressed, the constructed Soviet threat to South Africa was no longer heard, and yes, the country is nominally at peace with each of its neighbors, but the obsession with state security and a state-centered understanding of regional community has not passed. This, as we noted in Chapter 5, accounts for South Africa's decision to spearhead the SADC's intervention in Lesotho in September 1998 to restore security, order, and democracy. In choosing this particular route to regional community-making, postapartheid South Africa has closed off the option of building a different kind of southern Africa to the one we know, which colonialism authored, capitalism made possible, and apartheid fostered.

The example of the Himba people suggests that this approach has delivered great pain to the region's people and, if anything, appears to have closed off the search for sustainable security and community. The irony of this, however, is that the key to overcoming the self-enclosing rituals of security studies in southern Africa lies in countless other stories—in archaeology, in the environment, in church history—to mention only three among literally hundreds that lie scattered in other knowledge centers. These perspectives construct the region in entirely different ways than do the champions of boundaries who enthusiastically populate the mainstream of international relations and security studies. This point is illustrated in the strong and determined search for a southern African literature, which, to drive home a technique that has been repeatedly used in this text, can be strongly contrasted to security studies.[60] Southern African literature has many roots, but a rich impulse draws on the work of the exiled South African feminist writer Bessie Head. Her borderlands writing draws directly upon indigenous culture and transborder affiliations, both of which are located below the state, which is why her stories, although "set in a Botswanan village, convey a powerful sense of the ceaseless border crossings of imperialists, missionaries, refugees, migrant workers, prostitutes, school children, teachers and armies that score Southern Africa as a region."[61]

The emancipatory potential of her work rests in the distinction she draws between these communities (and their histories) and the violence attached to "the governing forms of historical narration as symptoms and agents of colonial violence."[62] Bessie Head mapped an entirely different southern African community than the maps hanging in schoolrooms, conference centers, and cabinet rooms. Her communities are not enclosed by the power represented by borders; they *challenge* borders in order to sustain and build community. So although her writing kneads the same historical material as boundary-makers, it gives rise to an entirely different understanding of community in southern Africa. In Ludwig Wittgenstein's terms, Bessie Head uses a different grammar from the great tradition of colonial historiography that privileges boundary-making as the only path to southern African community.

The ideas scattered throughout this chapter confirm that the basic social science in southern Africa is, certainly, very complex, but they also suggest that the intellectual and other risks undertaken by church histori-ans, anthropologists, and novelists have yielded new understandings of community in a part of the world in which the norm has been conflict and strife. Their work powerfully shows that beyond the barricades that are formed, forced, and often fudged by the rituals of state power, there is a new southern Africa in the offing.

The end of this chapter is in sight: let us again pause, this time to reflect on the arguments that have brought us here. The path to the opti-mistic and assertive conclusion that follows is nested in four self-support-ing arguments:

- Community-building in southern Africa has rested on a series of derived understandings that states in the region are the natural order of things.
- This is the result of orthodox security discourses that have impris-oned understandings of the region and entirely excluded other paths to its ways.
- Alternative conceptions of community in the region do exist, how-ever. Water and its management offer means to mediate between state-centered and alternative forms of the idea of community in the region, but security routines insist on capturing the emancipa-tory potential offered by water as a form of sovereignty.
- The emancipatory potential of community in the region, however, is to be found in new ways of remembering the region's hidden past.

We have one final task to complete, which involves not misrepresent-ing the embeddedness of current regional practices. Because the habit of states has taken hold in the region, states—and the system they have cre-ated—cannot be wished away. Put differently, the epochal will not be washed by words or wished away by other approaches to knowing. As we look forward, we know that "the future is always already populated with certain possibilities derived from the past."[63] States represent only one dimension of a continuing southern Africa, however, and I have tried to show how uneasily this resides with the local.

To bring theory to bear on practice is to suggest that self-reflective interpretations of contemporary southern Africa can, and have, produced evidence that is irrefutable: the region's people are in search of communi-ties that lie beyond the privileges that have until now been accorded to the region's states and their governing elites. State-building in southern Africa has been a manipulative process in which many identities have been massaged to suit the purposes of communities contrived, constructed, and exploited for narrow political and economic purposes. Appreciating this brings us finally to the purpose of this chapter: as Marx reminded us in his celebrated Eleventh Thesis on Feuerbach, "the philosophers have only interpreted the world in various ways; the point however is to change it."[64] By exploring the alternatives that lie beyond the narratives that both founded and constructed the region, we have moved in that direction.

7

Primus Inter Pares?

The world will NOT be contained:
It will only be loved
—Oskar Wolberheim

Although security and community begin in the past, it is faith in the future that provides both with form and content. This explains why the transaction moment between past and future is the focus of much of the recent writing on memory.[1] This work suggests a far more delicate social ecology than that previously thought possible or, from a practical point of view, necessary. What we remember is not stable but is continuously recast by amnesia or privileging—or both. So despite what we have been taught to believe, we can (and mostly do) remake the past in the present. Recognizing this provides an endless challenge to the world of practical ideas, because in the process of remaking the past, understandings of security and community (to borrow an idea from Pauline Rosenau) have become forms of terror.[2] By critically engaging South Africa's understandings of regional security, this book has aimed to prevent future terror in southern Africa.

The easy isolation of terror as a metaphor so late in this book might well be thought to be misplaced; upon reflection, this is not so. Any close reading of security texts suggests how powerfully the metaphor has conquered particular forms of applied social science (a point, incidentally, that has gone entirely unregistered in the study of southern African security and one to which I have tried to exercise great sensitivity).[3] To touch this issue is to give early notice that this chapter will pay close attention to issues of discourse and speech in the making of security knowledge. We have once again reached a little ahead of ourselves, and we must return to the power of the chapter's second image: terror.

The region's first state, the unequal continuously fingered in this book, once employed state terror equal in magnitude to that practiced by

Latin America in its dark decades.[4] The trope itself serves to remind us of two other themes that have run the course of the writing: historically, terror has been the tool of the strong, not the weak; and words construed to serve ideological ends, words like "terror," are mighty weapons in the arsenals of power.[5] Ordinarily, these thoughts might pass the reader by, but the developments associated with the attacks on the United States on September 11, 2001, give them a deeper salience, and the reader pause for thought. Those events have certainly altered many landscapes—but not the need for critical approaches to security. Indeed, the reckless use of the word "terror" in the speeches of the world's most powerful suggests how important critical approaches and attentiveness to language have become in a world increasingly disciplined by the routines of orthodox security studies.

Although this chapter bristles with practical matters, the argument turns on three enabling ideas—theory, history, and emancipation—that have run throughout the course of this writing; not strange, this, as different ideas would certainly have yielded another southern Africa and an alternative understanding of its security. We are very close here to the ideas that were traded in the book's earliest pages. To recall them here is to refocus our attention on epistemology and ontology. Colonial history and colonizing cartographers constructed southern Africa around a powerful South Africa; although this rendition of southern Africa has dominated the discourses of security, the critical inquiry that has been brought to bear has shown how it lives under increasing conceptual siege.

Using immanent critique—a method that judges society by the very norms of freedom and happiness that it professes to accept—this chapter will look forward to ways in which security and community in another form of the region may be possible.[6] The technique, as before, turns on posing question upon question: easy to ask, surely, but devilish—as every policymaker claims—to answer.

Because this is so, a brief text note that was prompted by Terry Eagleton, the literary theorist, clarifies the teleological goal of this chapter. Throughout this writing, I have vigorously used social theory to ask questions; in following this technique, my goal has not been to further some minor art form but rather to use theory to boldly raise "fundamental questions to which people would appreciate some answers."[7] The emancipatory purpose this opens contrasts with the apartheid period, when discussions on security and on community were hurried, in the purported national interest, toward closure and violence.

The Task of Critical Theory

This book is only the latest in a line of ideas that have problematized, rather than applauded, the narrative that guides and guards South African discourses on southern Africa.[8] Although this form of critique has become more readily available, the task of conceptualizing new forms of security and community seems, paradoxically, to have been closed off by the events since the end of apartheid. So the opportunities promised to the region by liberal democracy and its policy twin, market economics, appear, if anything, to have rekindled South Africa's militarism, a militarism that was momentarily hidden by the immediate postapartheid gaze.[9]

In the early 1990s, the discovery and rediscovery of southern Africa by South Africa seemed set to run endlessly as academic disciplines, political agendas, and personal preferences for the region and its future opened up.[10] No immediate purpose is served in pointing to the possibilities that were offered to southern Africa during this celebration, but the reasons for the failure to deliver certainly need to be given. That accounting, however, must be in a place different from this. Our teleological goal is nonetheless served by isolating from that golden age the single strand of emancipation: how to liberate the region's "people from those constraints that stop them carrying out what they freely would choose to do."[11]

Pursuing this in the proverbial cold light of the postliberation day tells us much about the relationship between continuity and change in South Africa, as well as the country's discourses of security. In casting their idea of the region within a realist discourse, defined by sovereignty, postapartheid understandings of the region have failed to see that nationalism, which was once conceived of as the only form of freedom, "is really . . . destroying forms of ordinary life that many people know. The nation state prevents the development of free exchange between people."[12] This suggests why South Africa's policy toward the region, as it was under apartheid, is marked by intellectual and moral poverty (to retrieve Hedley Bull's famous phrase).

Derived from culturally specific assumptions, interests, and sensitivities, South Africa's regional policy is characterized by successive reifications: political control, state sovereignty, and regional order. But to borrow an idea from Theodor Adorno, reification of a certain past and the future that it promises is indistinguishable from amnesia. This explains why I have worried "about what lies beyond . . . borders [and about those items that have] been forgotten."[13]

Speaking this particular truth to power—the core responsibility of critical theory—is uncomfortable, but I have shown why rendering to states the exclusive right to define security silences all those that lie beyond the artificial borders of nationhood, facilitates only certain ways of knowing, and privileges only certain language and particular voices.

Security and Its Making

Security discourse emerges from the making and circulation of threats. But threats invariably idealized the idea of a stable past and promised an assured future. In realist security studies, this particular transaction moment is cast within the command of a statist narrative that allows no scope for hesitation or question. Two crucial questions follow. What rite of political passage guides this process? And why does an idea that allows such little scope for questioning so endlessly proliferate? To answer these questions, we must turn to the theory of pragmatics and the role of language in speech that we touched upon in Chapter 6.

The command to security action through speech has been innovatively explored in the work of Ole Wæver, who has drawn speech act theory toward the routines involved in the making of security knowledge.[14] Put simply, Wæver suggests that utterance of security and interaction are part of a single moment of both naming and making. An analogy drawn from the Old Testament helps to underline the power of the initial conceptual point and forcefully demonstrates its practical consequences. Much of what follows in Christian belief is contingent on the unquestioned acceptance of a single declaration—in the form of a speech act—that appears in the third verse of Genesis: "And God said, Let their be light: and there was light." This idea—*creatio ex nihito* (creating something out of nothing)—has been the subject of much scholarly interest by rhetoricians and Old Testament scholars. In an auxiliary sense, of course, the idea of making something from nothing has run the full course of this book. Linguistic representations created a form for the region and inculcated it with organizational attributes offered by the idea of states. The license afforded by this language permitted the region's states to pursue security within set binary rituals—territory, sovereignty, and geopolitics—determined by realist approaches to international relations.

But how are we to understand the making of a security something out of nothing? What does it mean in southern Africa?

Wæver genuflects toward the pioneering work of the moral philosopher J. L. Austin, and his move enables the isolation of three aspects of speech: (1) the act of saying or expressing the proposition; (2) the declarative aspect of the speech moment; and (3) the understanding of the speech act by the hearer.[15] Because of its mobilizing power, the second moment is (for these immediate purposes) of the greater interest. In the act of naming security, Wæver suggests, "a state-representative moves a particular development into a specific area, and thereby claims a special right to use whatever means are necessary to block it."[16] At the declaratory moment, then, an entirely new condition emerges in the mind of the hearer: in this, and following Wæver, the everyday processes of the social—including negotiation, mediation, and reconciliation—are set aside in pursuit of asserting state control over the social world. The result of this is clear: security is only possible inside; it is impossible outside the state.

The same causal chain enables the argument to move beyond Wæver's proposal that states are the only agent of "securitization"—the term he uses to describe the consequences of the speech act. In South Africa, the right to securitize has not been the exclusive domain of state power. As they have sought to tame the social world, various interest groups can be thought of as secondary sites of securitization. Although located outside the formal organs of the state, these secondary sites have securitized the social within an analytical frame that views the progress promised by the state as the best form of protection. This suggests that the purpose of securitization, whether primary or secondary, is to inculcate the region's life with the values of modernity.

But this is not all. As an issue is securitized, two collateral functions have emerged; both have impacted upon the discourse and the practice of regional security, and because both significantly influence the way in which the argument in this chapter unfolds, distinctive typographical markers best separate them.

• Secondary sites offer particular ways to understand the declared threat in order to exact delivery from it. In his work on southern Africa, David Chidister suggests that Christianity once provided both the explanation and the means of delivery.[17] More recently, the cause represented by empire both explained and promised to deliver the threatened. The force of empire, of course, was used to justify the Boer War but was also used to expand the progress that the British Empire—through the influence of Cecil Rhodes, in particular—promised the region.

• On an independent axis, secondary sites of securitization identify derivative threats in order to assist the state to exercise control over fresh areas of the social world. Evidence of the latter is everywhere to be found in South Africa: as the region's people shifted from the countryside to its cities, the derivatives of security turned the latter into a series of gated communities. The spatial organization and reorganization of these communities lay at the very core of apartheid, a policy that was first conceived by a cohort of Afrikaner ideologues. In more recent times, gated suburbs—the successor condition of the sealed-off communities of apartheid—have proliferated and have helped personal security become the country's fastest growing industry.[18] Other social problems were similarly collaterally securitized: health issues like bubonic plague in the early 1900s, tuberculosis, malaria, and, most recently, HIV/AIDS have been constructed as security threats, as has the issue of habit-forming drugs.[19] The power offered by securitization has also been used to draw a range of additional social issues toward the orbit of the state: the environment, desertification, and pollution are the most recent.[20]

Dissolving an issue once it has been securitized and then stemming the expansion into further sites of securitization are nearly impossible because the master narrative insists that states (and their imputed power) are the only means to security. In southern Africa, state interest is reinforced by sovereignty—a purportedly neutral condition that orders and controls the social by delivering the successful exclusion of an alien outside and the total incorporation of a safe and secure inside. This, as we noted, is Rob Walker's famous Inside/Outside series. However, sovereignty in southern Africa has acted more as fiction than fact, thereby rendering itself unstable. Domestically, sovereignty has been rooted in bimodal racial practice that has generated more domestic than external conflict. The practice of the frontier, and the resulting frontier mentality, enabled South Africa to effectively use multiple renditions of sovereignty to secure its own position in the region at the expense of its unequals. Rehabilitating a securitized item once it has been cast within the framework of sovereignty is often complicated by the proliferation of controlling metaphors. So although the discourse of state security is ostensibly thought to represent the modernizing force of progress (by offering sovereignty as the only acceptable form of mediation between politics and agency), emancipatory change is entirely thwarted.[21]

But how has the old security discourse become the new?

Agents of continuity—fingered, as we have seen, by Antonio Gramsci in his prison notebooks—have transported ideologized notions of sovereignty, within the same retinues of cultural practice, from the apartheid moment to the next.

As apartheid's Total National Strategy embraced a widening of the security agenda, for instance, so South Africa's new security doctrine has followed the same expansionist trajectory; a crucial difference now, however, is that the expanded notion, and the license it offers for further securitization, rests comfortably within the folds of democratic practice. The direction promised by the slide toward endless securitization includes the reimmersion of the military into everyday life and national culture through a reintroduction of the draft, because, as South Africa's minister of defcnse has put it, conscription is "a powerful tool [in] nation-building."[22]

This appropriation of old security practice and the revival of national security culture have provided a strong validation for South Africa's purchase of advanced and sophisticated weaponry, notwithstanding the claim that the country is nominally at peace with each of its neighbors. So, the language of Carl von Clausewitz and Viscount Palmerston, with its emphasis on the inevitability of war and the permanence of national interests, has been used to defend a controversial decision made at an obviously crucial moment in the postapartheid security state-making enterprise.[23] More prosaically, but no less effectively, perhaps, the policy outcome must be seen as the product of instrumentalist discourse and the incessant repetition of set security-making phrases that are all too often mistaken for policy alternatives, even, perhaps, for the truth. Whatever the immediate explanation, particular forms of speech that are (to recall a phrase from Walter Benjamin) filthy with dishonest use continue to make South Africa's security discourse.[24] Hopes that this could be halted, or even that a more interrogative opportunity could be provided to engage the idea of regional security and its cardinal referent, states, have been stymied by other policy initiatives in postapartheid South Africa.

A notable one in the political history of regional security in South Africa is the otherwise laudable effort to increasc access to education by replacing traditional disciplinary codes of knowledge with broader forms of interdisciplinary knowledge.[25] Drawing on the theory of Mode Two knowledge production developed by the U.S. educationalist Michael Gibbons and his colleagues, South Africa labor legislation has established quasigovernmental bodies, called Sector Education and Training Authorities (SETAs), to accomplish the goal.[26] One of these is known by the acronym DIDTEA (for Diplomacy, Intelligence, Defence, and Trade Education and Training Authority) and claims to represent "the Sovereignty of the State."[27] The purposive rationality represented by this ordering of knowledge can only further locate the idea (and the defining and refining) of both sovereignty and security within the privilege of state. The implications of this institutionalization are wide-ranging and, indeed, long-term: universities anxious to gain access to SETA-distributed tax funding have unhesitatingly accepted the idea that the study of security should be ordered in this manner. The result is a veritable profusion of academic courses that seek to draw the academic study of security closer to the routines of power and the exercise of management skills to manipulate state sovereignty. Let me provide an example: the University of Pretoria offers a postgraduate degree called Master of Security Studies as the "ideal qualification for those participating or planning to participate in the conduct of [state] security affairs."[28]

This trend toward command, a development reflected throughout the unfolding of many policy discourses in the new South Africa, betrays the reflexive calling to explore the social emancipatory potential that was promised to the region beyond apartheid.

The Dimly Witted Power of Intellectuals

Few things in the new South Africa have been more frightening than the increased status of "scientifically minded brain trusters in the councils of government."[29] Especially important have been sites that manufacture security knowledge. Their rise to prominence within the politics of transformation confirms how quickly the idea of national security is able to reassert itself between possible junctures.

The ending of apartheid in South Africa was thought to open the way for a profusion of politics. The moment was marked, however, not by the emancipatory discourse that had driven (and been driven by) the rhetoric of liberation but by an institutionalizing rationality that demanded immediate policy answers. The resulting process, which has dominated the political landscape since then, has been characterized by the ever-present power of think tanks that have produced policy around crafted options in much the same way that conventional industries produce material goods.[30] Using the reconciliation that marked South Africa's transition to democracy as a moment to engage, security studies championed continuity as the only commonsense contribution that it could make to the efficiencies that purportedly would be delivered to South Africa's national interest by the market. If this was one level of debate, policy outcomes themselves, as South Africa's decision to refurbish its military demonstrates, were only to be negotiated within the limited world of "bureaucrats, credential experts, and interest group elites."[31] This is a phrase that we have read before.

As a result, the prospect for open dialogue on possible futures, let alone Jürgen Habermas's ideal speech situation, was ended before it began. Importantly for our immediate purposes, the possibility—and nothing more—that a new form for regional security might emerge was ended as the conversation on South Africa's transition commenced. The result, as we have seen, is that recycled understandings of regional security perfected during the apartheid years have been reinserted into the practice of liberal democracy.[32] This illustrates a wider point about political change: the most influential forms of transitional knowledge are not the politics of the new but power represented by the old. Despite understandings to begin again, an immediate bad experience—even (or especially) when this deeply troubled people, as it certainly was in apartheid South Africa—often provides the only certain clue to both manufacturing and managing the future. For many in South Africa and in the region, this has been a painful, often inexplicable, development.[33] In comparative terms, however, it is no different than what had happened in Germany fifty years earlier, when the "repressive environment of [the] Federal Republic [enabled] ex-Nazi's [to] return to power [and to] present themselves as mere Realists while socialists and even left liberals were excluded (even from the universities) as ideological."[34]

Gramsci pointed out the force of continuity over the promise of change; a (slightly edited) paragraph captures his insight and points to the carrying power of what he called "organic intellectuals":

> Every "essential" social group that emerges into history out of the preceding economic structure, and is an expression of a development of this structure, has found . . . categories of intellectuals already in existence and which seem indeed to represent an historical continuity uninterrupted even by the most complicated and radical changes in political and social forms. These various categories [constitute] an uninterrupted historical continuity . . . they put themselves forward as autonomous and independent of the dominant social group. This self-assessment is not without consequences in the ideological and political field, consequences of wide-ranging import. The whole idealist philosophy can easily be connected with this position assumed by the social complex of intellectuals and can be identified as the expression of social utopias by which intellectuals think of themselves as "independent," autonomous, endowed with a character of their own etc.[35]

The ready accessibility of these defense and military ideologues to a public hungry for assurances about security both inside and outside suggested that they understood that effective communication (to use an entirely appropriate metaphor) represents the true map coordinates in the battle for ideas.[36] Not surprisingly, there has been no place within this industry for sustained, or even mild, critique.[37] Instead, the established techniques, as in the past, have been applied social science, punditry, and everyday reportage within a state-centric ontology. What is new and entirely different in this slash-and-burn approach to security is slick presentation, which is cast within the unfolding keywords of late modernity: democracy, accountability, and good governance. By marrying these to the continuities represented by the idea of sovereignty, epistemic communities have become powerful secondary sites of securitization. In becoming effective managers of their public image as experts, they also have removed themselves from the criticism that is commonly provided by open and interrogative speech processes and so avoided rigorous scrutiny of both their method and controlling purpose.[38] Freed of the constraints of democracy, accountability, and good governance—which they have insisted on from others—their policy work and their energetic public interventions have helped to locate them at the apex of securitization first within South Africa and then, as events unfolded, within the wider region. The latter development is not strange: intellectuals from hegemonic states with more resources invariably have a disproportionate influence on how political space is represented.[39]

Although rooted within the spirit of the new South Africa, these epistemic communities stand in direct lineage to the nascent communities of security intellectuals and policy analysts that emerged during the apartheid years. It is therefore necessary, perhaps, to point out that the Total National Strategy—apartheid's response to the perceived threat represented by the total onslaught—issued forth from a generation of South African intellectuals who were located within closed, and ideologically committed, universities in the 1970s and 1980s and who used the controlling codes of late apartheid to structure their world.[40]

The power exercised by the new generation of intellectuals suggests why the much-anticipated peace dividend in southern Africa has not been available to all its peoples. Roughly a decade after the ending of apartheid, the discourse on the region's state system continues to rely on the narrow binaries that are characterized by uncritical and unhistoricized understandings of sovereignty; as I have shown, these offer inclusion and exclusion as the only explanations of, and solutions to, southern Africa's complex lifeworld. Moreover, their continued reliance on the explanatory techniques offered by political hierarchy and their fatalistic acceptance of uneven economic outcomes are structural constraints to the attainment of lasting security for the poor, for the marginalized,

and especially for women and children. Recognizing the dulling force
this representation of the past offers to the future recalls Hannah Arendt's
famous indictment of brain-trusters made more than thirty years ago:
"the trouble is not that they are cold-blooded enough to 'think the
unthinkable,' but that they do not think."[41]

This offers a compelling insight into the power of dissonance. The
most significant exchange in the region's history on the role of South
Africa's public intellectuals on the issue of regional security was made
when apartheid's security intellectuals were at the height of their power.[42]
If anything, then, this book resurrects a tradition of dissent with the way
in which think tanks and their ideologues have championed the cause of
power relations in the region.

Recognizing the importance of dissent will not, however, end the
power that states present in the region, and as we turn toward the future
we must consider a question that offers a powerful insight into the region's
state system: If states were so late in coming to southern Africa, why has
their narrative power nearly silenced all other lifeworlds?

Prior to the ending of colonialism, minority rule, and apartheid, manifestations of insecurity and war were at the core of the region's discursive
formation. Through this, realist security studies was presented as the only
means to understand the future of social organization in the region; this,
in turn, strengthened the power that this discourse exercised over a political lexicon that used gloomy tropes and hollow patriotism to reinforce the
idea that the region belonged not to its people but to its states. So the
assertion by colonial authorities that they spoke on behalf of majorities,
and its flipside (minority claims to privilege), were contested in a regional
struggle that was entirely cast within the discourse not of individual rights
but of sovereignty and security.[43] The lasting effect of this was discovered
with the ending of apartheid; for all the declarations of a new tradition of
multilateralism, southern Africa's sense of community stretched only as
far as individual interpretations of state sovereignty permitted, and this—
as truth was increasingly told in the 1990s—was no farther than the
immediate borders of each individual state.[44] South Africa has played an
inordinately powerful role in determining the outcome: a process that has
been preoccupied with the assertion of national difference.

No event has exposed the hold of sovereignty and security on the
affairs of the region more plainly, and with more pain, than South Africa's
1998 incursion into Lesotho (see Chapter 5). Although ostensibly aimed
at restoring democracy to that country, and conducted under the auspices
of the new spirit of multilateralism, the action destroyed the possibility
that a security community could easily be established in southern Africa

along the lines famously suggested by Karl Deutsch in the 1950s.[45] Indeed, if anything, South Africa's approach on regional security—exemplified by the Lesotho episode—has increased the sense that the trend will be in the opposite direction, that is, toward the fateful and fatalistic security dilemma, a condition in which states, striving to seek security, in John Herz's words, "are driven to acquire more and more power to escape the impact of the power of others."[46]

Overcoming the despair conditioned by this interpretation of the region's past and the tragedy it promises in the future will be achieved by discovering, retrieving, and nurturing that which remains hidden in a place other than its states. But where is this place?

Toward Emancipation

Like other critique, this writing insists that state-formation in southern Africa reflects not preordained truths but particular representations of history. But as South Africa's recent past suggests, recognition of difference, even its formal resolution, is not the same as emancipation. If anything, the ending of apartheid clouded the possibility for a critical transformation of society, providing instead the recovery of old habits. This raises a core question in critical theory: How is the bridge between theory and political practice to be crossed?

In southern Africa, the key to this lies in developing new understandings of the idea of region. The goal must be to shift thinking on both security and community beyond the simple taxonomy that has produced community by social engineering.[47] This can be achieved by thinking of the region's multiple lifeworld not "as temporary, exotic, abnormal [but] thinking of its implications as an entirely self-sufficient, mobile, internal revival community: the underground as a definition of our future."[48] Security, community, and southern Africa's future, therefore, lie in turning from the instrumental and technological method of states that has been championed by realist discourse toward the life that lies beyond state sovereignty.

To switch lenses thus is to immediately recognize that there is a region of people; not to see this is to hanker for the vision offered by southern Africa's own dark decades.[49] There is great creativity in the region's cross-border life: art, literature, the multiple trade links and many informal economies, and the political discourse of the everyday.[50] Cross-border activity is driving a great human experience: marijuana smugglers are ignoring national boundaries (and the long arm of the law) to trade in the region's most important cash crop;[51] new Trekboers, driven by selective interpretations of their own history, appear to be seeking out frontier-life fundamentalism like those who settled on the banks of the Orange River two centuries ago;[52] reciprocally, Zimbabwean farmworkers are carrying agricultural production in South Africa's Limpopo Province; a long and almost entirely forgotten Zanzibari diaspora has made its appearance;[53] women traders are using unauthorized and unguarded paths to crisscross borders;[54] and indigenous Christian movements, which throughout the apartheid years nervously conducted their cross-border activities, have been afforded a new lease on evangelical life. Although nominally outside the mainstream, this cross-border agitation has convincingly impacted the region's formal political practice. Let just one example make the point: when Zimbabwean president Robert Mugabe first savaged the common-law rights of homosexuals in that country, South Africa's vociferous and confident gay community took to the streets.[55] Their protests during a meeting of the region's political elites entirely silenced Mugabe, at that time one of the region's most influential leaders.[56]

To see this other region is to understand that the region's people carry an idea of a different southern Africa. This is at odds with the shape that has been constructed by its states. There is an irony here—an irony that has run throughout this text, off these pages, and, yes, out into the region's streets and fields: the region's people often lived and experienced a community that is uncluttered by the discourses of state and sovereignty. For them, therefore, there is no need to erase national borders; those borders have simply not existed in any meaningful sense. Their faith in southern Africa's future is born in the memories of the borderless region that they live every day. Understanding this profoundly challenges the operating principles of realism in southern Africa.

To recast the region's security discourse, one core understanding is necessary: lasting community cannot be built on representations of sovereignty.[57] Orthodox security studies will repudiate this move, so it seems worth pointing out that security and community, like sovereignty, are not stable but are a socially constructed concept. They are therefore subject to renegotiation and refutation, and, like all issues in social science, are vulnerable to changing objective conditions that affect the aspirations and capacities of collectives and individuals.[58]

In southern Africa, fortunately, political practice has championed problem-solving theory; this, and the common sense so readily sought by realists, suggest that we must permit—as realists seldom do—the real world to set the pace of lasting change. Consider this example: the idea of people's power lies close to the surface of the region's recent political experience.[59] This is especially so in South Africa, where the ending of apartheid was predicated on the mobilization of progressive (although not always critical) forms of politics from below, which is now silent.[60] Why? The layering of change, and its insertion into subsequent political practice, were unfortunately left to the "traditional orientation of the discipline of International Relations [with its bias] towards government politics and professional politicians."[61] This explains why the dynamic unleashed from below has slowed and also why the idea of regional multilateralism yields so few renovating projects to fire people's imaginations.[62]

In stark contrast, lasting imagination and courageous leadership will be needed to insert new maps into the discourse of the region and its security. In this, the role of intellectuals is not to offer the past as the future but to assist practitioners to conceptualize less violent ways of securing community and help them to

> deal with social change by [encouraging them to] see beyond the immediacy of what *is* at any particular moment to conceptualize something of what could be. This is not the same as utopian or any other kind of normative theorizing, though the same capacity facilitates normative theorizing. Rather, this is a critical analytical ability that shows the limits of sheer empiricism.[63]

Recognizing a common dependence on water, land, and food offers an obvious way forward, but to propose this blindly is to move to Barry Buzan's acclaimed idea of extending the security agenda into five sectors: military, political, economic, societal, and environmental.[64] Apartheid South Africa embraced an extended security agenda but remained, as southern Africa's people know all too well, strongly committed to traditional military means to exercise its needs. The result was the long and fatal destabilization of southern Africa, an episode that has run the full course of this writing and will continue to plague southern African affairs for the next century. If we extend the security agenda but retain the state as the core security referent, we will strengthen the view that the region's security past must become its security future. The purpose, rather, must be to position the issues of water, land, and food as security markers in a post-Westphalian region in which a series of overlapping loyalties continuously fashions and refashions human security concerns that lie close at hand.

Although recrafting security referents will help shift the focus of security in the region, the role of social formations remains paramount.

Here, the core task is to harness those critical forces that constantly challenge institutional structures, ways of life and thinking, as well as norms and moral codes.[65] Fortunately, the rediscovery of social movements has enabled a sustained deepening of efforts to "redress the impact of social disorganization and consequent personal disorganization" outside of formal frames.[66] Here, revisiting marginal groups theory can help further discovery of the social, but more probably the move toward a deeper understanding of grass-roots democratic associations will offer working alternatives to the state as the core of social organization.[67] By offering these voices, instead of the closed epistemic groupings that have drawn the past into the future, the making of security in southern Africa can move beyond national borders and closer to the many who most need security.[68] However, the theoretical keys to discovering and understanding the potential that this offers the region are to be found in the rich social theory that characterizes anthropology and sociology, both of which lie at some conceptual distance from realist security studies.

This brings us to our constant companions on this long journey: ontology and epistemology.

Using critique as a mode of inquiry, this book has sought to foster not another understanding of the region's set security pieces offered by, say, reinterpretations of SADC's rightly infamous SADC Organ on Peace and Security; rather, its intention has been to deepen the opportunities that the social world offers to the idea of security and community in southern Africa. The reason for this is clear: "daily life [in the region] is shot through with constant sharp reminders of past and continuing unequal access to resources."[69]

The epistemology offered by realist security studies genuflects toward the statist taxonomy that gave southern Africa its current form. This "powerful ensemble of science, the bureaucratic nation state, individualism and continuous advancement" offers no place for people, only for power.[70] It was the early acceptance of this as the only means to regional community that made apartheid a vicious, predatory, and cruel form of social control rooted in a series of applied social sciences.[71] And these ways of knowing were successively protected by the routines of their late-modern manifestations: strategic studies, military science, and, now, realist security studies. The same constructions of the region, using the same grammar and the same tropes, continue to function beneath the surface in the guise of liberal democracy and free markets of the new world order. Nowhere has this been more obvious than in efforts to explain and command the flow of migrants to postapartheid South Africa, an application of social science that the respected geographer Jonathan Crush (as we have seen) has rightly labeled "pseudoscience."

Fortunately, the cultural homogeneity and the methodological blindness that once sanctioned and then defended narrow scientistic constructions of the social world, in pseudo-routines of knowledge called eugenics, phrenology, even apartheid, are under epistemological attack by the rediscovery of social theory and reflexive techniques of contemporary social inquiry. However, as an old friend, Karl Marx, once noted, there is no royal road to science, which is why there are no quick answers; instead, there are only questions that promise an arduous search.

We are perilously near the end of this journey, but perhaps the most difficult task lies immediately before us. Discovering new ways to imagine, understand, and secure what we know as southern Africa will not be possible without recognizing the conceptual and practical ruptures caused by the initial confrontation between the hegemonic power of European knowing—backed by formidable firepower—that nearly obliterated an earlier lifeworld in the region. It was a drama of great consequence to the issues that have been discussed here because it entirely transformed representations of indigenous traditions of politics. Following European settlement, these were received "not in their own terms, but in the newly dominant ones, and not in their own right, but as *different* from European forms. In the new situation only, they became perceived as 'indigenous', as 'traditional', as 'African.' Formulated in the dichotomous vocabulary that accompanied European presence, one can only say that 'indigenous' Africa was a modern invention."[72] In Chapter 2, I drew attention to the challenges this presents to a new generation of scholars.

Superimposed on a particular cartography, this distortion gave southern Africa the form that determined a narrative of social control. Today, as we have repeatedly stressed, it lives under the continual threat of subversion by the uncovering of the precolonial past that is promised by Africanist epistemology. What this is called—"indigenous," "traditional," "African," "traditional knowledge"—is, I believe, suggestive of the epic political battles that will rage before any of it can (as it must) be recovered—certainly any that will assist to make people more secure or, indeed, more conscious of social community.[73] "The real issue today," Henk van Rinsum reports Paulin Hountondi, the African scholar as writing, "is how this so-called traditional knowledge can be actively, critically reappropriated in a way that does not entail traditionalism, passéism, or collective narcissism, but rather enables these societies to address the new challenges that face them."[74]

So where are we to find a new form for the region? Where is its form? What is its gender? As we ask and answer these questions, we turn to the lifeworld that has been so brutally hidden by generalizations, affirmations, repetitions, and reifications of realist security studies. South Africa's hopes for the security of the region dare not hinge on organizational rote, or rational returns, or national interest, or strategic options, which are the stock-in-trade of orthodox security studies; they must reflect the essence of local, of place, of identity, of community.

In the convention of critical theory, especially the sense of pessimism that marked the work of Theodor Adorno, I have frequently turned toward culture to map the terrains of both knowledge and social practice that lie beyond applied social science and, indeed, beyond the tracks to the future that are offered by social theory. Southern African literature, with its powerful use of image and imagination, often shines a solitary beam way, way ahead of the region's preoccupations, its continuously invented traditions (see Chapter 6 and the discussion of Bessie Head, the southern African novelist). These embellished a point by the novelist J. M. Coetzee, who described the Nobel laureate Nadine Gordimer as "a visitor from the future."[75] Gordimer herself has written of the discovery delivered by the literary voice: "in instances where time and history appear to have met before the event: the . . . imagination has visualized an ordering of human lives that seems to be attainable by the projection of a State not yet created."[76]

As social theorists consider the possibility of a different, less violent form for the place dominated by South Africa, representations of the social, the local, and the everyday must be allowed (in a phrase once championed in international relations) to merge, mingle, and mix with institutional structures, some of which, like South Africa and its unequals, are the product of bitter imposition. It will take generations to work the violence of states and their discourse out of the everyday assumptions of the region.[77] To achieve this, a transaction moment must be provided by critical scholarship, not the compliance of status quo realism. The novelist Zoë Wicombe has provided an early vision of how remaking the past can be turned into a promising and vibrant future through the exploration of multiple belongings in a postcolony. Her thoughts on a southern African hybridity are offered here as the cornerstone in a new regional ontology and a new way to secure its people:

Instead of denying history and fabricating a totalising [community] "multiple belongings" could be seen as an alternative way of viewing a culture where participation in a number of . . . micro-communities whose interests conflict and overlap could become a rehearsal of a cultural life in the larger [South/southern] African community where we learn to perform the same kind of negotiations in terms of identity within a lived culture characterised by difference.[78]

In the Afterword that follows, I will provide the finishing strokes that will fully explain the implications of the social theory that is the basis of my analysis.

Afterword

A cliché suggests that ending is infinitely more difficult than beginning, so let me offer a few lines on the direction we came from and where it is that we will end. In Chapter 1, I began this book a number of times over, and so it seems best to end it not once but a number of times. As the title suggests, this is not so much a chapter as an afterthought, more accurately a collection of afterthoughts on the main text. It is preoccupied with four closely interlinked goals: a rehearsal of the chief arguments in each of the chapters; a drawing-together of some threads that remain hanging from the text; an effort to again address the theory-practice divide; and an anticipation of some of the more obvious critiques that will be aimed at the book.

*   *   *

Following the forceful insights promised by theoretical consciousness, this book critiques the discourses on security that have been unleashed by South Africa's position in southern Africa. The idea of southern Africa is the product of modernity: although positioned on the periphery of the international system, the region evinces a symbolic importance entirely out of proportion with its marginality. This is the result of the attention that has been enjoyed by South Africa, a bridgehead of Western influence in a distant corner of Africa.

In Chapter 1, the theoretical perspectives that underpin the argument and its writing are set down. Rather than pursuing any one specific critical mode, a poststructuralist lens guides the analysis: at various places, the text uses postmodernism as a point of analytical entry; at others, critical theory in the Frankfurt tradition is preferred. Chapter 2 interrogates the discursive formations that first permitted the establishment of states in southern Africa and asks why South Africa was positioned as the first among unequals (to use a phrase from Chapter 2). Laying out a genealogy, I suggest that sovereignty, upon which much of the discourse of regional security turns, is a weasel-word easily twisted to suit the purposes intended by the South African state, its builders, and its longtime patrons—capital. The results of this manipulation are addressed in Chapter 3, where the conversational rituals of South Africa's security behavior are considered. Both colonialism and apartheid established bad security habits, and the effects of these were to be felt with terrible violence as apartheid South Africa destabilized its neighbors in the 1980s.

Chapters 4 and 5 are case studies, the former preoccupied with the violent othering of foreigners and migrants in postapartheid South Africa. Here the analysis turns to renditions of history. South Africa was made by migrants, so recent migrants "represent only the latest in a line of vendors [who] have come from all over Africa, [who have escaped] war, natural disaster of flood, drought, and poverty by comparison with which we are a rich country, despite our share of the poor and the workless. . . . They are the latest arrivals of the endless no-nation of immigrants, forming and re-forming the world, a globalization that long, long predates any present concept."[1] Chapter 5 shines a light on the limits of liberal internationalism in southern Africa, especially the idea of peacekeeping. Using the fig leaf this offers, South Africa invaded Lesotho in September 1998. What was it that drove South Africa to this action? Confusion? Care? Courage? Or common-garden national interest?

The future is the interest of Chapter 6. If, as a core theme of the book suggests, states have failed to deliver community in southern Africa, then what can? Borrowing from anthropology, the argument points the way to the region's lifeworld in the sense suggested by Jürgen Habermas. This underbelly offers an alternative form of regional community, but its form makes it difficult to control, politically speaking, and therefore it is considered hostile by states and their makers. Chapter 7 returns to some irreconcilable themes in the text: the power of intellectuals, prospects for emancipatory politics, and the role of critical theory. Although the chapter closes with the cornerstones of a new ontological rendering of the region, this cannot disguise a deep interest in how speech all too often makes security out of nothing.

Issues of method are peppered throughout the text. This is intentional. The hand-me-down ideas regarding southern Africa and its security have flourished because scholarly accounts of the region have been entirely inattentive to social-science methodologies. In ways more real than symbolic, this inattention has marked all the social sciences in South Africa and southern Africa, but it is certainly true that international relations, security studies, and military science have been especially wayward. Conceived in closed and self-referential epistemes, these forms of knowledge, as the terrible experience with security under apartheid suggests, are readily prone to ideological manipulation.

What has also been of particular concern is the power of language and the word: the pseudosciences (to use a word purloined from Jonathan Crush), represented by particularistic and reductionist forms of knowing southern Africa and explaining its ways, have seldom been subjected to close scrutiny of the kind suggested by Iris Murdoch.

> The study of a language or any study that will increase and redefine our ability to *be* through words is part of a battle for civilization and justice and freedom, for clarity and truth, against fake-scientific jargon and spiritless slipshod journalese and tyrannical mystification.[2]

* * *

This book aims to teach many things, but none is more important than this: although modernity has delivered much to southern Africa, it has delivered only one way to order the political. As a project in community and security, southern Africa was late in taking form: early in the text, the point was repeatedly made that the South African state is only eight years older than Nelson Mandela, its first democratically elected president! But the roots of its ready assimilation into the codes of Westphalian political community are located in the early nineteenth century. The lasting effects of this buy-in (to use the homogenizing language of our times) were devastating: southern Africa's political life in the twenty-first century is reproduced by alien routines that are almost 200 years old. These were born of Comtean logic as well as the interpretations of life and the challenge of living offered by Comte's near-contemporary, Charles Darwin. The results of this are plain: community in southern Africa is said to be naturally represented by states, and they, following Thomas Hobbes, are caught in the never-ending struggle for survival. In southern Africa, this approach has bequeathed weak and embattled states that in place of regional community deliver poorly executed liberal multilateralism.

A central goal of critical theory is to change this world, this region, this life for southern Africans. This is why the arguments offered in these pages have delivered different explanations of events and offered alternative outcomes to the region's status quo.

No theme in this text is stronger than the force and influence represented by political power and its innumerable unfoldings. This is a process that began with understandings of superiority that drove othering and its historical twin: violent conquest. The abiding idea in the successive making of the region was that the land was plentiful and ready for the taking. Local inhabitants were rendered invisible by the combined power of civilizing codes and gunpowder. The fiction persisted for centuries, rather than decades, that southern Africa comprised empty lands waiting to be populated by whites in the name of God, empire, and the chartered company. But even the power of the insight offered by frontier theory missed a vital point: one man's frontier is another's home! Nevertheless, invisibility to the European gaze—certainly in this particular accounting—did not mean disappearance, so the proverbial natives returned to haunt the statist project in southern Africa over and over again as domestic security concerns became far greater than the threats posed by hostile neighbors.

This development was rich with irony: early South Africans (especially black but also white) knew that the region was not for settling. Indeed, its history, its archaeology, its anthropology suggest that migration was the natural order of regional things. Movement of water, animals, and people was a seasonal patterning of which the formal frames inserted by modernity were more irritants than reality. Today's epic fights with drought and flooding were certainly well-known long before the region was divided into states, but forms of coping perhaps caught in clan lore may have anticipated climatic cycles better than today. The erosion and corrosion of this lore, its legends, and many, many local languages have become the price the region has paid for modernity with its derived forms of inside/outside; its migratory patterns first of people and then of the idea represented by the control offered by sovereignty; and its assertions of xenophobia and derived nationalisms of a regional state system.

The idea of a system—subordinate state or otherwise—sets limits on the outcomes of the most crucial debates in contemporary social science: the structure-agency divide. The fatal acceptance of Westphalia in the region ended all possibility that agency, outside the states, has a life in regional politics, that it can deliver a more acceptable, more just, more equitable outcome to the current structural violence. Although it is presented in a different way in the book, the agency-structure divide goes to the heart of the argument. The ending of apartheid promised the region so very, very much. The reassertion of South Africa as the region's leader—the first among unequals—rendered these promises impotent. A "new" South Africa has not delivered a "new southern Africa," as old divides made by sovereignty, by wealth, and by envy continue. This explains why at the time of this writing, roughly a decade after the ending of apartheid, the debate on regional security in southern Africa is entirely preoccupied with the only purpose of realism: system maintenance. The conflict between people and this system maintenance is a strong subtext in these pages. The natural rhythm of the region's lifeworld has put a great distance between citizen and state; hidden from the formal eye, the region's people turn toward this for support.

But equally so, southern Africa's people can embrace the state for succor, support, and sustenance at moments of crisis or celebration. If anything, this opens the idea—which runs through these pages, too—that states in the region are both imagined and invented. It seems plausible to suggest, then, that had the region's states been less gobbling and more giving, the relationship between citizen and state might well have been different. After all, the epochalist "Cry Freedom" that moved nationalism throughout Africa was one of the great rallying cries of the twentieth century. But the region's states, as South Africa's history again and again reveals, are tied and bound to the power of foreign capital. Within this partnership, Westphalia and its many celebratory accoutrements represent a project for the privileged, not the poor; this is not a uniquely southern African story, for the story of state-building is the story of struggle and reform that deliberately closes points of access and the means to human agency.

If states are for neither people nor the poor, then how are we to understand communities? As this text has argued, this question lies close to the story of southern Africa and how its tale is constantly being retold. The power of this telling has privileged states not only as the natural order of regional things but also as the commonsensical path to the world of community. And yet the region's history is redolent with different forms of community—family, clan, tribe, business, trading, religious. Rediscovering these communities, excavating them, and recovering their form are not easy because they are embedded within the self-reinforcing truths of state and the closed scholarly techniques of international relations and security studies. This explains why it is difficult for policymakers to see a future that lies beyond the compass set by the region's states.

* * *

In addressing the book at the policy community, it has been my intention to draw the power of critique closer to the practice of security. Any cursory understanding of security studies—even after the events of September 11, 2001—suggests that the message of this book is not from the margins. At meetings of the International Studies Association and the British International Studies Association, the analysis used in this book is commonplace (certainly not exceptional). And yet in South and southern

Africa, work that reflects either theoretical or methodological adventures or critiques the unfolding codes of social control is thought to be taboo, its protagonists relegated to some kind of netherworld. The result is a closed conversation between experts (often erroneously called "civil society"), the policy community, and politicians. Indulging in a language conditioned by managerialism and statistics and mired in the rituals of rational choice, policymaking—especially in the field of security in South Africa—has become a macabre dance, the key words—"democracy," "governance," "accountability," "transparency"—offering a license to state behavior and indulgence of a kind thought possible only under a system like apartheid. There is no better example of this than the decision by South Africa's government to purchase roughly U.S.$6.5 billion worth of sophisticated weapons to reequip its defense force.

By rendering alternative understandings, critical theory explains why change in southern Africa is conservative rather than radical. Cast within liberal definitions of politics, the ending of apartheid has made southern Africa safe for statist democracy. Recognizing this represents a difficult moment for policymakers. The courage to move beyond this self-enclosing reality is the most impossible moment in the theory and practice of contemporary politics. At the practical level, it requires theoretical opening vistas to an understanding that the future can never be neutral. As the theorists and practitioners battle with this world, understandings of history and doubt are the only certain companions. Hannah Arendt invokes a parable from Franz Kafka at a bridge between the past and the future. Here it is:

> He has two antagonists: the first presses him from behind, from the origin. The second blocks the road ahead. He gives battle to both. To be sure, the first supports him in his fight with the second, for he wants to push him forward, and in the same way the second supports him in his fight with the first, since he drives him back. But it is only theoretically so. For it is not only the two antagonists who are there, but he himself as well, and who really knows his intentions? His dream, though, is that some time in an unguarded moment—and this would require a night darker than any night there has ever been yet—he will jump out of the fighting line and be prompted, on account of his experience in fighting, to the position of umpire over his antagonists in their fight with each other.[3]

All too often, of course, the practitioner cannot indulge in this struggle as the busy demands of policymaking envelop the daily routine. So simple-minded constructions of political events and change, crafted in the language of progress and celebration, close even the most inquisitive of minds. This has been the graveyard of activists-turned-politicians and -policymakers and reinforces the wisdom and power of Rob Walker's observation, which we first noted in Chapter 3: "grand visions of the future have been linked to promises made by particular groups to effect change after gaining power, promises that have been broken either by the nature of the struggle for power itself or by the nature of the power that is attained. Too many revolutions have been swallowed by all powerful states."[4]

The sense in which theory has been used in these pages is not in the administrative, management, guide-to-action sense trumpeted by schools of public administration and government where problem-solving matters more than life itself. No, the role for theory is clear: it must guide practice by offering new possibilities, in changed circumstances, by helping practitioners to see what lies beyond the immediate horizon, by recognizing that statistics make particular kinds of facts and that facts are social constructions.

*   *   *

Many will see this book as a political text, a point frequently made in Chapter 2. But its purpose is to open up options, not to further close minds that are already half-shut. Essentially, the aim has been to promote thinking on both security and on southern Africa outside of the formal frames presented and represented by states and their behavior. Drawing upon the power of closure that lies in the routines of nations and national interests, mainstream thinking on security in southern Africa has not strayed far from its early confrontation with the other notwithstanding the ending of apartheid.

What has helped this closure is the power that has been exerted by defense and security intellectuals. There will be some criticism of the view that those who made apartheid's security rituals continue to do so in the new South Africa.

Put in the form of a question: Have I exaggerated the role that is played in the making of security policy by closed security think tanks like the Institute for Security Studies and the South African Institute of International Affairs? Let me be plain about this. It may certainly be true that at particular moments in the making of security policy in the new South Africa the hand of the ISS was frequently absent, for instance, in the defense white papers. Nevertheless, the overall power exerted by the ISS—through its capacity to successfully securitize issues—has been widely felt throughout South African society. This is a major feature of the country's life in the postapartheid period. This is not to suggest that there has been no tension between the ISS and South Africa's formal military establishment; quite the opposite, there have been moments of obvious tension, but the overall influence of the ISS (and to a lesser degree the SAIIA) on the debate on security cannot be sufficiently stressed. If a single thread joins regional relations, domestic politics, parliamentary procedure, gender, children, HIV/AIDS, agriculture, and regional peacekeeping, it is the thread of security, a thread made and remade by the formidable energy within security epistemes and the influence upon them of foreign funds. Unraveling this ontological thread and placing security within the perspectives needed to deal with the many opportunities it offers to policymakers represent two of the central challenges to serious scholarship in South Africa. There is a lesson here for other societies in transition: beware of the security discourse in changing times. Ask these questions: Who is driving them? Whose interests do they serve? Who funds the perpetuation of particular forms of security discourse? What impact is this having on wider public policy and societal change? And remember the power of the Shona proverb mentioned in Chapter 3: a hide is best folded when it is raw and wet.

Some eyebrows will be raised at my unwillingness to address the work of alternative voices, like the Military Research Group, during South Africa's transition, voices that were drawn from antiapartheid groupings and that helped to develop the new South Africa's security policy. Here two points are important. First, as to the central topic of this book—security relations in the region—these groupings were largely silent. Second, the work of this grouping, although directed toward peace studies, unquestioningly accepted the region's states as the core security referent. The ideas that other forms of security community were desirable in the region, and that these offered an alternative to states, were introduced into the South African debate by Ken Booth only in 1994.[5]

Outside of the state-directed argument, little attention has been directed to the imported force of realist discourse. This is certainly a lacuna in an argument that has been determined to make theoretical points with deep practical implications. The power of the exiled experience has been underestimated in contemporary explanations of South Africa, especially in discussions of security. Understanding exile through multiple conceptual lenses is work that beckons a coming generation of scholars. As they look into this experience, a helpful research project will be to map where the exiled leadership and defense cadres learned their brand of security studies. The link between this and the realist behavior of South

Africa's neighbors also requires further exploration. This emerging research agenda faces an important dilemma, however: Will these questions be cast within the traditional mold of regional security and the study of it, or will these questions be cast within the more searching points of entry provided by critical security studies?

*   *   *

Have I romanticized the power of the everyday, the potential offered by social movements, and the discourse of the local? After all, southern Africa's polity has been formed, its states displaying all its features, including, of course, parliaments, parties, and politicians. Faced with this, what hope is there that mobilizing opposition to these polities can take place and, importantly, what threat to emancipation is posed by the dark side of the everyday? Even the day-to-day unfolding of events in southern Africa shows that the glass is not half-empty but rather half-full. Although the hope for immediately realized and realizable popular democracy seems impossible in all but a few of the region's states, the region's people continue to display an impressive capacity both to mobilize and resist. Interestingly, this facility is shown in the daily struggles of individual people, especially women, to provide security and stability for families who have been rent asunder by the region's states and the system that is of their making. This lived world has been devastatingly affected by the HIV/AIDS pandemic that has swept through the subcontinent; here again, women, not men, have borne the brunt of the assault. But popular resistance to the virus is everywhere to be seen, nowhere more powerfully than in South Africa, where the government's policy on the disease has been contested in both the public and the private domains. The experience of struggle to apartheid, we best remember, is close to the surface of South African politics and will be drawn upon again and again to contest state policies.

This raises a near-hidden question in an argument that requires an answer: Why have South Africans supported their state in its assault on migrants? Hidden in the folds of this book the answers are to be found. Let us recall them. The othering of migrants was linked to feelings of superiority derived from the sense of economic development that had been built on apartheid and inflated by the success of South Africa's transition; paradoxically, however, it has constructed another underclass around the selfsame conceptual primitives upon which apartheid had once rested. And yet here is the irony: the transformative capacity of migrants on South Africa has been immense. The force of this has been particularly relevant in the cultural field. Let two examples both make and carry the case. First, the most easily recognizable face in South Africa (after that of Nelson Mandela) belongs to the Nigerian academic Kole Omotoso, whose visage has helped to launch and market the country's second fastest growing economic sector, the cellular phone industry. The second example also begins with the country's former president, Nelson Mandela, but ends in the country's classrooms, conference rooms, and chambers of state. Mandela's evocative dress code, especially his famous shirts, entirely changed the approach to attire, formal and informal, in South Africa. These cultural turning points, as we might call them, will not immediately end the national chauvinism that has driven the South African state to hound migrants, but the power of culture will break the barriers between locals and migrants. Recognizing this fingers a moment of extreme poverty for structural approaches to regional security: they can never, outside of bureaucracy, identify moments of significant cultural change and situate them within wider moments of transformation. Neither can they reach, as we noted in Chapter 6, beyond the simple war-determining hypothesis that guides their thinking. This failure—a failure of imagination, of method, of humanity—prevents them from using the life-giving essence of, say, water as a means to make community rather than as a tool to break community.

What about the dark side of the local? There is, quite frankly, no answer to this. South Africa's newspapers all too often feed on the frenzy of popular stories and tales of a return to the primitive. And yet any comparative work knows that the use of dark practices to serve the interests of science, even in the most developed and sophisticated societies, is commonplace. Think of the stories that emerged from Britain and New Zealand reporting on the removal of organs from deceased children for use in medical science. Where does this primeval behavior leave the idea of the economically rational, the policy focused, the politically accountable—indeed, where does it leave the very idea of security in the home of the most ordered state?

*   *   *

Finally, what is southern Africa? Who's in—and who's out? Structuralists will worry that this text is seemingly not interested in offering a definition of the region. There is no suggestion, for instance, that southern Africa means the inner periphery of Botswana, Lesotho, Namibia, and Swaziland—the states that make for the Southern African Customs Union. Indeed, in the discussion of migration, the text seems overly adventurous: Congolese, all too often at the sharp end of South Africa's xenophobia, are obviously counted in. But the question Where does the region end? entirely disregards the fact that the study of security is a social process that is difficult to pin down, except in efforts to exercise social control. These invariably end in violence. Social constructions of southern Africa are made and remade through intricate forms of human interaction. This is why looking beyond states for new forms of community promises to deliver an entirely new understanding of what constitutes region and why the region's hope for security may lie in the social theory that has run the course of these pages.

Notes

Chapter 1

1. Jason Frank and John Tambornio, "Introduction," in Frank and Tambornio, eds., *Vocations of Political Theory*, p. x.
2. Richard Devetak, "Critical Theory," in Burchill et al., eds., *Theories of International Relations*, p. 146.
3. Said, *Culture and Imperialism*, p. 336.
4. Wyn Jones, "'Message in a Bottle'?" pp. 299–319.
5. Said, *Representations of the Intellectual*, p. 84.
6. Quoted in Sole, "The Witness of Poetry."
7. Tony Morphet, "My Life Was a Transfer," in *Vintage Kenton*, p. 286.
8. Ramano, "It's Time for 'Comparative Intellectuals,'" p. B10.
9. *The Project "Training for Peace in Southern Africa,"* pp. 32–33.
10. See Walker, "Security, Sovereignty, and the Challenge of World Politics," p. 8; Walker, *Inside/Outside*, pp. 138–140.
11. Cited in Steve Smith, "The Self-Images of a Discipline," in Booth and Smith, eds., *International Relations Theory Today*, p. 2.
12. See Wyn Jones, "'Message in a Bottle'?" pp. 306–308.
13. My own earlier work on regional security represents a good example of this kind of fuzzy thinking; see Vale, *Southern African Security*, pp. 32–47.
14. Rosenau et al., *Global Voices*, p. 22.
15. See Hugh Gusterson, "Missing the End of the Cold War," in Weldes, ed., *Cultures of Insecurity*, pp. 319–345.
16. For an excellent summary, see Mittelman, ed., *Globalization*, p. 25.
17. Richard Devetak, "Critical Theory," in Burchill et al., eds., *Theories of International Relations*, p. 146.
18. See "Timothy Keegan Responds." http://uni-ulm.de/~rturrell/ sarobnewhtml/keegan.html (May 7, 1998).
19. For a discussion of this move, see Smith et al., *International Theory*.
20. Gibson, *Critical Theory and Education*, p. 15.

21. Steve Smith, "The Self-Images of a Discipline," in Booth and Smith, eds., *International Relations Theory Today,* p. 3.

22. From epigraph quoting David Campbell and Michael Dillon in Simon Dalby, "Contesting an Essential Concept," in Krause and Williams, eds., *Critical Security Studies,* p. 3.

23. Berger and Luckham, *The Social Construction of Reality.*

24. Walt, "International Relations," p. 40.

25. See Burchill et al., eds., *Theories of International Relations*; Booth and Smith, eds., *International Relations Theory Today.* See Krause and Williams, eds., *Critical Security Studies*; Walker, *One World, Many Worlds.*

26. "The philosophers have only 'interpreted' the world, in various ways; the point, however, is to *change* it." See Singer, *Marx,* p. 32. Hoffman, "Critical Theory and the Inter-Paradigm Debate," pp. 231–249.

27. Ibid., p. 233.

28. Craig Calhoun, "Social Theory and the Public Sphere," in *The Blackwell Companion to Social Theory,* p. 429. Richard Devetak, "Critical Theory," in Burchill et al., *Theories of International Relations*, p. 146.

29. Tim Luke, "Touring Hyperreality," in Wexler, ed., *Critical Theory Now*, p. 22.

30. Booth and Vale, "Security in Southern Africa," pp. 285–304.

31. Sheldon A. Wolin, "Political Theory," in Frank and Tambornio et al., *Vocations of Political Theory.*

32. See Michael C. Williams and Keith Krause, "Preface," in Krause and Williams, eds., *Critical Security.*

33. R.J.B. Walker, quoted in Terriff et al., *Security Studies Today,* p. 102.

34. This has happened elsewhere, too, of course. See Tilly, *Coercion, Capital, and European States.*

35. For example, see Geldenhuys, *South Africa's Search for Security Since the Second World War.*

36. Exactly how long and how influential a peace dividend might be is a matter for some speculation: orthodox strategic studies seemingly believes it should be brief. See, for example, Freedman, *The Revolution in Strategic Affairs*, p. 5.

37. Simon Dalby, "Contesting an Essential Concept," in Krause and Williams, eds., *Critical Security Studies*. J. Ann Tickner, "Re-visioning Security," in Booth and Smith, eds., *International Relations Theory Today.* Wæver, *Concepts of Security.*

38. As an example of this, see Mills, *South Africa and Security Building in the Indian Ocean Rim,* pp. 7–9.

39. On these efforts, see "Security Is Still 'Devillish,'" *Mail and Guardian* (Johannesburg), March 14–19, 1997.

40. Bowman, "The Subordinate State System of Southern Africa," pp. 231–261. However, the book that confirmed and advanced the idea of a state system was Potholm and Dale, eds., *Southern Africa in Perspective.* Steve Smith, "The Self-Images of a Discipline," in Booth and Smith, eds., *International Relations Theory Today,* p. 4.

41. J. Ann Tickner, "Re-visioning Security," in Booth and Smith, eds., *International Relations Theory Today*, p. 177.

42. See Booth and Vale, "Security in Southern Africa," pp. 285–304.

43. Simon Dalby, "Contesting an Essential Concept," in Krause and Williams, eds., *Critical Security Studies*, p. 5.

44. Robert Cox, "Critical Political Economy," in Cox et al., *International Political Economy*, p. 31.

45. The phrase is said to originate with the ethnographer Bronislaw Malinsowski. Recent work seems to suggest that Malinsowski's approach to this issue was more subtle than that usually assumed. See Otto, *Social Practice and the Ethnographic Circle,* p. 3.

46. Martin, *The Dialectical Imagination.*

47. Wyn Jones, "'Message in a Bottle,'" p. 313.

48. For an example of this kind of thinking, see Butts and Thomas, *The Geopolitics of Southern Africa.*

49. The social historian Charles van Onselen captures this condition in southern Africa with this line from his fine study of the African Highveld sharecropper Kas Maine: "in the long run insecurities weigh more heavily in landless tenants than they do on property-owning families." See van Onselen, *The Seed Is Mine,* p. 6. For a brief critical review of this work, see Gary Minkley and Ciraj Rasool, "Orality, Memory, and Social History in South Africa," in Nuttall and Coetzee, eds., *Negotiating the Past*, pp. 89–99.

50. Because jargon often confounds, let me explain a term that refers to the way in which "persons subjectively experience, understand and interpret their world. For Habermas, and for the sense it used in this book, it consists of implicit cultural-linguistic assumptions, norms, and habits that form the shared background of action and thought. The life world is constituted through the medium of communicative action, which is itself largely responsible for the organisation of family and the public sphere, the principal domains shaping life experience." See Ingram, *Critical Theory and Philosophy*, p. 222.

51. See Booth, "Security in Anarchy," p. 535.

52. Booth and Vale, "Security in Southern Africa," pp. 85–304.

53. Dr. Tony Holiday helped me think my way around this.

54. See Booth, "Security in Anarchy," p. 535.

55. Schama, *The Embarrassment of Riches,* p. 8.

56. Booth, "Security in Anarchy," p. 537.

57. Keith Krause and Michael C. Williams, "From Strategy to Security," in Krause and Williams, eds., *Critical Security Studies,* p. 35.

58. Simon Dalby, "Contesting an Essential Concept," in Krause and Williams, eds., *Critical Security Studies,* p. 24.

59. Bauman, *Modernity and the Holocaust,* p. x.

60. See Peter Vale, "'Whose World Is It Anyway'?" in Dyer and Mangasarian, eds., *The Study of International Relations,* pp. 201–220.

61. "TRC Deal with Military Allowed Truth to Slip Away," *Sunday Independent* (Johannesburg), September 11, 2001.

62. Tony Morphet, "My Life Was a Transfer," in *Vintage Kenton,* p. 283.

Chapter 2

1. Rotberg, "Centripetal Forces," p. 9.
2. Some of these images are drawn from Vale, *South Africa and Southern Africa*.
3. Ibid.
4. Said, *Culture and Imperialism*, p. 133.
5. David Mutimer, "Reimaging Metaphors: The Metaphors of Proliferation," in Krause and Williams, eds., *Critical Security Studies*, p. 205.
6. This is the basis of the infamous Kissinger National Security Study Memorandum (NSSM) 39 tilt toward the White South that was made by the U.S. National Security Council in 1969. See Cohen and El-Khawas, *The Kissinger Study of Southern Africa*.
7. This was the basis for South Africa's deepening involvement in southern Africa throughout the 1970s and 1980s—the infamous policy of destabilization. See Grundy, *The Rise of the South African Security Establishment*, pp. 51–68. For a powerful journalistic account, see Hanlon, *Beggar Your Neighbours*.
8. This has been the essence of the debate in the postapartheid situation. A major concern has been the seeming determination of the so-called Frontline States, led by Zimbabwe, to keep South Africa at some distance from decision-making in matters of security. See Solomon and Cilliers, "Southern Africa and the Quest for Collective Security," pp. 191–205.
9. See "Mugabe the Hawk Puts the Region at Risk," *Sunday Independent* (Johannesburg), August 23, 1998.
10. Walker, *Inside/Outside*, p. 15.
11. This work is exemplified in Hussein Solomon, "Realism and Its Critics," in Vale, ed., *Theory, Change, and the Future of Southern Africa*, pp. 34–57.
12. Gutteridge and Spence, eds., *Violence in Southern Africa*.
13. Bauman, *Modernity and the Holocaust*, p. 3.
14. See the important study by Comaroff and Comaroff, *Of Revelation and Revolution*.
15. For example, see Roskam, *Grenselose Oorlog*. For example, see Meyns, *Konflikt und Entwicklung im Südlichen Afrika* (Conflict and development in southern Africa). For example, see Oden, *Southern African Futures*, p. 15. Consider these two examples: Arlinghaus, ed., *African Security Issues*, and Clough, ed., *Changing Realities in Southern Africa*.
16. See MacKenzie, ed., *Imperialism and the Natural World*. On southern Africa, see Dubow, ed., *Science and Society in Southern Africa*.
17. Turner, *Orientalism, Postmodernism, and Globalism*, p. 31.
18. On the issue of imperial bargains, see Ellis, "Africa After the Cold War," pp. 1–28.
19. Strange, *States and Markets*, p. 18.
20. The Southern African Customs Union is the oldest economic integration scheme in the region. Established in 1910 and renegotiated in 1969, the Union comprises South Africa, Botswana, Lesotho, Swaziland, and, since 1990, Namibia. It provides for free movement of goods and services among members

through a common tariff. Customs and excise duties collected are paid into a common pool administered by the South African Reserve Bank. Revenues accruing to these states are paid annually in proportion to the amount of goods and services that entered their borders. See Development Bank of Southern Africa, *The Southern African Customs Union.*

21. *A Dictionary of South African History,* p. 154.

22. Keegan, *Colonial South Africa and the Origins of the Racial Order,* p. 255.

23. Ibid., p. 262.

24. For this see Kalley, *South Africa's Treaties in Theory and Practice, 1806–1998,* p. 28.

25. Christopher Saunders, "Political Processes in the Southern African Frontier Zones," in Lamar and Thompson, eds., *The Frontier in History,* p. 150.

26. For a brief discussion of Portuguese colonial states in Mozambique, see Christopher, *The Atlas of States,* p. 48.

27. R.B.J. Walker, "International Relations and the Concept of the Political," in Booth and Smith, eds., *International Relations Theory Today,* p. 319.

28. Dubow, "The War for South Africa," p. 1.

29. Richard Falk, "Sovereignty," in *The Oxford Companion to Politics of the World,* p. 789.

30. Walker, *Inside/Outside.*

31. Alexander B. Murphy, "The Sovereign State System as Political-Territorial Ideal," in Biersteker and Weber, eds., *State Sovereignty as Social Construct,* pp. 81–120.

32. See Bamyeh, *The Ends of Globalization,* p. 6.

33. Almost entirely forgotten now, but nevertheless closely bound up with the idea of creating the idea of southern Africa, is the role played by the idea of the region in the popular mind. See the annual publication entitled *Year Book and Guide to Southern Africa.*

34. See Mundazi, *The Struggle for Social Change in Southern Africa.*

35. There is an important theoretical debate in South African historiography over the Mfecane and interpretations of it that was sparked by the work of the historian Julian Cobbing. I believe that this debate and the excavation of material on premodern southern Africa have much to teach us about the search for the region's future security. This future work will be deeply influenced by interpretations of the Mfecane. On the latter, see Hamilton, ed., *The Mfecane Aftermath.* For an impressive and authoritative account of the origins of the Mfecane, see Pieres, *The Dead Will Arise.* But the Sotho term *difaqane,* which means "hammering" and "forced migration," is equally evocative in the idea of security and community.

36. Holiday, "Conversations in a Colony," p. 8.

37. Torodov, *The Conquest of America.*

38. Bamyeh, *The Ends of Globalization,* p. 107.

39. Chidester, *Savage Systems,* p. 9.

40. There is a fine critical exploration of these ideas in Leslie Witz, "Beyond van Riebeeck," in Nuttall and Michael, eds., *Senses of Culture Studies*, pp. 318–339.

41. Chidester, *Savage Systems*.

42. See Lamar and Thompson, eds., *The Frontier in History*.

43. Legassick, "The Griqua, the Sotho-Tswana, and the Missionaries"; and Martin Legassick, "The Frontier Tradition in South African Historiography," in Marks and Atmore, eds., *Economy and Society in Pre-industrial South Africa*, pp. 44–79.

44. Chidester, *Savage Systems*, pp. 20–21.

45. Keegan, *Colonial South Africa and the Origins of the Racial Order*, p. 27.

46. Chidester, *Savage Systems*, pp. 20–21.

47. Keegan, *Colonial South Africa and the Origins of the Racial Order*, p. 27.

48. See, for instance, "Does Pretoria Have a Cape Card to Play," *The Times* (London), September 1, 1986.

49. See du Toit, "Puritans in Africa?" pp. 209–240.

50. Davenport, "Kruger, Paul."

51. Thompson, *The Political Mythology of Apartheid*.

52. Ibid., p. 173.

53. Elphick and Davenport, eds., *Christianity in South Africa*, p. 56.

54. Suransky-Dekker, "A Liberating Breeze of Western Civilization," p. 106.

55. Norval, *Deconstructing Apartheid Discourse*, p. 93.

56. See Hanna, *The Story of the Rhodesias and Nyasaland*.

57. See Hyam, *The Failure of South African Expansion*.

58. See, for instance, Smuts, *Plans for a Better World*, pp. 243–254.

59. Hirson and Williams, *The Delegate for Africa*, p. 140.

60. See, for example, Wells, *Southern Africa*.

61. "Lost Trails of the Kruger Park," by Tim Couzens, *Sunday Times Lifestyle* (Johannesburg), May 23, 1999, p. 6.

62. Garson, "South Africa and World War I," p. 68.

63. Ruggie, "Territoriality and Beyond," p. 163.

64. See Martin, "Region Formation Under Crisis Conditions."

65. Grundy, *Defense Legislation and Communal Politics*.

66. Fourie, *Evolving Experience in Decisions for Defence*.

67. Elphick and Davenport, eds., *Christianity in South Africa*, p. 56.

68. Andrews et al., *South Africa in the Sixties*, pp. 128–129.

69. Campbell, *Writing Security, United States Foreign Policy, and the Politics of Identity*.

70. Hobden, "State Formation and Development in Southern Africa."

71. For the fiction around this policy, see Malan and Hattingh, *Black Homelands in South Africa*; for their search for international recognition, see Letlaka, "The Republic of Transkei and the International Community," pp. 79–83.

72. See *Keesing's Record of World Events*, vol. 29 (January 1983).

73. Kapuściński, *Another Day of Life*, p. 129.

74. In other work I have told these three stories a number of times. See, for example, *South Africa and Southern Africa,* and "Dissenting Tale," in Vale et al., *Theory, Change, and Southern Africa's Future,* pp. 17–33.

75. Ibid., p. 383.

76. Dingake, *My Fight Against Apartheid.*

77. "Africa's Poverty Threatens SA," *The Star* (Johannesburg), May 1, 1996.

78 Harries, "The Roots of Ethnicity," p. 26; from Dubow, *Scientific Racism in Modern South Africa,* p. 77.

79. Ruggie, "Territoriality and Beyond," p. 151.

Chapter 3

1. Some of the early ideas in this chapter were embedded in my monograph *Of Laagers, Lepers, and Leanness.*

2. See media briefing by Joe Modise, South African minister of defense, Cape Town, February 12, 1998; parliamentary media briefing by the minister of defense, August 3, 1998; and address by the minister of defense, Joe Modise, on the occasion of the defense budget vote in the National Assembly, May 22, 1997.

3. Der Derian and Shapiro, eds., *International/Intertextual Relations,* p. 13.

4. AMLIVE SAFm 104–107, September 17, 1998.

5. Dubow, *Scientific Racism in Modern South Africa,* p. 281.

6. See Spence, *The Strategic Significance of Southern Africa*; Bowman, "The Strategic Importance of South Africa to the United States," pp. 159–191.

7. Jaster, *The Defence of White Power.*

8. Debbie Posel, "A 'Battlefield of Perceptions,'" in Cock and Nathan, eds., *War and Society,* p. 272.

9. Crampton, "The Voortrekker Monument, the Birth of Apartheid, and Beyond," pp. 228–229.

10. This was just one of innumerable ways in which the military inserted itself in the life of apartheid power. See "Laundry, Canned Goods, and Rape," A34–A36.

11. See "Why This Violence, Reform, and Unrest Go Together," *Sunday Tribune* (Durban), March 2, 1996.

12. Grundy, *Soldiers Without Politics.*

13. The measuring of this is found not in political text but in the powerful flourishing of literature around these themes, particularly in the Afrikaans language, that occurred throughout the 1980s. For this work, see Strachen, *'N Wereld Sonder Grense* (A world without borders); Prinsloo, *Jonkmanskas* (Youngman's treasure); Prinsloo, *Hemel Help Ons* (Heaven help us). For an assessment, see Coetsee, *Letterkunde en die Krisis* (Literature and the crisis). For a commentary of this work written in the English language, see H. E. Koornhof, "Works of Friction: Current South African War Literature," in Cock and Nathan, eds., *War and Society,* pp. 275–282.

14. See Hugo, "Towards Darkness and Death," pp. 567–596.

15. Njabulo Ndebele, "Memory, Metaphor, and the Triumph of Narrative," in Nuttall and Coetzee, eds., *Negotiating the Past,* p. 23.

16. See McSweeney, *Security, Identity, and Interests.*

17. Graebner, ed., *The National Security,* p. v.

18. Hoffman, "An American Social Science," pp. 41–60.

19. At the time, he was director of the Foreign Policy Research Institute of South Carolina. See *Military Review*, November 1965, p. 107. Harrigan, *Defence Against Total Attack.*

20. Professor Marius J. Swart, a leading Afrikaner public intellectual, recommended this to the publisher in a review of the book. See letter from Marcus de Jong to Herman Steyler of Nasionale Boekhandel dated January 11, 1966.

21. On the Cold War and culture, see Bacon, *Flannery O'Connor and Cold War Culture.*

22. Harrigan, *Defence Against Total Attack,* p. 89.

23. Ibid.

24. Ibid., p. 92.

25. Ibid., p. 95.

26. There are various South African examples that I might have chosen, beginning, perhaps, with the massive doctoral thesis of Lukas Daniël Barnard, once a professor of political studies at the University of the Orange Free State, who was to become South Africa's spymaster during the final years of apartheid, and who continued to occupy positions of authority in the new South Africa as the chief of the bureaucracy of the Cape Province. See Barnard, *Die Magsfaktor in Internasionale Verhoudinge* (The power factor in international relations). One might, perhaps, have continued with the work of the German-born, U.S.-trained Dirk Kunert, once the Jan Smuts Professor of International Politics at the University of Witwatersrand. An homage to Kunert and his work (including a sample of his writing) is to be found in Vale and van den Ende, eds., *The Loss of Innocence.* For a policy-oriented sample of this kind of work, see Maritz, "Pretoria's Reaction to the Role of Moscow and Peking in Southern Africa," pp. 321–344.

27. Book Discussion: "Defence Against Total Attack," by Anthony Harrigan, *SABC Survey, Current Affairs*, January 28, 1966, 7:15 P.M., English Service.

28. "Whose World Is It Anyway?" in Dyer and Mangasarian, eds., *The Study of International Relations,* p. 208.

29. Rosenau et al., *Global Voices,* p. 13.

30. There are many examples of this, but let this single one stand for others; see Clifford-Vaughan, *Force and Peace.*

31. Louw, ed., *National Security.*

32. Ibid.

33. Book reviews, *International Affairs Bulletin* 2, 1 (1978): 49.

34. Williams, "South African Foreign Policy," pp. 73–91.

35. Robert Thornton, "The Potentials of Boundaries in South Africa," in Werbner and Ranger, eds., *Postcolonial Identities in Africa,* p. 139.

36. Guelke, "The Impact of the End of the Cold War on South African Transition," pp. 87–100; Guelke, *South Africa in Transition*. See also Daniel, "A Response to Guelke," pp. 101–104.

37. Theodore Draper, "Is the CIA Necessary?" *New York Review of Books,* August 14, 1997, p. 21.

38. This thought is borrowed from Doctorow, *Poets and Presidents*, pp. x–xi.

39. The controversy over the Battle of Cuito Cuanavale is most often used to advance this argument. See Breytenbach, "Cuito Cuanavale Revisited," pp. 54–62. See also Horace Campbell, Cuito Cuanavale, *The Oxford Companion to Politics of the World,* pp. 187–188. The influential newspaper of the powerful Nederduitse Gereformerde Kerk published an editorial in July 1988 that raised questions about the role of South African troops in Angola. "Troepe in Angola" (Troops in Angola), *Die Kerkbode* (Cape Town), July 8, 1988.

40. Fraser, *The Strategy of the Revolutionary.*

41. See "Harmony over Mandela," *Financial Mail* (Johannesburg), June 24, 1988.

42. See Margaret Thatcher's message to P. W. Botha in Prinsloo, *Stem Uit die Wilderness,* p. 312.

43. These issues are discussed in Allen, "Financial Globalisation, Debt Negotiations, and Reform in South Africa."

44. See Pottinger, *The Imperial Presidency.*

45. The background to this policy and the machinations that made it are carefully described in Seegers, *The Military in the Making of Modern South Africa,* esp. pp. 161–170. Although Seegers is a careful student of the South African military, she is surprisingly contemptuous of theoretical inquiry, particularly that of a critical nature. See Southall's significant review of her book, "A Review of A. Seegers' *The Military in the Making*," pp. 523–526.

46. See "Shadow Role Expanding," *Eastern Province Herald* (Port Elizabeth), July 20, 1987.

47. In presenting evidence before South Africa's Truth and Reconciliation Commission, Clive Derby-Lewis (convicted in the conspiracy to kill the Communist Party leader Chris Hani) repeatedly referred to the circumstances of white South Africa and his belief that "the Bible teaches that it is our duty as Christians to fight the Antichrist in what ever way we can. The act of war I was prompted into doing could also be justified in terms of my Christian beliefs." *Cape Times* (Cape Town), August 14, 1997.

48. Gibson, *Critical Theory and Education*, p. 11.

49. See Mary Crewe, "Sunny Skies and Total Onslaught—Youth Preparedness and Veld Schools on the Highveld," in Morrow, ed., *The Proceedings of the Kenton Conference 1985*, pp. 129–146.

50. See Hayward R. Alker, "International Systems," in *The Oxford Companion to Politics of the World,* pp. 423, 428–429.

51. There is neat discussion of these issues by Craig Calhoun, "Social Theory and the Public Sphere," in *The Blackwell Companion to Social Theory,* p. 436–439.

52. For a recent discussion of these issues, see Fowler and Bunck, "What Constitutes the Sovereign State?" pp. 381–405.

53. Mazrui, "The African State as a Political Refugee," p. 23.

54. See Suttner and Cronin, *30 Years of the Freedom Charter.*

55. Patterson, "Institutions for Global Environmental Change," pp. 175–177.

56. Galbraith, "The Autonomous Military Power," p. 40.

57. O'Meara, *Forty Lost Years,* p. 423.

58. Ibid., p. 424.

59. "Development and Underdevelopment," by Claude Ake, in *The Oxford Companion to Politics of the World,* pp. 218–221.

60. Rostow, *The Stages of Economic Growth.*

61. Norval, *Deconstructing Apartheid Discourse,* p. 255.

62. The Free Market Foundation published a book that sought to promote the virtues of the free market, federal devotion toward a canton system, and negotiations. See Louw and Kendall, *South Africa: The Solution.*

63. For a preliminary view of this process, see Beare and Bell, "For All We Know," pp. 136–141.

64. Tucker and Scott, eds., *South Africa.*

65. African Development Bank, *Economic Integration in Southern Africa,* p. 16.

66. See "Krygkor Kry Groot Uitvoer-Kontrakte" (Armscor gets export contracts), *Beeld* (Johannesburg), July 5, 1996; "Open for Business," *Salut,* January 1977, pp. 22–24; "Armscor Turns Its Guns on the Global Market," *Sunday Times Business Times,* December 31, 1995. For an alternative perspective, see Frank Smyth, "Deadly Opportunities: New Markets for South Africa's Arms Industry," *Multinational Monitor,* May 1994, pp. 13–15.

67. Habermas, "The Normative Content of Modernity," in *The Polity Reader in Social Theory,* p. 151.

68. The idea of nationalization continued in liberation rhetoric until well into the 1990s. More popular slogans—"No education before Liberation" and "One settler; one bullet"—represented another mood of the country's politics.

69. One of the most prescient observers of South Africa, Frederik Van Zyl Slabbert, in an address to the Pretoria Press Club in August 1995, called South Africa a "deal-driven" society.

70. *The Reconstruction and Development Programme,* p. 1.

71. See Marais, "The RDP," pp. 1–19.

72. For a discussion of how this happened, see Lodge, "Policy Processes Within the African National Congress and the Tripartite Alliance," pp. 5–32.

73. For a fairly typical example, see "Trimming Socialism to Cut Cloth for Fiscal Measurements," *Business Report* (Johannesburg), February 17, 1997.

74. See, for example, "The Battle to Control the Soul of the ANC," *Sunday Tribune* (Durban), March 30, 1997.

75. George, *Discourses of Global Politics.*

76. Walker, *One World, Many Worlds,* p. 116.

77. Bardill, *Sources of Domestic Insecurity in Southern African States.*

78. See *The Southern African Institute.*

79. See Peter Vale, "Backwaters and Bypasses," in Swatuk and Black, eds., *Bridging the Rift*, pp. 71–84.

80. Murphree, "Strategic Considerations for Enhancing Scholarship at the University of Zimbabwe," p. 7.

Chapter 4

1. See Ran Greenstein, "Identity, Race, History: South Africa and the Pan-African Context," in Greenstein, ed., *Comparative Perspectives on South Africa*, pp. 1–32.

2. Doty, "Immigration and National Identity," p. 240.

3. In 1986, the apartheid government erected a 137-kilometer electric fence along South Africa's northern border with Zimbabwe. Eleven years later, South Africa's first postapartheid minister of defense, Joe Modise, threatened to turn on the electric fence separating South Africa and Mozambique to "lethal" mode to stem the flow of illegal migrants from that country. McDonald, ed., *On Borders*, p. 2, quoting from *The Star* (Johannesburg), May 6, 1997. See also "Talk of Turning up the Power Again as Illegal Immigrants Flood Through the Fence into South Africa," *Sunday Independent* (Johannesburg), August 13, 1995.

4. Some of this is not delivered directly by man, although certainly it is constructed by the conditions of the only politics that is currently on offer, as this small example shows. In June 1998, it was reported that a "pride of lions" had attacked and killed a suspected Mozambican migrant in South Africa's Kruger National Park. In ghoulish fashion, it was reported that game rangers, after rushing to the scene, found "only the deceased head and a few ribs." "Lions Kill Illegal Migrant," *The Citizen* (Johannesburg), June 3, 1998.

5. "Train from Hell to Irene Station," *Pretoria News*, September 4, 1998. For a wider description of these kinds of practice, see *Prohibited Persons*.

6. "Horror Deaths of 18 Illegals," *The Star* (Johannesburg), October 23, 1998; "Death-truck Survivors Tell of Ordeal," *The Star* (Johannesburg), October 27, 1998; "Embassy Slammed over Zim Women's Death," *The Citizen* (Johannesburg), October 27, 1998;

7. "Lions, Hyenas Eat Illegal Immigrant," *The Citizen* (Johannesburg), October 27, 1998.

8. From Peter Baehr, "Editor's Introduction," in *The Portable Hannah Arendt*, p. xxv. On the Hannah Arendt and Eichman trial, see Sela Benhabib, "Arendt's Eichman in Jerusalem," in *The Cambridge Companion to Hannah Arendt*, pp. 65–85, 74.

9. For a discussion of early policy, see Kotze and Hill, "Emergent Migration Policy in a Democratic South Africa," pp. 5–32.

10. See Ryan Sinclair, "I Know a Place That Is Softer Than This," pp. 465–481.

11. For an example of this, see the collection of essays in Spiegel and McAllister, eds., *Tradition and Transition in Southern Africa*.

12. Benjamin, *Illuminations*, p. 258.

13. On this theme, see Peter Vale, "Backwaters and Bypasses," in Swatuk and Black, eds., *Bridging the Rift,* pp. 71–84.

14. The trauma of this life in contemporary urban South Africa is described in Mpe, *Welcome to Our Hillbrow.*

15. For a discussion of migration in Africa as a localized issue, see van Hear, "Refugees and Displaced People in Africa."

16. Weiner, "Security, Stability, and International Migration," pp. 91–126.

17. Weiner, *The Global Migration Crisis.* See Solomon, "Defending Borders," pp. 9–13.

18. Huntington, "The West," pp. 28–46.

19. Huntington, "Reform and Stability in a Modernizing, Multi-ethnic Society," pp. 8–26.

20. Huntington, *The Clash of Civilizations and the Remaking of World Order.*

21. Schlesinger, *The Disuniting of America.*

22. Kennedy, *Preparing for the Twenty-first Century.*

23. It is certainly true that these were not the only voices on the issue; for example, the liberal academic and journalist Sanford Ungar published a book in which he argues that to be American "is being part of an ever more heterogeneous people" and taking part in the constant redefinition of its fabric. See "Mixed Reception," *The Economist* (London), November 4, 1995, p. 109.

24. Ayoob, *The Third World Security Predicament,* pp. 173–175. For a recent South African articulation of the same position, see Annette Seegers, "The New National Security Doctrine."

25. Ayoob, *The Third World Security Predicament.*

26. See Vale and Daniel, "Regional Security in Southern Africa in the 1990s," pp. 84–93.

27. Brettell and Hollifield, *Migration Theory,* p. 154.

28. Solomon, *Towards the Free Movement of People in Southern Africa*, p. 2.

29. Solomon, "Defending Borders," p. 10.

30. In June 1998, the Institute for Strategic Studies at the University of Pretoria (ISSUP) arranged a workshop on border control and protection under this title: "The Illegal Movement of People and Goods: Where Is South Africa Heading and How Can It Be Managed?" The only non–South African speaker was the country attaché of the U.S. Department of Justice.

31. See Mandela, "South Africa's Future Foreign Policy."

32. See Danso and McDonald, *Writing Xenophobia.*

33. Messina, "The Not So Silent Revolution," p. 152.

34. Jonathan Crush, "Migrations Past," in McDonald, ed., *On Borders,* p. 22.

35. The surveillance of migrants to the new South Africa has, in some cases, been as viciously executed as that used against the apartheid regime. For an insight into these techniques, see Minaar and Hough et al., *Who Goes There?* pp. 164–171.

36. Writing on this issue, Marion Ryan Sinclair says: "The migration research that has been conducted within South Africa since the beginning of the decade, and particularly over the past two years, has revolved largely around the discus-

sions of migration as a societal response to state policies and action, explaining migration primarily in terms of national sovereignty and security, as a phenomenon to control, contain and export." Ryan Sinclair, "Community, Identity, and Gender in Migrant Societies of Southern Africa," p. 341.

37. "Foreign Influx: Mbeki Takes a Soft Line," *Cape Times* (Cape Town), October 13, 1994.

38. Ann Bernstein, "Influx Control in Urban South Africa," in Giliomee and Schlemmer, eds., *Up Against the Fences*, p. 85.

39. *The Argus* (Cape Town), September 2, 1994. The alien theme was taken up a few years later. See Maharaj and Rajkumar, "The 'Alien Invasion' in South Africa," pp. 255–273.

40. A survey conducted by an NGO-sponsored project on migration to South Africa reported that "anti-foreigner sentiments are more rampant among White than Black South Africans, with more Whites favouring a prohibitionist migration policy." See "Anti-foreigner Feelings 'Run High Among Whites,'" *The Star* (Johannesburg), September 25, 1998.

41. Quoted in James F. Hollifield, "The Politics of International Migration," in Brettell and Hollifield, eds., *Migration Theory,* p. 154.

42. See Hussein Solomon, "From Accommodation to Control, to Control and Intervention," in Rotberg and Mills, eds., *War and Peace in Southern Africa*, pp. 122–148.

43. Consider this quote from "Illegal Immigration Getting Worse," *The Citizen* (Johannesburg), January 10, 1996: the "'problem [of migrants] is far worse than it should be,' says [Minister of Home Affairs] Buthelezi. The United States drug enforcement agency head, Thomas Constantine had exchanged views with Buthelezi on border control problems. Several South African government departments would visit the United States to study cross-border drug trafficking and the related problem of illegal immigration. Chief Buthelezi says the US had extensive experience with illegal immigration from Mexico."

44. See Schutte, *Migration,* p. 8. See also Venter, ed., *Migrancy and AIDS*.

45. Ingrid de Kok, "Cracked Heirlooms," in Nuttall and Coetzee, eds., *Negotiating the Past*, p. 70.

46. "Border Security: A Major Concern for SA?" *Cape Times* (Cape Town), December 14, 1994.

47. In 1989, it was introduced at a meeting of the then–Institute for Democracy in South Africa by the public intellectual and businessman Fredrik van Zyl Slabbert.

48. Peter Vale, "A Farewell to Arms?" in Beukes et al., *Development, Employment, and the New South Africa*, pp. 3–23.

49. See, for example, Vale and Solomon, in "Migration and Global Change," *Migration,* pp. 2–22.

50. Mills, "Permeable Borders," p. 78.

51. Norval, *Deconstructing Apartheid Discourse*. For a discussion on the construction of national identity in South Africa, see Cross, *Imagery of Identity in South African Education, 1880–1990*.

52. Messina, "The Not So Silent Revolution," p. 141.

53. Ibid., p. 142.

54. See Prah, *Beyond the Colour Line.*

55. Bowman, "The Subordinate State in Southern Africa," pp. 231–361.

56. See Booth and Herring, *Keyguide to Information Resources on Strategic Studies*, pp. 23–26.

57. Strik, *Critical Theory, Politics, and Society*, p. 71.

58. For an example of the official approach to the issue, see "Immigration and Emigration," in *South Africa 1976*, pp. 289–296.

59. *Official Year Book of the Union of South Africa and of Basutoland, Bechuanaland, and Swaziland*, p. 1099. Although no details exist for the source of these migrants, it is possible to suggest that many of these were of the Jewish faith who, fearing the persecution that eventually followed, were drawn to the promise of South Africa. The rich texture of South African life, and, indeed, its passage to change, has been marked in significant ways by the contributions of South Africa's Jewish community. See Lazerson, *Against the Tide*, pp. 82–99.

60. Messina, "The Not So Silent Revolution," p. 153.

61. Soguk, *States and Strangers*, p. 71.

62. Davenport, *South Africa*, pp. 21–22.

63. Soguk, *States and Strangers*, p. 72.

64. Manzo, "Global Power and South African Politics," p. 23.

65. See Bhana and Brain, *Setting Down Roots.*

66. See Yap and Man, *Colour, Confusion, and Concession.*

67. See, for example, Porter, *The Origins of the South African War.*

68. Drawn from the entry "Migration," in *The Blackwell Dictionary of Twentieth Century Social Thought.*

69. Solomon, "Immigration and Security in South Africa," p. 4.

70. These notions of the migrant as the force for disruption of local politics have made many appearances in contemporary times, too. In his powerful analysis of refugees and statecraft, Nevzat Soguk reports this 1993 paragraph from the pen of Polish columnist Witold Pawloski: "Another blow has struck [generating] another major problem: of refugees. . . . All over the world, the problem, of refugees, is a kind of tax levied on democracy and prosperity. Every state avoids the refugees like the plague, even if they travel in escorted carriages." Soguk, *States and Dangers*, p. 31.

71. The best book on these issues remains, in my view, De Klerk, *The Puritans in Africa.*

72. There are many examples of this work. See, for instance, Murray, *South African Capitalism and Black Political Opposition.* See O'Dowd, *South Africa.*

73. Jonathan Crush, "Migrations Past," in McDonald, ed., *On Borders,* pp. 12–13.

74. Wilson, "Minerals and Migrants," p. 104.

75. Donnan and Wilson, *Border's Frontiers of Identity, Nation, and State*, p. 6.

76. Crush, "Fortress South Africa and the Deconstruction of Apartheid's Migration Regime," p. 5.

77. A happy email exchange with Dr. Marion Ryan Sinclair on May 25, 2001, clarified these points.

78. For a brief summary discussion of these issues, see Crush, "Fortress South Africa and the Deconstruction of Apartheid's Migration Regime."

79. Shapiro, "Narrating the Nation," p. 6.

80. The clearest, and certainly the most accessible, presentation of this is Johnstone, "Most Painful to Our Hearts," pp. 5–26.

81. Here are a few random examples of this work: Wilson, *Labour in the South African Gold Mines, 1911–1969*; Johnstone, *Class, Race and Gold*; Lacey, *Working for Boroko*; Crush, Jeeves, and Yudelman, *South Africa's Labour Empire*; James, *Our Precious Metal*.

82. Deborah Potts, "The Hanging Geography of Southern Africa," in Chapman and Baker, eds., *The Changing Geography of Africa and the Middle East*, p. 30.

83. *Apartheid*, p. 43.

84. Worden, *The Making of Modern South Africa*, p. 43.

85. Gary Minkley, "Corpses Behind Screens," in Judin and Vladislavić, eds., *Blank: Architecture, Apartheid, and After*, D11.

86. Jonathan Crush, "Migrations Past," in McDonald, ed., *On Borders*, p. 13.

87. Cited in Mark Laffey, "Adding an Asian Strand," in Weldes, ed., *Cultures of Insecurity*, p. 234.

88. Grundy's pioneering work *Confrontation and Accommodation in Southern Africa* is "interested in the impact of these . . . [migrant] . . . patterns on regional international relations," p. 67.

89. The best study on this remains Lake, *The "Tar Baby" Option*.

90. Minnaar, "Ours for the Taking?" pp. 23–30.

91. See, for example, First, *Black Gold*. See also the update in Centro de Estudos Africanos, *O Mineiro*. See Coplan, *In Time of Cannibals*. See, for example, Nkomo, *Migrant Labor Economic Theory and National Development Policy;* Whiteside, *Labour Migration in Southern Africa*.

92. Harries, *Work, Culture, and Identity*, p. xv.

93. Arendt, *The Origins of Totalitarianism*.

Chapter 5

1. Many of the early cadences of this chapter and its discursive direction are informed by my chapter "Peace in Southern Africa—Time for Questions," in Sorbo and Vale, eds., *Out of Conflict*, pp. 39–53.

2. Mayall, ed., *The New Interventionism, 1991–1994*.

3. See Held, *Democracy and the Global Order*, p. 71.

4. Craig Calhoun, "Social Theory and the Public Sphere," in *The Blackwell Companion to Social Theory*, p. 462.

5. The issue of peacekeeping was discussed, for instance, in the transitional substructure that was concerned with foreign affairs. The main feature of this dis-

cussion was South Africa's rejoining of the United Nations. Telephone interview with Professor John Barratt, June 15, 2001.

6. *Keesing's Record of World Events,* vol. 38 (April 1992).

7. For a detailed account of this, see Anglin, "The Life and Death of South Africa's National Peacekeeping Force," pp. 21–52.

8. From Steve Smith, "Is the Truth Out There?" in Paul and Hall, *International Order and the Future of World Politics,* p. 111.

9. Since its founding in 1991, this institution has had three names; each reflects a metamorphosis toward expanding the idea of security and, quite naturally, its own role in naming sketching an epistemology for "security" in the countries. So the Institute for Defence Politics became the Institute for Defence Policy (IDP) and then became the Institute for Security Studies (ISS). On this, see the document by Cilliers, *The Establishment of the Institute for Security Studies (ISS).*

10. See, for example, Solomon and Cilliers, "Southern Africa and the Quest for Collective Security," pp. 191–205.

11. See Williams, *Intellectuals and the End of Apartheid.*

12. Haas, "Introduction," pp. 1–36.

13. See Said, *Representations of the Intellectual,* p. 7.

14. Craig Calhoun, "Social Theory and the Public Sphere," in *The Blackwell Companion to Social Theory,* 1996, p. 454.

15. *The Project "Training for Peace in Southern Africa,"* pp. 26–27.

16. See Cock and Nathan, eds., *War and Society.* A fine example of this work and an effort to cast a feminist eye on the evolving debate is to be found in Cock, *Colonels and Cadres: War and Gender in South Africa.* Notwithstanding limited external funding, some work has appeared. See Cock and McKenzie, eds., *From Defence to Development.*

17. This idea is drawn from Booth, *A Security Regime in Southern Africa,* p. 23.

18. Whitworth, "Gender, Race, and the Politics of Peacekeeping," p. 7.

19. This is, of course, drawn from Robert W. Cox's essay, "Social Forces, States, and World Orders," in Keohane, ed., *Neorealism and Its Critics,* pp. 208–209.

20. On the Cold War as an eschatological issue, see Ken Booth, "Cold Wars of the Mind," in Booth, ed., *Statecraft and Security,* pp. 29–53.

21. On similar categories, see Debrix, *Re-Envisioning Peacekeeping,* pp. 61–62.

22. Maynes, "Relearning Intervention," p. 97.

23. Habermas, *The Past as the Future,* p. 144.

24. Ibid., pp. 9–10.

25. "SA World Peacekeeping Role 'Inevitable,'" *The Argus* (Cape Town), October 27, 1994.

26. See "Focus on SA Role as Ethnic Conflict Boils up in Burundi," by Stephen Laufer, *Business Day* (Johannesburg), July 15, 1996.

27. "Battle of the 'Blue Helmet' Troops," *Weekly Mail and Guardian* (Johannesburg), December 2, 1995.

28. Chase, Hill, and Kennedy, "Pivotal States and U.S. Strategy," pp. 33–51.

29. Drawn from Evans et al., *Penguin Dictionary of International Relations,* p. 220.

30. See "The Economist Sees SA as a Potential Uplifter of Neighbours," *Sunday Independent* (Johannesburg), August 13, 1995. Jeffrey Herbst, "South Africa," in Chase et al., *The Pivotal States,* p. 152.

31. Mastanduno, "Preserving the Unipolar Moment," pp. 84–88. Habermas, *The Past as the Future,* p. 147.

32. Simon, "Trading Spaces," pp. 383, 385.

33. Maynes, "Relearning Intervention," p. 97.

34. Mills, ed., *From Pariah to Participant.*

35. Conrad Strauss, "Preface," in Mills, Begg, and van Nieuwkerk, eds., *South Africa in the Global Economy,* p. v. It must be said that the bank of which Strauss is head, the Standard Bank of South Africa, was the chief sponsor of the publication in which his words appear.

36. See "Guardian Angel or Global Gangster," pp. 123–135.

37. Huntington, *The Third Wave.* For a critical perspective on this trend, see Good, *Realizing Democracy in Botswana, Namibia, and South Africa.*

38. For a good summary of this process, see Ohlson, *Power Politics and Peace Politics,* pp. 88–95.

39. Ibid., pp. 64–65.

40. I cannot resist putting in this quotation, the first paragraph of a book on peacekeeping, because it captures the seeming innocence of the endeavor and the good-neighborliness, order, and normative drift of these interventions: "This monograph has been commissioned by the *Training for Peace in Southern Africa* project. The project was established through an agreement reached at the end of 1995 between three participatory organizations, namely IDP (Institute for Defence Policy), NUPI (Norwegian Institute of International Affairs) and ACCORD (African Centre for the Constructive Resolution of Disputes), and the Royal Norwegian Ministry for Foreign Affairs, which is funding the project. The purpose of the project is to contribute to the establishment of a viable regional capacity for conducting peace operations in Southern Africa. The project's immediate objective is to equip participants from the departments of Defence and Foreign Affairs in as many SADC countries as possible, plus NGOs involved in peacekeeping operations, with the necessary knowledge and skills for engaging in their complementary and mission-specific roles within the broad ambit of peacekeeping operations." From Malan, ed., *New Partners in Peace,* p. 5.

41. See Pule, "Power Struggles in the Basutoland Congress Party, 1991–1997," pp. 1–30. Lesotho's situation in the region is well described in Weisfelder, "Lesotho and the Inner Periphery in the New South Africa," pp. 643–668.

42. "Regional Break-through as SA Invited to Help Lesotho Mutiny Taskforce," http://southscan.gn.apc.org/oldindexes/scanindexes/V09index.html.

43. On these endeavors, see "Lesotho King Faces Sanctions Pressure from Pretoria and Region," *SouthScan* (London), August 26, 1994.

44. See Southall and Petlane, eds., *Democratisation and Demilitarisation in Lesotho;* Matlosa, "The Recent Political Crisis in Lesotho and the Role of Exter-

nal Forces"; Garba and Herskovits, *Militaries, Democracies, and Security in Southern Africa*, pp. 12–18. See *Cape Times* (Cape Town), September 15, 1994.

45. "Threat of Military Intervention in Lesotho Recedes," *SouthScan* (London), September 2, 1994.

46. There is a brief account of these tactics, which included the overflight of South African fighter planes of Lesotho airspace and parachute drops on the South African border side of the border, in "Military and Economic Pressure from SA Forces King to Yield," *SouthScan* (London), September 16, 1994.

47. See "SA and Others Keep Wary Eye on Deal After King Capitulates," *SouthScan* (London), September 23, 1994. For an official account of South Africa's view of these events, see L. H. Evans, "Preventative Diplomacy in Lesotho and Mozambique," in Cilliers and Mills, eds., *Peacekeeping in Africa.*

48. "MPs Applaud Lesotho Deal," *Cape Times* (Cape Town), September 15, 1994.

49. Held, *Democracy and the Global Order*, p. 78.

50. *Keesing's Record of World Events*, vol. 40 (September 1994).

51. See "SADC Organ Formed to Ensure Stability," *Business Day* (Johannesburg), July 29, 1996; Cilliers, *The SADC Organ for Defence, Politics, and Security*; Malan and Cilliers, *SADC Organ on Politics, Defence, and Security.* "President Ketumile Masire of Botswana has proposed that [Southern African Development Community] member states should establish a permanent army." SABC Safm radio, Johannesburg, in English 1500 GMT, April 23, 1996.

52. See "A Blueprint to Meet the Challenge of Africa's Regional Demands," *Business Day* (Johannesburg), October 11, 1990.

53. See "Is SA Ready for International Role?" *The Star* (Johannesburg), September 24, 1998.

54. Andrew Hurrell, "Regionalism in Theoretical Perspective," in Fawcett and Hurrell, eds., *Regionalism in World Politics*, pp. 37–73.

55. *Keesing's Record of World Events*, vol. 41 (February 1995).

56. Peter Vale, "Regional Strategy," in Blumenfeld, ed., *South Africa in Crisis*, pp. 176–194.

57. There are countless examples of this kind of nonstate conflict; for tension in Zambia, for instance, see "Unita Barter May Supply Arms to Lozi Successionists," *SouthScan* (London), March 10, 1995, p. 79.

58. This document is to be found at http://www.polity.org.za/govdocs/white_papers/.

59. Habermas, *The Past as the Future*, p. 146.

60. Barry Smart, "Postmodern Social Theory," in *The Blackwell Companion to Social Theory*, p. 411.

61. See Rosenau, ed., *Global Dialogues*, p. 9.

62. See Cilliers, *To Sell or Die*. "SANDF a Top Dollar Earner Says Modise," *The Star and SA Times International* (Johannesburg), May 1, 1996. In July 1996, South Africa's defense procurement agency, called Armscor, offered to take on a similar task for the countries of the region. See "Armscor Offers Procurement Services to SADC States," *Sunday Independent* (Johannesburg), July 7, 1996.

63. "Illegal Exports of SA Arms Fuels Bloodshed in Rwanda and Burundi," *The Star* (Johannesburg), July 28, 1996.

64. See, for instance, "National Interest," *Business Day* (Johannesburg), April 24, 1996.

65. Peter Vale, "Some Conceptual Concerns for Policy Makers," in Shaw and Cilliers, eds., *South Africa and Peacekeeping in Africa*, p. 17.

66. See Debrix, *Re-Envisioning Peacekeeping*, p. 53.

67. This section's title, of course, is taken from the famous quote, "Pobre Mexico, tan lejos de Dios y tan cerca de los Estados Unidos (Poor Mexico so far from God, so close to the United States), attributed to General Porfirio Díaz (1830–1915), president of Mexico (1877–1880 and 1884–1911).

68. This election is discussed in Sekatle, "The Lesotho General Election of 1998," pp. 31–45.

69. Khabele Matlosa, "The Dilemma of Security in Southern Africa," in Poku, ed., *Security and Development in Southern Africa*, p. 95.

70. For a recent discussion of this, see Rok Ajulu, "Survival in a Rough Neighbourhood," in Adar and Ajulu, eds., *Globalization and Emerging Trends in African States' Foreign Policy-Making Process,* pp. 51–70.

71. See "Mufamadi Lays Down the Law on Lesotho," *Business Day* (Johannesburg), September 22, 1998. "Militêre Ingryping in Lesotho Is die Laaste Uitweg—Mufamadi" (Military action in Lesotho is the last option—Mufamadi), *Beeld* (Johannesburg), September 22, 1998.

72. A copy of the letter is to be found at http://gopher.anc.org.za/anc/newsbrief/1998/news0923.

73. Khabele Matlosa, "The Dilemma of Security in Southern Africa," in Poku, ed., *Security and Development in Southern Africa*, p. 96.

74. See "King of Lesotho Wasn't Consulted, Says Brother," *The Citizen* (Johannesburg), October 3, 1998. "Letsie Is Part of the Problem," *The Star* (Johannesburg), September 23, 1998.

75. Communication from Khabele Matlosa to Peter Vale, April 6, 2002.

76. "Buthelezi Took the Decision to Go In," *The Star* (Johannesburg), September 23, 1998. For some aspects of the decision process, see "I Consulted the King: Buthelezi," *The Citizen* (Johannesburg), October 3, 1998.

77. "Cabinet Endorses Decision to Send Troops," *The Star* (Johannesburg), September 24, 1998.

78. Molomo, "External Military Intervention in Lesotho's Recent Political Crisis," pp. 133–162.

79. Khabele Matlosa, "The Dilemma of Security in Southern Africa," in Poku, ed., *Security and Development in Southern Africa*, p. 96.

80. Gearóid Ó Tuathail and John Agnew, "Geopolitics and Discourse," in Tuathail, Dalby, and Routledge, eds., *The Geopolitics Reader*, p. 83.

81. See "Blunders of the Raid on Lesotho," *The Star* (Johannesburg), September 24, 1998. "Die Prys van Swak Intelligensie" (The cost of poor intelligence), *Beeld* (Johannesburg), September 24, 1998. "Foray Lacks Clear Doctrine," *The Star* (Johannesburg), September 23, 1998. "Lesotho Intervention Wasn't

Strictly Legal," *Sunday Independent* (Johannesburg), October 4, 1998. See "Ebony and Ivory, Side by Side," *The Star* (Johannesburg), September 25, 1998.

82. "Top Brass Slam Action in Lesotho," *Pretoria News*, October 1, 1998.

83. "Has SA's Impartiality Met Its End in Lesotho?" *Pretoria News*, September 23, 1998.

84. "The SANDF's Baptism of Fire," *Bulletin*, October 22, 1998, www.mil.za/News&Events/News/Bulletins/Bulletins1997_1998/22October1998.htm.

85. "Critics of SA's Role in Lesotho Are Ignorant, Says Mandela," *The Star* (Johannesburg), September 25, 1998. See "Pahad Rejects Criticism as Bordering on Treason," *Business Day* (Johannesburg), November 3, 1998. See "Defending Regional Democracy," by Fink Haysom (President Nelson Mandela's legal adviser), *The Star* (Johannesburg), October 14, 1998.

86. See Said, *Representations of the Intellectual*, pp. 4–6. "Orwellian Ring to Lesotho Saga," *The Star* (Johannesburg), October 1, 1998.

87. "Parties Slam Govt over Lesotho Move," *The Sowetan* (Johannesburg), September 23, 1998. "South African Socialists Condemn Lesotho Incursion," *International Viewpoint* (London), September 1998. Under the banner "Say NO to the South African invasion of Lesotho," a protest was organized at Cape Town's parade on September 26, 1998. "Cross-border Intervention Is Intolerable, Say Churchmen," *The Star* (Johannesburg), September 23, 1998. "Num to Start Fund to Help Lesotho," *The Citizen* (Johannesburg), October 3, 1998.

88. See Makoa, "The Challenges of the South African Military Intervention in Lesotho After the 1998 Elections," pp. 84–109.

89. *Beeld* (Johannesburg), September 25, 1998.

90. von Hippel, *Democracy by Force*, p. 101.

91. Ibid., pp. 101–103.

92. George, *Discourses of Global Politics*, p. 205.

93. See "Lesotho in the Grip of Anarchy," *The Star* (Johannesburg), September 22, 1998; "Alarm as Lesotho Government Teeters," *Pretoria News*, September 22, 1998; "Lesotho in Crisis as Peace Efforts Fail," *The Sowetan* (Johannesburg), September 22, 1998.

94. See "SA Troop Alert as Maseru Mutinies," *Mail and Guardian* (Johannesburg), September 18, 1998.

95. Richmond, "Towards a Genealogy of Peacemaking."

96. Ibid., p. 3.

97. Von Hippel, *Democracy by Force*.

98. Matlosa, "The Dilemma of Security in Southern Africa," in Poku, ed., *Security and Development in Southern Africa,* p. 95.

99. The surname literally means "lover of hearts." "Colonel Was Also in Angolan Battle," *Business Day* (Johannesburg), September 29, 1998.

100. "Hartslief Sedert Skooldae 'Lief vir Skiet'" (From [his] schooldays, Hartslief loved to shoot), *Naweek-Beeld* (Johannesburg), October 3, 1998.

101. "The Cordite of Co-operation," *Financial Mail* (Johannesburg), October 2, 1998, pp. 38–39, 41.

102. These are a reworking of lines from Held, *Democracy and the Global Order*, p. 125.

103. *The Sowetan* (Johannesburg), September 23, 1998.

104. See Söderbaum, "The New Regionalism in Southern Africa," pp. 75–94.

105. Shotter, *Cultural Politics of Everyday Life,* p. 33.

106. Some of these are discussed in Vale and Motlasa, "Beyond the Nation State," pp. 34–37, 83–84.

107. Andrew Linklater, "The Achievements of Critical Theory," in Smith, Booth, and Zalewski, eds., *International Theory,* pp. 279–280.

108. "Move Over, Shrinks," *Times Higher Education Supplement* (London), April 14, 2000.

Chapter 6

1. See Jenny Parsley, *Free Markets, Free Women?*

2. Bauman, *Community,* pp. 1–2.

3. Charles Tilly, "International Communities," in Adler and Barnett, eds., *Security Communities,* pp. 397–412.

4. Williams, *Keywords: A Vocabulary of Culture and Society* (1996), p. 66.

5. Bauman, *Community,* p. 54. See "Crime Wave Robs Some, Pays Others," *Sunday Times Business Times* (Johannesburg), July 22, 2001, p. 6.

6. Bauman, *Community,* p. 54.

7. Ibid., pp. 37–38.

8. Plank, "Dreams of Community," pp. 13–20.

9. I have taken some of the arguments in this chapter from Peter Vale, "The Way We Remember," in Booth, ed., *Security, Community, and Emancipation.*

10. Geertz, *The Interpretation of Cultures,* p. 10.

11. Ibid., p. 20.

12. This is taken from Otto, *Social Practice and the Ethnographic Circle,* p. 5.

13. Ibid., p. 4.

14. Exceptions are Booth and Vale, "Securing Southern Africa," pp. 285–304, and Thompson and Leysens, "Changing Notions of Human Security in the Southern African Region," pp. 1–24.

15. Geertz, *The Interpretation of Cultures,* p. 243.

16. My colleague Suren Pillay rightly took me to task on the power of binaries when he commented on a draft of this chapter at a history seminar at University of the Western Cape on August 17, 1999. There is a neat discussion of the trap of binaries in Mamdani, *Citizen and Subject,* p. 9.

17. Geertz, *The Interpretation of Cultures,* p. 241.

18. Ibid., p. 243.

19. Ibid., p. 243.

20. Smith, *National Identity,* pp. 23–25.

21. Charles Tilly, "International Communities," in Adler and Barnett, eds., *Security Communities,* pp. 398–399. Jonathan Rèe, "Cosmopolitanism and the

Experience of Nationality," in Cheah and Robbins, eds., *Cosmopolitics,* pp. 82–83.

22. For early inroads into this, see Ndebele, "The Rediscovery of the Ordinary," pp. 143–157. Sole, "The Witness of Poetry." He quotes the development economist David Korten, who states it is those "who live ordinary lives far removed from the corridors of power who have the clearest perception of what is happening, but they don't speak out."

23. Ernesto Laclau, "Universalism, Particularism, and the Question of Identity," in Wilmsen and McAllister, eds., *The Politics of Difference,* pp. 45–58.

24. See Kunnie, *Is Apartheid Really Dead?*

25. This issue has been underresearched, in my view. Interesting historical artifacts exist, however. See, for example, Malan, *Naar Congloland.*

26. For an example of this state creation, see Rotberg, *The Rise of Nationalism in Central Africa*; Mulford, *Zambia,* pp. 362; for a more recent interpretation, see Wright, "An Old Nationalist in New Nationalist Times," pp. 339–351.

27. Rob Nixon, "Rural Transnationalism," in Darian-Smith, Gunnar, and Nuttall, eds., *Text, Theory, and Space,* pp. 243–254.

28. Mahmood Mamdani has presented a fine refutation of the exceptionalist perspective, especially as it emanates from South African scholarship. See Mamdani, *Citizen and Subject,* pp. 27–32. For an interesting discussion of the idea of apartheid and national liberation in the making of South Africa, see Nimer, "National Liberation and the Conflicting Terms of Discourse in South Africa: An Interpretation," pp. 313–353.

29. See "Miracle in Africa," *Sunday Times* (Johannesburg), September 30, 2001; "Maputo Corridor to Benefit All Parties," *The Star* (Johannesburg), June 5, 1997; "Corridor to Maputo May Start in 1997," *Saturday Star* (Johannesburg), May 24, 1997; "Maputo-netwerk Bring Groei in Mpumalanga" (Maputo network generates growth in Mpumalanga), *Rapport* (Johannesburg), May 25, 1997; "Die Maputo-korridor Moet Bewys Daar Is Nog Lewe in Afrika" (The Maputo corridor must show that there is still life in Africa), *Beeld* (Johannesburg), May 9, 1996; "South Africa–Mozambique Development Corridor," p. 12480. See "Pooling of Electrical Power Benefits Southern Africa," *Business Day* (Johannesburg), March 9, 1998; "Eskom Lights the Way in Africa with Regional Power Grid," *Sunday Times Business Times* (Johannesburg), May 3, 1998; "Power Pool Needs Political Harmony."

30. See Vale, "A Drought Blind to the Horrors of War," pp. 51–52, 57. On the consequences of recent floods, see Christie and Hanlon, *Mozambique and the Great Flood of 2000.* The best publication on this issue remains Bryant, ed., *Poverty, Policy, and Food Security in Southern Africa.*

31. Solomon, ed., *Sink or Swim?*

32. Larry Swatuk, "Southern Africa Through Green Lenses," in Vale et al., *Theory, Change, and Southern Africa's Future,* pp. 272, 288.

33. Rockström, "Green Water Security for the Food Makers of Tomorrow," pp. 71–78.

34. See, for example, Solomon, ed., *Sink or Swim?*

35. There is a good summary of this approach in Ole Wæver, "Securitization and Desecuritization," in Lipschutz, ed., *On Security,* pp. 46–86.

36. See Solomon and Turton, eds., *Water Wars.*

37. See Maluwa, "Disputed Sovereignty over Sidudu (or Kasikili) Island (Botswana-Namibia)," pp. 18–22.

38. For details, see Larry A. Swatuk, "Environmental Co-operation for Regional Peace and Security in Southern Africa," in Conca and Dabelko, eds., *Environmental Peacemaking.*

39. See Larry Swatuk and Peter Vale, "Sovereignty, States, and Southern Africa's Future," in Thompson, ed., *Critical Perspectives on Security and Sovereignty,* pp. 1–25.

40. Booth and Vale, "Security in Southern Africa."

41. Geertz, *The Interpretation of Cultures,* p. 244.

42. Plank, "Dreams of Community," p. 15.

43. Robert J. Gordon, "Serving the Volk with Volkekunde," in Jansen, ed., *Knowledge and Power in South Africa,* pp. 79–97.

44. See Dubow, *Scientific Racism in Modern South Africa.* See John Lazar, "Verwoerd Versus the 'Visionaries,'" in Bonner, Delius, and Posel, *Apartheid's Genesis, 1935–1962,* pp. 362–392.

45. See Cherry, "Development, Conflict, and the Politics of Ethnicity in South Africa's Transition to Democracy," pp. 613–631.

46. Lye and Murray, *Transformations on the Highveld,* p. 20.

47. See Vale and Matlosa, "Beyond the Nation State," pp. 34–37, 83–84.

48. Elphick and Davenport, eds., *Christianity in South Africa,* 1997.

49. Hennie Pretorius and Lizo Jafta, "'A Branch Springs Out,'" in Elphick and Davenport, eds., *Christianity in South Africa,* p. 226.

50. In interesting ways the study of religion and the study of international relations seem to be drawn increasingly toward each other. See, for example, "Special Issue: Religion and International Relations," *Millennium* 29, 3 (2000).

51. Marty, *Pilgrims in Their Own Land.*

52. John E. Kaemmer, "Southern Africa," in Stone, *The Garland Encyclopaedia of World Music,* vol. 1, p. 701.

53. See James, "Musical Form and Social History," pp. 309–312, and James, *Songs of the Women Migrants.*

54. Kubik, *Malawian Music.*

55. Ivor Neumann has, apparently, used this same idea. See Hall, "Applying the 'Self/Other' Nexus in International Relations," p. 104. Neumann argues that the literature neglects the fact that regions are no less "imagined communities" than are nations.

56. There are, unfortunately, other examples in the region of treatment of minorities. For example, Kenneth Good has offered a stunning indictment of the treatment of the San people by Botswana, the state with the highest per capita income in southern Africa. See Good, "The State and Extreme Poverty in Botswana," pp. 185–205. On the legal arguments around this issue, see Harring, "'God Gave Us This Land.'"

57. See "Namibia's Huge New R2,5bn Monument to Independence," *Business Report on Sunday* (Johannesburg), January 24, 1999.

58. "Dam That Spells Death for One of Africa's Last Tribes," *Sunday Telegraph* (London), February 22, 1998.

59. The phrase was used by the BBC's Jim Clarke in a program broadcast by SAfm's 104–107 on July 8, 2001, at 18h00–18h30.

60. Chapman, *Southern African Literatures.*

61. Rob Nixon, "Rural Transnationalism," in Darian-Smith, Gunnar, and Nuttall, eds., *Text, Theory, and Space,* p. 244.

62. Ibid., p. 246.

63. Wendy Brown, "Spectres and Angels at the End of History," in Frank and Tambornino, eds., *Vocations of Political Theory,* p. 36.

64. Singer, *Marx,* p. 32.

Chapter 7

1. See Nuttall and Coetzee, eds., *Negotiating the Past.*

2. Rosenau, *Post-modernism and the Social Sciences,* p. 78.

3. Steen, *Understanding Metaphor in Literature,* p. 5. On the metaphor in security studies, see David Mutimer, "Reimaging Metaphors," in Krause and Williams, eds., *Critical Security Studies,* pp. 187–221.

4. On apartheid state terror, see Friedland, "South Africa and Instability in Southern Africa," pp. 95–105.

5. "What Is Terrorism?" *The Economist* (London), March 2, 1996.

6. Bronner and Kellner, eds., *Critical Theory and Society,* p. 19.

7. Eagleton, *Literary Theory,* p. 206.

8. For recent examples, see Thompson and Leysens, "Changing Notions of Human Security in the Southern African Region," pp. 1–24; Lisa Thompson, "Feminist Theory and Security Studies in Southern Africa," in Vale, Swatuk, and Oden, eds., *Theory, Change, and Southern Africa's Future,* pp. 237–265; Anthony Leysens, "Critical Theory, Robert Cox, and Southern Africa," in Vale, Swatuk, and Oden, eds., *Theory, Change, and Southern Africa's Future,* pp. 219–236. The most comprehensive, certainly, is Williams's recent Ph.D. thesis, "Intellectuals and the End of Apartheid."

9. These issues are explored in Latham, *The Liberal Moment.*

10. See, for example, the collection by Venter, ed., *Prospects for Progress.*

11. Booth, "Security in Anarchy," p. 539.

12. "Lessons from the 12th Century," an interview with Amitav Ghosh, *Newsweek,* European edition (December 13, 1993).

13. Richard Wyn Jones, "'Travel Without Maps,'" in Davis, ed., *Security Issues in the Post–Cold War World,* p. 208.

14. See Ole Wæver, "Securitization and Desecuritization," in Lipschutz, ed., *On Security,* pp. 46–86.

15. Austin, *How to Do Things with Words.*

16. Ole Wæver, "Securitization and Desecuritization," in Lipschutz, ed., *On Security,* p. 55.

17. Chidester, *Savage Systems.*

18. "Security Firms Offering Vital Services," *Zambia Daily Mail* (Lusaka), August 17, 1998; also Mark Shaw, "Profitable Policing," in Scharf and Nina, eds., *The Other Law*, pp. 208–224, and Shaw, *Crime and Policing in Post-Apartheid South Africa.*

19. Christopher, *The Atlas of Changing South Africa*, p. 33. See Heineken, "AIDS," pp. 12–15. See Grove, "The Drug Trade as a National and International Security Threat"; Parry, "The Illegal Narcotics Trade in Southern Africa," pp. 38–70; *The Illegal Drug Trade in Southern Africa.*

20. Hough, "Crime as a National Security Issue in South Africa," pp. 56–71. Schönteich, "The Impact of HIV/AIDS on South Africa's Internal Security."

21. David Mutimer, "Re-imaging Metaphors," in Krause and Williams, eds., *Critical Security Studies,* p. 204.

22. This included programs that aimed to alert schoolchildren to the threats facing the state. For a discussion of these, see Mary Crewe, "Sunny Skies and Total Onslaught," in Morrow, ed., *The Proceedings of the Kenton Conference, 1985,* pp. 129–146. "Lekota Says National Service Will Help Bridge Racial Divide," *Sunday Independent* (Johannesburg), September 24, 2000.

23. Vale and Daniel, "Regional Security in Southern Africa in the 1990s."

24. Ibid.

25. For the background to this process, see Kraak, *Competing Education and Training Policies.*

26. Dr. Tahir Wood of the University of the Western Cape offered some early thoughts on this paragraph. Gibbons et al., *The New Production of Knowledge.* See Kraak, *Competing Education and Training Policies.* Also "Department of Labour—SETAS Review," *Business Report* (Johannesburg), October 4, 2001.

27. Diplomacy, Intelligence, Defence, Trade Education, and Training Authority, *Update,* p. 1.

28. Brochure entitled "University of Pretoria. Faculty of Arts. Department of Political Sciences. Master of Security Studies (MSS)." http://www.up.ac.za/acamemic/polsci.

29. Arendt, *On Violence,* p. 6.

30. Sheldon S. Wolin, "Political Theory," in Frank and Tambornio, eds., *Vocations of Political Theory,* p. 9.

31. Craig Calhoun, "Social Theory and the Public Sphere," in *The Blackwell Companion to Social Theory,* p. 454.

32. On the limits of this in the security sector, see *Parliamentary Oversight of the Security Sector in the Commonwealth.*

33. A deluge of books on the failure to change will certainly follow. For an early example of this, see Bell, *Unfinished Business.*

34. Craig Calhoun, "Social Theory and the Public Sphere," in *The Blackwell Companion to Social Theory,* p. 449.

35. Gramsci, *Selections from Prison Notebooks of Antonio Gramsci*, pp. 6–8.

36. Easterbrook, "Ideas Move Nations," p. 80.

37. Any reading of the more than ten volumes of the *African Security Review*, the flagship journal of the Institute for Security Studies, proves this point.

38. This said, it seems wise to bear in mind a warning from Hannah Arendt: "nothing is more important to the integrity of the universities than a rigorously enforced divorce from war-oriented research and all connected enterprises," Arendt, *On Violence, pp.* 16–17.

39. Gearóid Ó Tuathail and John Agnew, "Geopolitics and Discourse," in Tuathail, Dalby, and Routledge, *The Geopolitics Reader,* p. 82.

40. For a brief explanation of this, see Meyns, *Konflikt und Entwicklung im Südlichen Afrika,* pp. 61–65. See du Toit, "Facing Up to the Future," pp. 1–27.

41. Arendt, *On Violence*, p. 6.

42. See Geldenhuys, "Some Strategic Implications of Regional Economic Relationships for the Republic of South Africa"; Davies and O'Meara, "Total Strategy in Southern Africa," pp. 183–211; and Davies, "The Military and Foreign Policy in South Africa," pp. 313–315.

43. See Millar, *South Africa and Regional Security.*

44. The limits of the sovereignty, in my opinion, were illustrated by the proposal to establish a regional parliament in southern Africa. SABC SAfm radio (Johannesburg), in English, 1110 GMT, March 14, 1996.

45. See Nolutshungu, *Southern Africa in a Global Context*. Deutsch et al., *Political Community in the North Atlantic Community.*

46. See "Security Dilemma," by Bruce Russett, in *The Oxford Companion to Politics of the World,* pp. 760–761.

47. On social engineering of states versus the power of the writer's imagination, see Gordimer, *Living in Hope and History*, pp. 191–206.

48. Berrigan, *America Is Hard to Find,* p. 97.

49. On this kind of hankering and the secondary securitization of the region's lifeworld, see Rotberg and Mills, eds., *War and Peace in Southern Africa.*

50. See Adams, ed., *We Came for Mandela*. See Mpe, *Welcome to Our Hillbrow*. See, for instance, Rogerson, "African Immigrant Entrepreneurs and Johannesburg's Changing Inner City," pp. 265–273.

51. For efforts to control this, see "Cross-border Dagga Control Planned," *The Star* (Johannesburg), September 16, 1999. "Securing Our Borders," *Salut* (Pretoria), July 1998, pp. 26–27.

52. "Zuid-Afrikaanse Boeren Trekken Weer Verder" (South African farmers trek further), *De Telegraaf* (Amsterdam), July 18, 1996; "Afrikaner Farmers Discover a 'Promised Land' in Congo," *International Herald Tribune* (Paris), September 23, 1996; "Accord Paves the Way for SA Farmers," *Pretoria News*, February 19, 1996.

53. See 1996 SABCTV series on South Africa's Zanzibari community and "Unshackling the Zanzibari," *Mail and Guardian* (Johannesburg), February 16, 1996.

54. "Smuggling Brings Home the Bacon," *Sunday Independent* (Johannesburg), August 30, 1998.

55. See Dutton and Palmberg, *Human Rights and Homosexuality in Southern Africa;* "Uncle Bob's in for a Gay Old Time," *The Star* (Johannesburg), August, 25, 1995.

56. See ibid.

57. See the challenging piece by Mbembe, "At the Edge," pp. 4–15.

58. Sam C. Nolutshungu, "Introduction," in Nolutshungu, ed., *Margins of Insecurity,* p. 14.

59. Booth, "Security in Anarchy," p. 537.

60. Albrecht, "The Role of Social Movements in the Collapse of the German Democratic Republic," p. 157.

61. Ibid.

62. "Love Among the Ruins: An Interview with Octavio Paz," *Observer Review* (London), June 23, 1996.

63. Craig Calhoun, "Social Theory and the Public Sphere," in *The Blackwell Companion to Social Theory,* p. 436.

64. Buzan, *People, States, and Fear.*

65. *The Blackwell Dictionary of Twentieth-Century Social Thought,* p. 596.

66. Sheldon Stryker, Timothy J. Owens, and Robert W. White, "Social Psychology and Social Movements," in Stryker, Owens, and White, eds., *Self, Identity, and Social Movements,* p. 2.

67. See Nolutshungu, ed., *Margins of Insecurity.* On the potential for this, see Owusu, "Democracy and Africa," pp. 369–396. For examples of this, see Bukurura, "The Maintenance of Order in Rural Tanzania," pp. 1–29, and Bukurura, "Combatting Crime Among the Sukuma and Nyamwezi of West-Central Tanzania," pp. 257–266. For the region's experience, see Chingono, *The State.*

68. See Moore, "Contesting Terrain in Zimbabwe's Eastern Highlands," pp. 380–401.

69. Erica Burman et al., "Power and Discourse," in Burman, ed., *Culture, Power, and Difference,* p. 5.

70. van Hensbroek, *African Political Philosophy,* p. 20.

71. Dubow, *Scientific Racism in Modern South Africa.* See Banks, "Of 'Native Skulls' and 'Noble Caucasians,'" pp. 387–403.

72. Van Hensbroek, "African Political Philosophy," pp. 13–14.

73. Examples of this search are to be found in Prah, *Beyond the Colour Line;* Mbembe, *On the Postcolony;* Mudimbe, *The Invention of Africa;* and Owomoyela, *The African Difference.*

74. Van Rinsum, "Slaves of Definition," p. 155.

75. See "Gordimer Explores the Globalisation of Vulnerability," *Sunday Independent* (Johannesburg), October 28, 2001. See also Atwell, *Doubling the Point.*

76. Gordimer, *Living in Hope and History,* p. 193.

77. See Smith, "New Geographies," p. 29.

78. Zoë Wicombe, "Shame and Identity," in Attridge and Jolly, eds., *Writing South Africa,* p. 105.

Afterword

1. "What News on the Rialto," *Sunday Independent* (Johannesburg), July 15, 2001.

2. "The Pleasure of Iris Murdoch," *New York Review of Books* 48, 18 (November 15, 2001), p. 25.

3. Reproduced in Craig Calhoun, "Social Theory and the Public Sphere," in *The Blackwell Companion to Social Theory*, p. 437.

4. Walker, *One World, Many Words*, p. 116.

5. Booth, *A Security Regime in Southern Africa*.

Bibliography

Adams, K. *We Came for Mandela: The Cultural Life of the Refugee Community in South Africa.* Cape Town: Footprints Publishing, 2001.

Adar, Korwa Gombe, and Rok Ajulu, eds. *Globalization and Emerging Trends in African States' Foreign Policy-Making Process: A Comparative Perspective of Southern Africa.* Aldershot, UK: Ashgate, 2002.

Adler, Emanuel, and Michael Barnett, eds. *Security Communities.* Cambridge, UK: Cambridge University Press, 1998.

African Development Bank. *Economic Integration in Southern Africa: Executive Summary.* Harare, Zimbabwe: African Development Bank, 1994.

Albrecht, Ulrich. "The Role of Social Movements in the Collapse of the German Democratic Republic." *Global Society* 10, 2 (1996).

Allen, Michael. "Financial Globalisation, Debt Negotiations, and Reform in South Africa." Paper delivered to Annual Conference of the British International Studies Association. University of York, England, December 19–21, 1994.

Allison, Graham, and Gregory F. Treverton. *Rethinking America's Security: Beyond Cold War to New World Order.* New York: W. W. Norton for the American Assembly and the Council on Foreign Relations, 1992.

Andrews, H. T., et al. *South Africa in the Sixties: A Socio-Economic Survey.* Johannesburg: South Africa Foundation, 1962.

Anglin, Douglas G. "The Life and Death of South Africa's National Peacekeeping Force." *Journal of Modern African Studies* 33, 1 (1995).

Apartheid: The Facts. London: International Aid and Defense Fund Publications, 1991.

Arendt, Hannah. *On Violence.* London: Allen Lane and the Penguin Press, 1970.

———. *The Origins of Totalitarianism.* New York: Harcourt, Brace, 1951.

Arlinghaus, Bruce E., ed. *African Security Issues: Sovereignty, Stability, and Solidarity.* Boulder: Westview, 1984.

Attridge, Derek, and Rosemary Jolly, eds. *Writing South Africa: Literature, Apartheid and Democracy, 1970–1995.* Cambridge, UK: Cambridge University Press, 1998.

Austin, J. L. *How to Do Things with Words.* 2d ed. Oxford, UK: Oxford University Press, 1975.

Ayoob, Mohammed. *The Third World Security: Predicament, State Making, Regional Conflict, and the International System.* London: Lynne Rienner Publishers, 1995.

Bacon, Jon Lance. *Flannery O'Connor and Cold War Culture.* Cambridge, UK: Cambridge University Press, 1993.

Baehr, Peter, ed. *The Portable Hannah Arendt.* London: Penguin Books, 2000.

Bamyeh, Mohammed A. *The Ends of Globalization.* Minneapolis: University of Minnesota Press, 2000.

Banks, Andrew. "Of 'Native Skulls' and 'Noble Caucasians': Phrenology in Colonial South Africa." *Journal of Southern African Studies* 22, 3 (1996).

Bardill, John. *Sources of Domestic Insecurity in Southern African States: A Conference Report.* Backgrounder no. 12. Bellville, South Africa: Centre for Southern Africa Studies, University of the Western Cape, 1994.

Barnard, Lukas Daniël. "Die Magsfaktor in Internasionale Verhoudinge" Band 1 and 2 (The power factor in international relations, Vols. 1 and 2). Unpublished Ph.D. thesis, Faculty of Arts and Philosophy, University of the Orange Free State, 1975.

Barratt, John, and James Barber. *South Africa's Foreign Policy: The Search for Status and Security.* Cambridge, UK: Cambridge University Press, 1990.

Bauman, Zygmunt. *Community: Seeking Safety in an Insecure World.* Cambridge, UK: Polity, 2001.

———. *Modernity and the Holocaust.* Cambridge, UK: Polity, 1989.

Beare, Mark and Paul Bell. "For All We Know." *Leadership* (July 1997).

Bell, Terry, in collaboration with Duidsa Buhle Ntsebeza. *Unfinished Business: South Africa, Apartheid, and Truth.* Cape Town: RedWorks, 2001.

Benjamin, Walter. *Illuminations.* Rpt. Trans. Harry Zohn. London: Fontana-Collins, 1973.

Berger, Peter, and Thomas Luckham. *The Social Construction of Reality.* New York: Doubleday, 1967.

Berrigan, Daniel. *America Is Hard to Find.* London: Society for the Promotion of Christian Knowledge, 1973.

Beukes, E. P., et al., eds. *Development, Employment, and the New South Africa.* Innesdal, South Africa: Development Society of Southern Africa, 1991.

Bhana, Surendra, and Joy B. Brain. *Setting Down Roots: Indian Migrants in South Africa, 1860–1911.* Johannesburg: Witwatersrand University Press, 1990.

Biersteker, Thomas J., and Cynthia Weber, eds. *State Sovereignty as Social Construct.* Cambridge, UK: Cambridge University Press, 1996.

The Blackwell Companion to Social Theory. Ed Bryan S. Turner. Oxford, UK: Blackwell, 1996.

The Blackwell Dictionary of Twentieth Century Social Thought. Ed. William Outhwaite and Tom Bottomore. Oxford, UK: Blackwell, 1998.

Blumenfeld, Jesmond, ed. *South Africa in Crisis.* London: Croom Helm for the Royal Institute of International Affairs, 1987.

Bonner, Philip, Peter Delius, and Deborah Posel. *Apartheid's Genesis, 1935–1962.* Johannesburg: Witwatersrand University Press, 1993.

Booth, Ken. "Security in Anarchy: Utopian Realism in Theory and Practice." *International Affairs* 67, 3 (1991).

——. *A Security Regime in Southern Africa: Theoretical Consideration.* South-ern African Perspectives, Working Paper Series no. 30, Bellville, South Africa: Centre for Southern African Studies, University of the Western Cape, 1994.

Booth, Ken, ed. *An Introduction to Critical Security Studies: Security, Commu-nity, and Emancipation.* London: Lynne Rienner Publishers, forthcoming.

——. *Statecraft and Security: The Cold War and Beyond.* Cambridge, UK: Cambridge University Press, 1998.

Booth, Ken, and Eric Herring. *Keyguide to Information Resources on Strategic Studies.* London: Mansell, 1994.

Booth, Ken, and Steve Smith, eds. *International Relations Theory Today.* Cam-bridge, UK: Polity, 1995.

Booth, Ken, and Peter Vale. "Security in Southern Africa after Apartheid: Beyond Realism." *International Affairs* 71, 2 (1995).

Botha, P. W., and Daan Prinsloo. *Stem Uit die Wilderness: 'N Biografie oor Oud-Pres. PW Botha* (A voice from the wilderness: A biography of former presi-dent P. W. Botha). Mossel Bay, South Africa: Vaandel-Uitgewers, 1997.

Bowman, Larry W. "The Strategic Importance of South Africa to the United States: An Appraisal and Policy Analysis." *African Affairs* 81, 323 (1982).

——. "The Subordinate State System of Southern Africa." *International Stud-ies Quarterly* 12, 3 (1968).

Brettell, Caroline B., and James F. Hollifield. *Migration Theory: Talking Across Disciplines.* London: Routledge, 2000.

Brewer, J. D. *Can South Africa Survive? Five Minutes to Midnight.* New York: St. Martin's, 1989.

Breytenbach, Willie. "Cuito Cuanavale Revisited." *Africa Insight* 27, 1 (1997).

Bronner, Stephen Eric, and Douglas MacKay Kellner, eds. *Critical Theory and Society: A Reader.* London: Routledge, 1989.

Brown, Judith, and William Roger Louis, eds. *The Oxford History of the British Empire,* Volume 4: *The Twentieth Century.* Oxford, UK: Oxford University Press, 1999.

Bryant, Coralie, ed. *Poverty, Policy, and Food Security in Southern Africa.* Boul-der: Lynne Rienner Publishers, 1988.

Bukurura, Sufain Hemed. "Combatting Crime Among the Sukuma and Nyamwezi of West-Central Tanzania." *Crime, Law, and Social Change* 24 (1996).

——. "The Maintenance of Order in Rural Tanzania." *Journal of Legal Plural-ism and Unofficial Law* 34 (1994).

Burchill, Scott, and Andrew Linklater, et al. *Theories of International Relations.* London: Macmillan, 1996.

Burman, Erica, Amanda Kottler, Ann Levett, and Ian Parker, eds. *Culture, Power, and Difference: Discourse Analysis in South Africa.* Cape Town: University of Cape Town Press, 1997.

Butts, Kent Hughes, and Paul R. Thomas. *The Geopolitics of Southern Africa: South Africa as a Regional Super-Power.* Boulder: Westview, 1986.

Buzan, Barry. *People, States, and Fear: An Agenda for International Security Studies in the Post–Cold War Era.* 2d ed. Boulder: Lynne Rienner Publishers, 1991.

————. *People, States, and Fear: The National Security Problem in International Relations.* Brighton, UK: Wheatsheaf, 1983.

Cain, P. J., and A. G. Hopkins. *British Imperialism: Innovation and Expansion, 1688–1914.* London: Longman, 1993.

Callaghy, T. M., ed. *South Africa in Southern Africa: The Intensifying Vortex of Violence.* New York: Praeger, 1983.

The Cambridge Companion to Hannah Arendt. Ed. Dana Villa. Cambridge, UK: Cambridge University Press, 2000.

Campbell, David. *Writing Security, United States Foreign Policy, and the Politics of Identity.* Minneapolis: University of Minnesota Press, 1998.

Cawthra, G. *Brutal Force: The Apartheid War Machine.* London: International Defence and Aid Fund for Southern Africa, 1986.

Chapman, Graham P., and Kathleen M. Baker, eds. *The Changing Geography of Africa and the Middle East.* London: Routledge, 1992.

Chapman, Michael. *Southern African Literatures.* London: Longman, 1996.

Chase, Robert S., Emily B. Hill, and Paul Kennedy. "Pivotal States and U.S. Strategy." *Foreign Affairs* 75, 1 (1996).

Chase, Robert S., Emily B. Hill, and Paul Kennedy, eds. *The Pivotal States: A New Framework for U.S. Policy in the Developing World.* New York. W. W. Norton, 1999.

Cheah, Pheng, and Bruce Robbins, eds. *Cosmopolitics: Thinking and Feeling Beyond the Nation.* Minneapolis: University of Minnesota Press, 1998.

Cherry, Janet. "Development, Conflict, and the Politics of Ethnicity in South Africa's Transition to Democracy." *Third World Quarterly* 15, 4 (1994).

Chidester, David. *Savage Systems: Colonialism and Comparative Religion in Southern Africa.* Cape Town: University of Cape Town Press, 1996.

Chingono, Mark F. *The State: Violence and Development; the Political Economy of the War in Mozambique, 1975–1992.* Aldershot, UK: Avebury, 1996.

Christie, Frances, and Joseph Hanlon. *Mozambique and the Great Flood of 2000.* London: James Currey, 2001.

Christopher, A. J. *The Atlas of Changing South Africa.* London: Routledge, 2001.

————. *The Atlas of States: Global Change, 1900–2000.* Chichester, UK: John Wiley and Sons, 1999.

Cilliers, Jakkie. *The SADC Organ for Politics, Defence, and Security.* IDP Paper no. 10. Halfway House: Institute for Defence Policy, 1996.

————. "To Sell or Die: The Future of the South African Defence Industry." *University of Pretoria, Issue Bulletin* 1 (1994).

Cilliers, Jakkie, and Greg Mills, eds. *Peacekeeping in Africa.* Vol. 2. Johannesburg: Institute for Defence Policy and South African Institute of International Affairs, 1995.

Clifford-Vaughan, F. McA. *Force and Peace: Four Introductory Lectures on Strategic Studies.* Occasional Papers Series. Durban, South Africa: University of Natal, Department of Political Science, 1979.

Clough, Michael, ed. *Changing Realities in Southern Africa: Implications for American Policy*. Berkeley: University of California Press, 1982.

Clough, Michael, and J. Herbst. *South Africa's Changing Regional Strategy: Beyond Destabilization*. New York: Council on Foreign Relations, 1989.

Cock, Jacklyn. *Colonels and Cadres: War and Gender in South Africa*. Oxford, UK: Oxford University Press, 1991.

Cock, Jacklyn, and Penny McKenzie, eds. *From Defence to Development: Redirecting Military Resources in South Africa*. Cape Town: David Philip, 1998.

Cock, Jacklyn, and Laurie Nathan, eds. *War and Society: The Militarisation of South Africa*. Cape Town: David Philip, 1989.

Coetsee, Ampie. *Letterkunde en die Krisis*. Johannesburg: Tauris, 1990.

Cohen, Barry, and Mohammed A. El-Khawas. *The Kissinger Study of Southern Africa: National Security Study Memorandum 39 (Secret)*. Westport, CT: Lawrence Hill, 1976.

Comaroff, Jean, and John Comaroff. *Of Revelation and Revolution: Christianity, Colonialism, and Consciousness in South Africa*. Vol. 1. Chicago: University of Chicago Press, 1991.

Conca, Ken, and Geoffery D. Dabelko, eds. *Environmental Peacekeeping*. Baltimore: Johns Hopkins University Press, 2001.

Concise Dictionary of Sociology. Comp. Gordon Marshall. Oxford, UK: Oxford University Press, 1994.

Cooper, Andrew F., ed. *Niche Diplomacy: Middle Powers After the Cold War*. London: Macmillan, 1997.

Coplan, David B. *In Time of Cannibals: The Word Music of South Africa's Basuto Migrants*. Johannesburg: Witwatersrand University Press, 1994.

Cox, Robert, et al. *International Political Economy: Understanding Global Disorder*. London: Zed Books, 1995.

Crampton, Andrew. "The Voortrekker Monument, the Birth of Apartheid, and Beyond." *Political Geography* 20 (2001).

Cross, Michael M. *Imagery of Identity in South African Education, 1880–1990*. Durham, NC: Carolina Academic Press, 1999.

Crush, Jonathan. "Fortress South Africa and the Deconstruction of Apartheid's Migration Regime." *Geoforum* 30, 1 (1999).

Crush, Jonathan, Alan Jeeves, and David Yudelman. *South Africa's Labour Empire: A History of Black Migrancy to the Gold Mines*. Boulder: Westview, 1992.

Daniel, John. "A Response to Guelke: The Cold War Factor in South Africa's Transition." *Journal of Contemporary African Studies* 14, 1 (1996).

Danso, Ransford, and David A. McDonald. *Writing Xenophobia: Immigration and the Press in Post-Apartheid South Africa*. Migration Policy Series no. 17. Cape Town: IDASA for the Southern African Migration Project, 2000.

Darian-Smith, Kate, Liz Gunnar, and Sarah Nuttall, eds. *Text, Theory, and Space: Land, Literature, and History in South Africa and Australia*. London: Routledge, 1996.

Davenport, Rodney. "Kruger, Paul." *New Dictionary of South African Biography*, forthcoming 2004.

————. *South Africa: A Modern History.* 4th ed. London: Macmillan, 1991.

Davies, Robert. "The Military and Foreign Policy in South Africa: Review Article." *Journal of Southern African Studies* 12, 2 (1986).

Davies, Robert, and Judith Head. "The Future of Mine Migrancy in the Context of Broader Trends in Migration in Southern Africa." *Journal of Southern African Studies* 21, 3 (1995).

Davies, Robert, and Dan O'Meara. "Total Strategy in Southern Africa: An Analysis of South African Regional Policy Since 1978." *Journal of Southern African Studies* 11, 2 (1985).

Davis, M. Jane, ed. *Security Issues in the Post–Cold War World.* Cheltenham, UK: Edward Elgar, 1996.

Debrix, Francois. *Re-Envisioning Peacekeeping: The United Nations and the Mobilization of Ideology.* Minneapolis: University of Minnesota Press, 1999.

Der Derian, James, and Michael J. Shapiro, eds. *International/Intertextual Relations: Postmodern Readings of World Politics.* Lexington, MA: Lexington Books, 1989.

De Klerk, W. A. *The Puritans in Africa: A History of Afrikanerdom.* London: Penguin, 1983.

Deutsch, Karl W., et al. *Political Community in the North.* Princeton, NJ: Princeton University Press, 1957.

Development Bank of Southern Africa. *The Southern African Customs Union: A Review of Costs and Benefits.* Halfway House, South Africa: Development Bank of Southern Africa, 1994.

A Dictionary of South African History. Comp. Christopher Saunders and Nicholas Southey. Cape Town: David Philip, 1998.

Dingake, Michael. *My Fight Against Apartheid.* London: Kliptown Books, 1987.

Diplomacy, Intelligence, Defence and Trade Education, and Training Authority (DIDETA). Centurion, *Update* 1 (July 2001).

Doctorow, E. L. *Poets and Presidents: Selected Essays, 1977–1992.* London: Papermac, 1993.

Donnan, Hastings, and Thomas M. Wilson. *Border's Frontiers of Identity, Nation, and State.* Oxford, UK: Berg, 1999.

Doty, Roxanne Lynn. "Immigration and National Identity: Constructing the Nation." *Review of International Studies* 22, 3 (1996).

Dubow, Saul. *Scientific Racism in Modern South Africa.* Cambridge, UK: Cambridge University Press, 1995.

————. "The War for South Africa." Paper delivered at the Unisa Library Conference entitled "Rethinking the South African War, 1899–1902," Pretoria, South Africa, August 3–5, 1998.

Dubow, Saul, ed. *Science and Society in Southern Africa.* Manchester, UK: Manchester University Press, 2000.

Duffy, Rosaleen. "The Environmental Challenge to the Nation State: Superparks and National Parks in Zimbabwe." *Journal of Southern African Studies* 23, 3 (1997).

Dunn, Kevin C., and Timothy M. Shaw, eds. *Africa's Challenges to International Relations Theory.* London: Palgrave, 2001.

du Toit, Andre. "Facing Up to the Future: Some Personal Reflections on the Predicament of Afrikaner Intellectuals in the Legitimation Crisis of Afrikaner Nationalism and the Apartheid State." *Social Dynamics* 7, 2 (1981).

———. "Puritans in Africa? Afrikaner 'Calvinism' and Kuyperian Neo-Calvinism in Late-Nineteenth Century South Africa." *Comparative Studies in History and Society in History* 27, 3 (1985).

Dutton, Chris, and Mai Palmberg. *Human Rights and Homosexuality in Southern Africa*. Current African Issues no. 19. Uppsala, Sweden: Nordiska Afrikainstutet, 1996.

Dyer, Hugh C., and Leon Mangasarian, eds. *The Study of International Relations: The State of the Art*. London: Macmillan, 1989.

Eagleton, Terry. *Literary Theory: An Introduction*. 2d ed. Minneapolis: University of Minnesota Press, 1996.

Easterbrook. Gregg. "Ideas Move Nations." *Atlantic Monthly* (January 1986).

Ellis, Stephen. "Africa After the Cold War: New Patterns of Government and Politics." *Development and Change* 27, 1 (1996).

Elphick, Richard, and Rodney Davenport, eds. *Christianity in South Africa: A Political, Social, and Cultural History*. Cape Town: David Philip, 1997.

Fawcett, Louise, and Andrew Hurrell, eds. *Regionalism in World Politics: Regional Organization and International Order*. Oxford, UK: Oxford University Press, 1995.

Feldberg, Meyer, et al., eds. *Milton Friedman in South Africa*. Cape Town: University of Cape Town, Graduate School of Business, 1976.

First, Ruth. *Black Gold: The Mozambican Miner, Proletarian, and Peasant*. Brighton, UK: Harvester, 1983.

Foucault, Michel. *Power/Knowledge: Selected Interviews and Other Writings, 1972–1977*. New York: Pantheon, 1980.

Fourie, Deon. *Evolving Experience in Decisions for Defence: Consequences of Leaving the British Commonwealth*. Unpublished paper.

Frank, Jason A., and John Tambornio, eds. *Vocations of Political Theory*. Minneapolis: University of Minnesota Press, 2000.

Fraser, C. A. *The Strategy of the Revolutionary*. Johannesburg: South African Institute of International Affairs, 1969.

Freedman, Lawrence. *The Revolution in Strategic Affairs*. Adelphi Papers no. 318. London: International Institute for Strategic Studies, 1998.

Friedland, Elaine A. "South Africa and Instability in Southern Africa." *Annals of the American Academy of Political and Social Science* 463 (1982).

Galbraith, John Kenneth. "The Autonomous Military Power: An Economic View." *Disarmament* 19, 3 (1996).

Garba, Joseph Nanven, and Jean Herskovits. *Militaries, Democracies, and Security in Southern Africa*. Report of the Southern African Security Project. New York: International Peace Academy, 1997.

Garson, N. G. "South Africa and World War I." *Journal of Imperial and Commonwealth Studies* 8, 1 (1979).

Geertz, Clifford. *The Interpretation of Cultures: Selected Essays*. New York: Basic Books, 1973.

Geldenhuys, Deon. *The Diplomacy of Isolation: South African Foreign Policy Making.* Johannesburg: Macmillan, 1984.

———. "Rethinking Foreign Intervention: South Africa as a Case-study." *Strategic Review for Southern Africa* 15, 1 (1993).

———. "Some Strategic Implications of Regional Economic Relationships for the Republic of South Africa." University of Pretoria *ISSUP Strategic Review* (January 1981).

———. *South Africa's Search for Security Since the Second World War.* Occasional Paper. Johannesburg: South African Institute of International Affairs, 1978.

———. "Ten Crisis in South Africa's External Relations." *International Affairs Bulletin* 13, 3 (1989).

George, Jim. *Discourses of Global Politics: A Critical (Re)Introduction to International Relations.* Boulder: Lynne Rienner Publishers, 1994.

Gibbons, Michael, et al. *The New Production of Knowledge.* London: Sage, 1994.

Gibson, Rex. *Critical Theory and Education.* London: Hodder and Stoughton, 1986.

Giliomee, Hermann. "Survival in Justice: An Afrikaner Debate over Apartheid." *Comparative Studies in Society and History* 36, 3 (1994).

Giliomee, Hermann, and Lawrence Schlemmer, eds. *Up Against the Fences: Poverty, Passes, and Privilege in South Africa.* Cape Town: David Philip, 1985.

Gledhill, John. *Power and Its Disguises: Anthropological Perspectives on Politics.* 2d ed. London: Pluto Press, 2000.

Good, Kenneth. *Realizing Democracy in Botswana, Namibia, and South Africa.* Pretoria: Africa Institute of South Africa, 1997.

———. "The State and Extreme Poverty in Botswana: The San and Destitutes." *Journal of Modern African Studies* 37, 2 (1997).

Gordimer, Nadine. *Living in Hope and History: Notes from Our Century.* Cape Town: David Philip, 2000.

Graebner, Norman, ed. *The National Security: Its Theory and Practice, 1945–1960.* Oxford, UK: Oxford University Press, 1986.

Gramsci, Antonio. *Selections from Prison Notebooks of Antonio Gramsci.* Ed. and trans. Quinton Hoare and Geoffrey Nowell Smith. London: Lawrence and Wishart, 1986.

Greenstein, Ran, ed. *Comparative Perspectives on South Africa.* London: Macmillan, 1998.

Grovè, W. "The Drug Trade as a National and International Security Threat: Where Do We Stand?" University of Pretoria *ISSUP Bulletin* 7, 94 (1994).

Grovogui, Biba N. "Rituals of Power: Theory Languages and Vernaculars of International Relations." *Alternatives* 23, 4 (1998).

Grundy, Kenneth W. *Confrontation and Accommodation in Southern Africa: The Limits of Independence.* Berkeley: University of California Press for the Center on International Race Relations, University of Denver, 1973.

———. *Defense Legislation and Communal Politics: The Evolution of a White South African Nation as Reflected in the Controversy over the Assignment of*

Armed Forces Abroad, 1912–1976. Papers in International Studies no. 33. Columbus: Ohio University, Center for International Studies, 1978.

————. *The Rise of the South African Security Establishment: An Essay in the Changing Locus of State Power*. Johannesburg: South African Institute of International Affairs, 1983.

————. *Soldiers Without Politics: Blacks in the South African Armed Forces*. Berkeley: University of California Press, 1983.

Guelke, Adrian. "The Impact of the End of the Cold War on South African Transition." *Journal of Contemporary African Studies* 14, 1 (1996).

————. *South Africa in Transition: The Misunderstood Miracle*. London: I. B. Tauris, 1999.

Gupta, V. "Pressures Against Regional Cooperation: A Study of the SADCC." *International Studies* 26, 4 (1989).

Gutteridge, Willam, and J. E. Spence, eds. *Violence in Southern Africa*. London: Frank Cass, 1997.

Haas, Peter. "Introduction: Epistemic Communities and International Policy Coordination." *International Organization* 14, 1 (1992).

Habermas, Jürgen (interviewed by Michael Haller). *The Past as the Future*. Cambridge, UK: Polity, 1994.

Hall, Rodney Bruce. "Applying the Self/Other Nexus in International Relations." *International Studies Review* 3, 1 (2001).

Hallencreutz, Carl Fredrik, and Mai Palmberg. *Religion and Politics in Southern Africa*. Seminar Proceedings no. 24. Uppsala, Sweden: Scandinavian Institute of African Studies, 1991.

Hamilton, Carolyn, ed. *The Mfecane Aftermath: Reconstructive Debates in Southern African History*. Johannesburg: Witwatersrand University Press, 1995.

Hanlon, Joseph. *Beggar Your Neighbours: Apartheid Power in Southern Africa*. London: Catholic Institute for International Affairs in collaboration with James Currey, 1986.

Hanna, A. J. *The Story of the Rhodesias and Nyasaland*. London: Faber and Faber, 1965.

Harries, Patrick. "The Roots of Ethnicity: Discourse and the Politics of Language Construction in South-East Africa." *African Affairs* 87, 346 (1988).

————. *Work, Culture, and Identity: Migrant Labourers in Mozambique and South Africa, c. 1860–1910*. Johannesburg: Witwatersrand University Press, 1994.

Harrigan, Anthony. *Defence Against Total Attack*. Cape Town: Nasionale Boekhandel, 1965.

Harring, Sidney L. "'God Gave Us This Land': The OvaHima, the Proposed Epupa Dam, the Independent Namibian State, the Law, and Development in Africa." Undated manuscript.

Heineken, Lindy. "AIDS: The New Security Frontier." *Conflict Trends* 4 (2000).

Held, David. *Democracy and the Global Order: From Modern State to Cosmopolitan Governance*. Cambridge, UK: Polity, 1995.

Hirson, Baruch, and Gwyn A. Williams. *The Delegate for Africa: David Ivon Jones, 1883–1924*. London: Core Publications, 1995.

Hobden, Steve. "State Formation and Development in Southern Africa: A Framework for Analysis from Historical Sociology." Paper presented at the Conference entitled "Neither Great nor Good: The Genesis and Development of the Early State System in Southern Africa," held under the auspices of the Centre for African Studies, University of Porto, and the Centre for Southern African Studies, University of the Western Cape, Porto, Portugal, July 18–19, 1997.

Hoffman, Mark. "Critical Theory and the Inter-Paradigm Debate." *Millennium* 16, 2 (1987).

Hoffman, Stanley. "An American Social Science: International Relations." *Daedalus* 106 (supp. 1) (1977).

Holiday, Anthony. "Conversations in a Colony: Natural Language and Primitive Interchange." *Pretexts* 4, 2 (1993).

Hough, Mike. "Crime as a National Security Issue in South Africa." *Strategic Review for Southern Africa* 17, 2 (November 1995).

Hugo, Pierre. "Towards Darkness and Death: Racial Demonology in Southern Africa." *Journal of Modern African Studies* 26, 4 (1988).

Huntington, Samuel P. *The Clash of Civilizations and the Remaking of World Order*. New York: Simon and Schuster, 1996.

———. "Reform and Stability in a Modernizing, Multi-Ethnic Society." *Politikon* 8, 2 (1981).

———. *The Third Wave: Democratization in the Late Twentieth Century*. Norman: University of Oklahoma Press, 1991.

———. "The West: Unique, Not Universal." *Foreign Affairs* 75, 6 (1996).

Hyam, Ronald. *The Failure of South African Expansion, 1908–1948*. London: Macmillan, 1972.

The Illegal Drug Trade in Southern Africa: International Dimensions to a Local Crisis. Johannesburg: South African Institute of International Affairs with the assistance of the Swedish International Development Agency and the Embassy of the United States of America, Pretoria, 1998.

Ingram, David. *Critical Theory and Philosophy*. New York: Paragon House, 1990.

Ivison, Duncan, Paul Patton, and Will Sanders, eds. *Political Theory and the Rights of Indigenous Peoples*. Cambridge, UK: Cambridge University Press, 2000.

James, Deborah. "Musical Form and Social History: Research Perspectives on Black South African Music." *Radical History Review* 46/47 (1990).

———. *Songs of the Women Migrants: Performance and Identity in South Africa*. Johannesburg: Witwatersrand University Press, 1999.

James, Wilmot. *Our Precious Metal: African Labour in South Africa's Gold Industry, 1970–1990*. Cape Town: David Philip, 1990.

James, Wilmot, ed. *The State of Apartheid*. Boulder: Lynne Rienner Publishers, 1987.

Jansen, Jonathan D., ed. *Knowledge and Power in South Africa: Critical Perspectives Across the Disciplines*. Johannesburg: Skotaville, 1991.

Jaster, Robert Scott. *The Defence of White Power: South African Foreign Policy under Pressure*. London: Macmillan, 1988.

Johnstone, Frederick A. "Most Painful to Our Hearts: South Africa Through the Eyes of the New School." *Canadian Journal of African Studies* 16, 1 (1982).

Johnstone, R. *Class, Race, and Gold: A Study of Class Relations and Racial Discrimination in South Africa.* London: Routledge and Kegan Paul, 1976.

Judin, Hilton, and Ivan Vladislavić, eds. *Blank: Architecture, Apartheid, and After.* Cape Town: David Philip, n.d.

Kalley, Jacqueline A. *South Africa's Treaties in Theory and Practice, 1806–1998.* Lanham, MD: Scarecrow, 2001.

Kapuściński, Ryszard. *Another Day of Life.* London: Picador, 1987.

Keegan, Timothy. *Colonial South Africa and the Origins of the Racial Order.* Cape Town: David Philip, 1996.

Keller, E. J., and L. A. Picard, eds. *South Africa in Southern Africa: Domestic Change and International Conflict.* Boulder: Lynne Rienner Publishers, 1989.

Kennedy, Paul M. *Preparing for the Twenty-First Century.* New York: Random House, 1993.

Keohane, Robert O., ed. *Neorealism and Its Critics.* New York: Columbia University Press, 1986.

Kotze, Hennie, and Lloyd Hill. "Emergent Migration Policy in a Democratic South Africa." *International Migration* 35, 1 (1997).

Kraak, Andre. *Competing Education and Training Policies.* Occasional Papers. Pretoria: Human Sciences Research Council, 1998.

Krause, Keith, and Michael C. Williams, eds. *Critical Security Studies: Concepts and Cases.* Minneapolis: University of Minnesota Press, 1997.

Kubik Gerhard. *Malawian Music: A Framework for Analysis.* Zomba, Malawi: Centre for Social Research and the Department of Fine and Performing Arts, University of Malawi, 1987.

Kunnie, Julian. *Is Apartheid Really Dead? Pan-Africanist Working-Class Perspectives.* Boulder: Westview, 2000.

Lacey, Marion. *Working for Boroko: The Origins of the Coercive Labour System in South Africa.* Johannesburg: Ravan, 1981.

Lake, Anthony. *The "Tar Baby" Option: American Policy Towards Southern Rhodesia.* New York: Columbia University Press, 1976.

Lamar, Howard, and Leonard Thompson, eds. *The Frontier in History.* New Haven: Yale University Press, 1981.

Larsson, Anita, et al. *Changing Gender Relations in Southern Africa: Issues of Urban Life.* Roma: Institute of Southern African Studies, University of Lesotho, 1998.

Latham, Robert. *The Liberal Moment: Modernity, Security, and the Making of the Postwar International Order.* New York: Columbia University Press, 1997.

"Laundry, Canned Goods, and Rape: A Scholar Explores the Military's Impact on Women." *Chronicle of Higher Education* 14 (April 2000).

Lazerson, Joshua A. *Against the Tide: Whites in the Struggle Against Apartheid.* Boulder: Westview, 1994.

Legassick, Martin. "The Griqua, the Sotho-Tswana, and the Missionaries, 1780–1840: The Politics of a Frontier Zone." Unpublished Ph.D. thesis, Department of History, University of California–Los Angeles, 1969.

Letlaka, Tsepo. "The Republic of Transkei and the International Community." *International Affairs Bulletin* 1, 2 (1977).

Libby, R. T. *The Politics of Economic Power in Southern Africa.* Princeton, NJ: Princeton University Press, 1987.

Lippman, Walter. *U.S. Foreign Policy: Shield of the Republic.* London: H. Hamilton, 1943.

Lipschutz, Ronnie D., ed. *On Security.* New York: Columbia University Press, 1995.

Lodge, Tom. "Policy Processes Within the African National Congress and the Tripartite Alliance." *Politikon* 26, 1 (1999).

Louw, Leon, and Frances Kendall. *South Africa: The Solution.* Bisho, South Africa: Amagi, 1986.

Louw, Michael H.H., ed. *National Security: A Modern Approach.* Pretoria: University of Pretoria, 1978.

Lye, William F., and Colin Murray. *Transformations on the Highveld: The Tswana and Southern Sotho.* Cape Town: David Philip, 1980.

MacKenzie, John M., ed. *Imperialism and the Natural World.* Manchester, UK: Manchester University Press, 1990.

Maclennan, Don, and Norbert Nowotny. *In Memoriam: Oskar Wolberheim.* Cape Town: Balkema, 1971.

McDonald, David A., ed. *On Borders: Perspectives on International Migration in Southern Africa.* New York: St. Martin's for the Southern African Migration Project, 2000.

McSweeney, Bill. *Security, Identity, and Interests: A Sociology of International Relations.* Cambridge, UK: Cambridge University Press, 1999.

Maharaj, Brij, and Rinku Rajkumar. "The 'Alien Invasion' in South Africa: Illegal Immigrants in Durban." *Development Southern Africa* 14, 2 (1997).

Makoa, Francis K. "The Challenges of the South African Military Intervention in Lesotho After the 1998 Elections." *Lesotho Social Science Review* 5, 1 (1999).

Malan, D. F. *Naar Congoland: Een Reisbeschrijving* (To Congo: A travelogue). Stellenbosch, South Africa: De Christen-Studenten Vereening van Zuid-Afrika, 1913.

Malan, Mark, ed. *New Partners in Peace: Towards a Southern African Peacekeeping Capacity.* IDP Monograph Series no. 5. Halfway House, South Africa: Institute for Defence Policy, 1996.

Malan, Mark, and Jakkie Cilliers. *SADC Organ on Politics, Defence, and Security: Future Development.* ISS Paper no. 19. Halfway House, South Africa: Institute for Security Studies, 1997.

Malan, T., and P. S. Hattingh. *Black Homelands in South Africa.* Pretoria: Africa Institute of South Africa, 1976.

Maluwa, Tiyanjana. "Disputed Sovereignty over Sidudu (or Kasikili) Island Botswana-Namibia." *Southern Africa: Political and Economic Monthly* 6, 2 (November 1992).

Mamdani, Mahmood. *Citizen and Subject: Contemporary Africa and the Legacy of Late Colonialism.* Cape Town: David Philip, 1996.

Mandela, Nelson. "South Africa's Future Foreign Policy." *Foreign Affairs* 72, 5 (1993).

Manzo, Kate. "Global Power and South African Politics: A Foucauldian Analysis." *Alternatives* 17, 1 (1992).

Marais, Hein. "The RDP: Is There Life After GEAR." *Development Update* 1, 1 (1997).

Maritz, C. J. "Pretoria's Reaction to the Role of Moscow and Peking in Southern Africa." *Journal of Modern African Studies* 25, 2 (1987).

Marks, Shula, and Anthony Atmore, eds. *Economy and Society in Pre-Industrial South Africa.* London: Longman, 1980.

Martin, Jay. *The Dialectical Imagination: A History of the Frankfurt School and the Institute of Social Research, 1023–1950.* London: Heineman, 1973.

Martin, William G. "Region Formation Under Crisis Conditions: South Versus Southern Africa in the Interwar Period." *Journal of Southern African Studies* 16, 1 (1990).

Marty, Martin. *Pilgrims in Their Own Land: 500 Years of Religion in America.* New York: Harper and Row, 1984.

Marx, Karl. *Capital.* Vol. 1. Moscow: Progress, 1974.

Marx, Karl, and Friedrich Engels. *Selected Works in Three Volumes.* Moscow: Progress, 1969.

Mastanduno, Michael. "Preserving the Unipolar Moment: Realist Theories and U.S. Grand Strategy After the Cold War." *International Security* 21, 4 (1997).

Matlosa, Khabele. "The Recent Political Crisis in Lesotho and the Role of External Forces." *Africa Insight* 24, 4 (1994).

Mayall, James, ed. *The New Interventionism, 1991–1994: United Nations Experience in Cambodia, Former Yugoslavia, and Somalia.* New York: Cambridge University Press, 1996.

Maynes, Charles William. "Relearning Intervention." *Foreign Policy* 102 (1995).

Mazrui, Ali A. "The African State as a Political Refugee." *International Journal of Refugee Law* Special Issue (Summer 1995).

Mbembe, Achille. "At the Edge: Boundaries, Territoriality, and Sovereignty in Africa." *Codesria Bulletin* 3 and 4 (1999).

———. *On the Postcolony.* Berkeley: University of California Press, 2001.

Messina, Anthony M. "The Not So Silent Revolution: Postwar Migration to Western Europe." *World Politics* 49 (1996).

Meyns, Peter. *Konflikt und Entwicklung im Südlichen Afrika* (Conflict and development in southern Africa). Grundwissen Politik Band 27. Oplanden: Leske + Budrich, 2000.

Migration: Sources, Patterns, and Implications. Johannesburg: South African Institute of International Affairs, 1993.

Millar, Tom. *South Africa and Regional Security.* Bradlow Series no. 3. Johannesburg: South African Institute of International Affairs, 1985.

Mills, Greg. *South Africa and Security Building in the Indian Ocean Rim.* Johannesburg: South African Institute of International Affairs, 1998.

Mills, Greg, ed. *From Pariah to Participant: South Africa's Evolving Foreign Relations.* Johannesburg: South African Institute of International Affairs, 1994.

Mills, Greg, Alan Begg, and Anthonie van Nieuwkerk, eds. *South Africa in the Global Economy.* Johannesburg: South African Institute of International Affairs with the assistance of the Standard Bank Foundation, 1995.

Mills, Kurt. "Permeable Borders: Human Migration and Sovereignty." *Global Society* 10, 2 (1976).

Minnaar, Anthony. "Ours for the Taking? Crime and Illegals." *Information Update* 5, 4 (1995).

Minnaar, Anthony, and Mike Hough, et al. *Who Goes There? Perspectives on Clandestine Migration and Illegal Aliens in Southern Africa.* Pretoria: Human Sciences Research Council Publishers, 1996.

Mittelman, James, ed. *Globalization: Critical Reflections.* London: Lynne Rienner Publishers, 1997.

Molomo, Mpho G. "External Military Intervention in Lesotho's Recent Political Crisis." *Lesotho Social Science Review* 5, 1 (1999).

Moore, Donald S. "Contesting Terrain in Zimbabwe's Eastern Highlands: Political Ecology, Ethnography, and Peasant Resource Struggles." *Economic Geography* 69, 4 (1993).

Morrow, Wally, ed. *The Proceedings of the Kenton Conference 1985.* Bellville, South Africa: Faculty of Education, University of the Western Cape, 1986.

Morton, Nicola. "Parks That Cross the Borderline: Transnational Co-operation under the Ethical Umbrella of Sustainable Development." Unpublished M.A. diss., Department of Political Science, University of the Stellenbosch, 1999.

Mostert, Noel. *Frontiers: The Epic of South Africa's Creation and the Tragedy of the Xhosa People.* London: Pimlico, 1993.

Mpe, Phaswane. *Welcome to Our Hillbrow.* Pietermaritzburg, South Africa: University of Natal Press, 2001.

Mudimbe, V. Y. *The Invention of Africa: Gnosis, Philosophy, and the Order of Knowledge.* London: J. Currey, 1990.

Mulford, David. *Zambia: The Politics of Independence, 1957–1964.* Oxford, UK: Oxford University Press, 1967.

Mundazi, Dickson A. *The Struggle for Social Change in Southern Africa: Visions of Liberty.* New York: Crane Russak, 1989.

Murphree, M. W. "Strategic Considerations for Enhancing Scholarship at the University of Zimbabwe." *Zambesia* 24, 1 (1997).

Murray, Martin J. "'Blackbirding' at 'Crooks Corner': Illicit Labour Recruiting in the Northeastern Transvaal, 1910–1940." *Journal of Southern African Studies* 21, 3 (1995).

———. *South African Capitalism and Black Political Opposition.* Cambridge, MA: Schenkman, 1982.

Ndebele, Njabulo. "The Rediscovery of the Ordinary: Some New Writings in South Africa." *Journal of Southern African Studies* 12, 2 (1986).

The New Fontana Dictionary of Modern Thought. Ed. Alan Bullock and Stephen Trombley. London: HarperCollins, 1999.

Nimer, Benjamin. "National Liberation and the Conflicting Terms of Discourse in South Africa: An Interpretation." *Political Communication and Persuasion* 3, 4, 1986.

Nkomo, Sibusiso. *Migrant Labor Economic Theory and National Development Policy: The Case of Southern Africa and Lesotho.* Ph.D. diss., University of Delaware, 1985; available from Ann Arbor: University Microfilms International.

Nolutshungu, Sam C. *Southern Africa in a Global Context: Towards a Southern African Security Community.* Harare, Zimbabwe: South African Political Economy Books, 1994.

Nolutshungu, Sam C., ed. *Margins of Insecurity: Minorities and International Security.* Rochester, NY: University of Rochester Press, 1996.

Norval, Aletta J. *Deconstructing Apartheid Discourse.* London: Verso, 1996.

Nuttall, Sarah, and Carli Coetzee, eds. *Negotiating the Past: The Making of Memory in South Africa.* Oxford, UK: Oxford University Press, 1998.

Nuttall, Sarah, and Cheryl-Ann Michael, eds. *Senses of Culture: South African Culture Studies.* Oxford, UK: Oxford University Press, 2000.

O Mineiro Moçambicano: Um Estudo Sobre a Exportação de Mão de Obra em Inhambane (The Mozambican miner: a study on the export of labor in Inhambane). Grupo de revisão: Luís Covane, Colin Darch, David Hedges, Alpheus Manghezi. Maputo: Centro de Estudos Africanos, Universidade Eduardo Mondlane, 1998.

Oden, Bertil. *Southern African Futures: Critical Factors for Regional Development in Southern Africa.* Uppsala, Sweden: Nordiska Afrikainstitutet, 1996.

O'Dowd, Michael. *South Africa: The Growth Imperative.* Johannesburg: Jonathan Ball, 1991.

Official Year Book of the Union of South Africa and of Basutoland, Bechuanaland, and Swaziland. Issued by J. L. Raats. Pretoria: Bureau of Census and Statistics, 1954.

Ohlson, Thomas. *The New Is Not Yet Born: Conflict Resolution in Southern Africa.* Washington, DC: Brookings Institution Press, 1994.

———. *Power Politics and Peace Politics: Inter-State Conflict Resolution in Southern Africa.* Uppsala, Sweden: Department of Peace and Conflict Resolution, University of Uppsala, 1998.

O'Meara, Dan. "Destabilization in Southern Africa: Total Strategy in Total Disarray." *Monthly Review* (April 1986).

———. *Forty Lost Years: The Apartheid State and the National Party, 1948–1994.* Johannesburg: Ravan, 1996.

Orkin, M., ed. *Sanctions Against Apartheid.* New York: St. Martin's, 1989.

Otto, Ton. *Social Practice and the Ethnographic Circle: Rethinking the 'Ethnographer's Magic' in a Late Modern World.* Working Paper no. 1. Aarhus, Denmark: Department of Ethnography and Social Anthropology, Aarhus University, 1997.

Owomoyela, Oyekan. *The African Difference: Discourses on Africanity and the Relativity of Cultures.* Johannesburg: Witwatersrand University Press, 1996.

Owusu, Maxwell. "Democracy and Africa: A View from the Village." *Journal of Modern African Studies* 30, 3 (1992).

The Oxford Companion to Politics of the World. Ed. Joel Krieger. Oxford, UK: Oxford University Press, 2001.

Parliamentary Oversight of the Security Sector in the Commonwealth. London: Institute of Commonwealth Studies, 2000.

Parry, Charles D.H. "The Illegal Narcotics Trade in Southern Africa: A Programme for Action." *South African Journal of International Affairs* 5, 1 (1997).

Parsley, Jenny. "Free Markets, Free Women? Changing Conceptions of Citizenship and Gender Relations Among Women Cross-Border Traders in Contemporary Southern Africa." Unpublished M.A. diss., Department of Sociology, University of Witwatersrand, 1998.

Patterson, Matthew. "Institutions for Global Environmental Change." *Global Environmental Change* 7, 2 (1992).

Paul, T. V., and John A. Hall. *International Order and the Future of World Politics.* Cambridge, UK: Cambridge University Press, 1999.

Penguin Dictionary of International Relations. London: Penguin Books, 1998.

Pieres, J. B. *The Dead Will Arise: Nongqawuse and the Great Xhosa Cattle Killing Movement of 1856–1857.* Johannesburg: Ravan, 1989.

Plank, David N. "Dreams of Community." *Journal of Education Policy* Special Edition (*Yearbook of the Politics of Education Association*), part 1 (1996).

Poku, Nana, ed. *Security and Development in Southern Africa.* London: Praeger, 2001.

The Polity Reader in Social Theory. Cambridge, UK: Cambridge, Polity, 1995.

Porter, A. N. *The Origins of the South African War: Joseph Chamberlain and the Diplomacy of Imperialism, 1895–1999.* Manchester, UK: Manchester University Press, 1980.

Potholm, Christian P., and Richard Dale, eds. *Southern Africa in Perspective: Essays in Regional Politics.* New York: The Free Press, 1972.

Pottinger, Brian. *The Imperial Presidency: PW Botha the First 10 Years.* Johannesburg: Skotaville, 1988.

Prah, Kwesi Kwaa. *Beyond the Colour Line: Pan-Africanist Disputations.* Florida, South Africa: Vivlia, 1997.

Prinsloo, Koos. *Hemel Help Ons.* Johannesburg: Tauris, 1987.

———. *Jonkmanskas.* Cape Town: Tafelberg, 1982.

Prohibited Persons: Abuse of Undocumented Migrants, Asylum Seekers, and Refugees in South Africa. London: Human Rights Watch, 1998.

The Project "Training for Peace in Southern Africa: An Evaluation Report Prepared by FAFO." Evaluation Report 3/2000. Oslo: Norwegian Ministry for Foreign Affairs, September 2000.

Pule, Neville W. "Power Struggles in the Basutoland Congress Party, 1991–1997." *Lesotho Social Science Review* 5, 1 (1999).

Ramano, Carlin. "It's Time for 'Comparative Intellectuals.'" *Chronicle of Higher Education* 17 (November 2000).

The Reconstruction and Development Programme: A Policy Framework. Johannesburg: African National Congress, 1994.

Richmond, Oliver P.A. "Genealogy of Peacemaking: The Creation and Recreation of Order." *Alternatives* 26 (2001).

Rockström, Johan. "Green Water Security for the Food Makers of Tomorrow: Windows of Opportunity in Drought-Prone Savannahs." *Water Science and Technology* 43, 4 (2001).

Rogerson, Chris. "African Immigrant Entrepreneurs and Johannesburg's Changing Inner City." *Africa Insight* 27 (1997).

Rosenau, James N., et al. *Global Voices: Dialogues in International Relations*. Boulder: Westview, 1993.

Rosenau, Pauline. *Post-Modernism and the Social Sciences: Insights, Inroads, and Intrusions*. Princeton, NJ: Princeton University Press, 1992.

Roskam, Karel. *Grenselose Oorlog: Suid Afrika Tegen de Buurlande* (War without borders: South Africa against its neighbors). Amsterdam: Jan Mets, 1984.

Ross Fowler, Michael, and Julie Marie Bunck. "What Constitutes the Sovereign State." *Review of International Studies* 22, 4 (1996).

Rostow, W. W. *The Stages of Economic Growth: A Non-Communist Manifesto*. Cambridge, UK: Cambridge University Press, 1971.

Rotberg, Robert I. "Centripetal Forces: Regional Convergence in Southern Africa." *Harvard International Review* 17, 4 (1995).

———. *The Rise of Nationalism in Central Africa: The Making of Malawi and Zambia, 1873–1964*. Cambridge, MA: Harvard University Press, 1967.

Rotberg, Robert I., and Greg Mills, eds. *War and Peace in Southern Africa: Crime, Drugs, Armies, and Trade*. Washington, DC: Brookings Institution Press and the World Peace Foundation, 1998.

Ruggie, John Gerard. "Territoriality and Beyond: Problemizing Modernity in International Relations." *International Organization* 47, 1 (1993).

Ryan Sinclair, Marion. "Community, Identity, and Gender in Migrant Societies of Southern Africa: Emerging Epistemological Challenges." *International Affairs* 74, 2 (1998).

———. "'I Know a Place That Is Softer Than This': Emerging Migrant Communities in South Africa." *International Migration Quarterly Review* 37, 2 (1999).

Said, Edward W. *Culture and Imperialism*. London: Vintage, 1993.

———. *Representations of the Intellectual: The 1993 Reith Lectures*. London: Vintage, 1994.

Säkerhet och Utveckling i Africa (Security and development in Africa). Stockholm: Utrikes-depatementet, 1996.

"The SANDF's Baptism of Fire." *U.S. Department of State Bulletin* 76 (October 1998).

Schama, Simon. *The Embarrassment of Riches: An Interpretation of Dutch Culture in the Golden Age*. London: Fontana, 1991.

Scharf, Wilfried, and Daniel Nina, eds. *The Other Law: Non-State Ordering in South Africa*. Cape Town: Juta, 2001.

Schlesinger, Arthur M. *The Disuniting of America: Reflections on a Multicultural Society*. Larger Agenda Series. New York: Whittle Direct Books, 1998.

Schönteich, Martin. "The Impact on HIV/Aids on South Africa's Internal Security." Paper delivered at the first Annual Conference of the South African Association of Public Administration and Management, CSIR Conference Centre, Pretoria, November 23, 2000.

Schutte, D.P.A. *Migration: The Status Quo and Prospects for Southern Africa*. Address delivered to a meeting of the Institute for Strategic Studies, University of Pretoria, June 3, 1993.

Seegers, Annette. *The Military in the Making of Modern South Africa*. London: I. B. Tauris, 1996.

————. "The New National Security Doctrine: The South African Experience." Paper delivered to the Inter-University Seminar on Armed Forces and Society, Biennial International Conference, Baltimore, Maryland, October 22–24, 1999.

Sekatle, Pontšo. "The Lesotho General Election of 1998." *Lesotho Social Science Review* 5, 1 (1999).

Shapiro, Michael. "Narrating the Nation, Unwelcoming the Stranger: Anti-Immigration Policy in Contemporary 'America.'" *Alternatives* 22, 1 (1997).

Shaw, Mark. *Crime and Policing in Post-Apartheid South Africa: Reforming Under Fire*. London: Hurst, and Cape Town: David Phillip, 2001.

Shaw, Mark, and Jakkie Cilliers, eds. *South Africa and Peacekeeping in Africa*. Halfway House, South Africa: Institute for Defence Policy, 1995.

Shotter, John. *Cultural Politics of Everyday Life*. Buckingham, UK: Open University Press, 1993.

Simon, David. "Trading Spaces: Imagining and Positioning the 'New' South Africa Within the Regional and Global Economies." *International Affairs* 77, 2 (2001).

Simons, Jack. *Struggles in Southern Africa for Survival and Equity*. Cape Town: Macmillan, 1997.

Singer, Peter. *Marx*. New York: Oxford University Press, 1980.

Smith, Anthony D. *National Identity*. Las Vegas: University of Nevada Press, 1991.

Smith, Neil. "New Geographies: Old Ontologies." *Radical Philosophy* 106 (2001).

Smith, Steve, Ken Booth, and Marysia Zalewski. *International Theory: Positivism and Beyond*. Cambridge, UK: Cambridge University Press, 1996.

Smuts, Jan Christian. *Plans for a Better World: Speeches of Field-Marshal, the Right Honourable J.C. Smuts, P.C., C.H., K.C., D.T.D*. London: Hodder and Stoughton, 1942.

Söderbaum, Fredrik. "The New Regionalism in Southern Africa." *Politeia* 17, 3 (1998).

Soguk, Nevzat. *States and Strangers: Refugees and Displacements of Statecraft.* Borderlines no. 11. Minneapolis: University of Minnesota Press, 1999.

Sole, Kelwyn. "The Witness of Poetry: Economic Calculation, Civil Society, and the Limits of Everyday Experience in a Liberated South Africa." *New Formations* 45 (2001–2002).

Solomon, Hussein. "Defending Borders: Strategic Responses to Illegal Immigrants." *Indicator SA* 13, 3 (1996).

———. "Immigration and Security in South Africa." Undated mimeo.

———. *Towards the Free Movement of People in Southern Africa.* ISS Paper no. 18. Halfway House, South Africa: Institute for Strategic Studies, 1997.

Solomon, Hussein, ed. *Sink or Swim? Water, Resource Security, and State Cooperation.* ISS Monograph Series no. 6. Halfway House, South Africa: Institute for Security Studies, 1996.

Solomon, Hussein, and Jakkie Cilliers. "Southern Africa and the Quest for Collective Security." *Security Dialogue* 28, 2 (1997).

Solomon, Hussein, and Anthony Turton, eds. *Water Wars: Enduring Myth or Impending Reality.* African Dialogue Monograph Series no. 2. Durban, South Africa: ACCORD, 2000.

Sorbo, Gunnar, and Peter Vale, eds. *Out of Conflict: From War to Peace in Africa.* Uppsala, Sweden: Nordiska Afrika Institutet, 1997.

Sources of Domestic Insecurity in Southern African States, a Conference Report. Comp. John Bardill. Backgrounder no. 12. Bellville, South Africa: Centre for Southern African Studies, University of the Western Cape, 1994.

"South Africa–Mozambique: Development Corridor." *Africa Research Bulletin: Economic, Financial, and Technical Series* 33, 2 (February 1996).

South Africa 1976: Official Yearbook of the Republic of South Africa. 3d ed. Pretoria: Department of Information, 1976.

Southall, Roger. "Review of A. Seegers' *The Military in the Making.*" *Journal of Modern African Studies* 53, 3 (1997).

Southall, Roger, and Tsoeu Petlane, eds. *Democratisation and Demilitarisation in Lesotho.* Pretoria: Africa Institute of South Africa, 1995.

The Southern African Institute: A Forum for Security and Development Concerns: The Lupogo Report. Arusha Papers no. 4. Bellville, South Africa: Centre for Southern African Studies, University of the Western Cape, 1995.

"Special Issue: Religion and International Relations." *Millennium* 29, 3 (2000).

Spence, J. E. "South Africa's Foreign Policy: The Evolution, 1945–1986." *Energos* 14 (1986).

———. *The Strategic Significance of Southern Africa.* London: Royal United Services Institute, 1970.

Spiegel, A. D., and P. A. McAllister, eds. *Tradition and Transition in Southern Africa: Festschrift for Philip and Iona Mayer.* Johannesburg: Witwatersrand University Press, 1991.

Steen, Gerard. *Understanding Metaphor in Literature.* London: Longman, 1994.

Stone, Ruth M. *Africa. The Garland Encyclopaedia of World Music.* Vol. 1. New York and London: Garland Publishing, 1998.

Strachan, Beth. *Angola, the Struggle for Power: The Political, Social, and Economic Context, 1980–1993, a Select and Annotated Bibliography*. SAIIA Bibliographical Series no. 28. Johannesburg: South African Institute of International Affairs, 1994.

Strachen, Alexander. *'N Wereld Sonder Grense*. Cape Town: Tafelberg, 1984.

Strange, Susan. *States and Markets*. 2d ed. London: Pinter, 1998.

Strik, Peter M.R. *Critical Theory, Politics, and Society: An Introduction*. London: Pinter, 2000.

Stryker, Sheldon, Timothy J. Owens, and Robert W. White, eds. *Self, Identity, and Social Movements*. Minneapolis: University of Minnesota Press, 2000.

Suransky-Dekker, Caroline. "'A Liberating Breeze of Western Civilization': A Political History of Fundamental Pedagogics as an Expression of Dutch-Afrikaner Relationships." Unpublished D.Ed. thesis, Department of Curriculum Studies, University of Durban–Westville, 1998.

Suttner, Raymond, and Jeremy Cronin. *30 Years of the Freedom Charter*. Johannesburg: Ravan, 1986.

Swatuk, Larry, and David Black, eds. *Bridging the Rift: The "New" South Africa in Africa*. New York: Westview, 1997.

Tamarkin, M. "South Africa's Regional Options: Policy Making and Conceptual Environment." *International Affairs Bulletin* 7, 3 (1983).

Terriff, Terry, and Stuart Croft, et al. *Security Studies Today*. Cambridge, UK: Polity, 1999.

Thomas, Scott. *The Diplomacy of Liberation: The Foreign Relations of the African National Congress Since 1960*. London: Tauris Academic Studies, 1996.

Thompson, Leonard. *The Political Mythology of Apartheid*. New Haven: Yale University Press, 1985.

Thompson, Lisa, ed. *Critical Perspectives on Security and Sovereignty: Perspectives from the South*. Bellville, South Africa: Centre for Southern African Studies, University of the Western Cape, 2001.

Thompson, Lisa, and Anthony Leysens. "Changing Notions of Human Security in the Southern African Region." *Transformation: Critical Perspectives on Southern Africa* 43 (2000).

Tilly, Charles. *Coercion, Capital, and European States, A.D. 990–1990*. Cambridge, MA: Basil Blackwell, 1990.

Torodov, Tzveran. *The Conquest of America: The Question of the Other*. New York: Harper and Row, 1984.

Tuathail, Gearóid Ó, Simon Dalby, and Paul Routledge, eds. *The Geopolitics Reader*. London: Routledge, 1998.

Tucker, Rob, and Bruce R. Scott, eds. *South Africa: Prospects for Successful Transition*. Cape Town: Juta, 1992.

Turner, Bryan S. *Orientalism, Postmodernism, and Globalism*. London: Routledge, 1994.

Vale, Colin, and Irene van den Ende, eds. *The Loss of Innocence: International Relations Essays in Honour of Dirk Kunert*. Pretoria: Human Sciences Research Council, 1994.

Vale, Peter. "A Drought Blind to the Horrors of War (and the Challenge of Peace)." *Die Suid-Afrikaan* 40 (1992).

———. *Of Laagers, Lepers, and Leanness: South Africa and Regional Security.* Bergen, Norway: Christian Michelsen Institute, 1995.

———. "Regional Security in Southern Africa." *Alternatives* 21, 3 (1996).

———. "South Africa and Southern Africa: Theories and Practice, Choices and Ritual." Inaugural Lecture, UNESCO Africa Chair, Faculteit der Letteren at the Universiteit Utrecht, 1996.

———. *Southern African Security: Some Old Issues, Many New Questions: Confidence- and Security-building Measures in Southern Africa.* Disarmament Topical Papers no. 14. New York: United Nations, Department of Political Affairs, 1993.

Vale, Peter, and John Daniel. "Regional Security in Southern Africa in the 1990s: Challenging the Terms of the Neo-Realist Debate." *Transformation* 28 (1995).

Vale, Peter, and Khabele Motlasa. "Beyond the Nation State: Rebuilding Southern Africa from Below." *Harvard International Review* 17, 4 (1995).

Vale, Peter, Larry A. Swatuk, and Bertil Oden, eds. *Theory, Change, and Southern Africa's Future.* London: Palgrave, 2001.

Van Hear, Nicholas. "Refugees and Displaced People in Africa." *Africa Contemporary Record* 22 (1989–1990).

Van Hensbroek, Pieter Boele. "African Political Philosophy, 1860–1995." Unpublished Ph.D. thesis, Department of Philosophy, University of Groningen, the Netherlands, 1998.

Van Onselen, Charles. *The Seed Is Mine: The Life of Kas Maine, a South African Sharecropper, 1894–1985.* Cape Town: David Philip, 1996.

Van Rinsum, Henk J. "Slaves of Definition: In Quest of the Unbeliever and the Ignoramus." Unpublished Ph.D. thesis, Faculty of Social Sciences, University of Utrecht, the Netherlands, 2001.

Van Wyk, K., and S. Radloff. "Symmetry and Reciprocity in South Africa's Foreign Policy." *Journal of Conflict Resolution* 37, 2 (1993).

Venter, Minnie, ed. *Migrancy and AIDS: Conference Proceedings December 1994.* Cape Town: Medical Research Council, 1994.

———. *Prospects for Progress: Critical Choices for Southern Africa.* Cape Town: Maskew Miller Longman, 1994.

Vintage Kenton: A Kenton Education Association Commemoration 21. Comp. Wendy Flanagan et al. Cape Town: Maskew Miller, 1994.

Visvanathan, Shiv. "A Celebration of Difference: Science and Democracy in India." *Science* 280 (April 3, 1998).

von Hippel, Karin. *Democracy by Force: US Military Intervention in the Post–Cold War World.* Cambridge, UK: Cambridge University Press, 2000.

Wæver, Ole. *Concepts of Security.* Copenhagen: Institute of Political Science, University of Copenhagen, 1997.

Walker, R.B.J. *Inside/Outside: International Relations as Political Theory.* Cambridge, UK: Cambridge University Press, 1993.

————. *One World, Many Worlds: Struggles for a Just World Peace.* Boulder: Lynne Rienner Publishers, 1998.

————. "Security, Sovereignty, and the Challenge of World Politics." *Alternatives* 15, 1 (1990).

Walt, Stephen M. "International Relations: One World, Many Theories." *Foreign Policy* 110 (1998).

Weiner, Myron. *The Global Migration Crisis: Challenge to States and Human Rights.* New York: HarperCollins College Publishers, 1995.

————. "Security, Stability, and International Migration." *International Security* 17, 3 (1992/1993).

Weisfelder, Richard. "Lesotho and the Inner Periphery in the New South Africa." *Journal of Modern African Studies* 30, 4 (1992).

Weldes, Jutta, et al. *Cultures of Insecurity: States, Communites, and the Production of Danger.* Borderlines no. 14. Minneapolis: University of Minnesota Press, 1999.

Wells, A. W. *Southern Africa: Today—and Yesterday.* Rev. ed. London: J. M. Dent and Son at the Aldine Press, 1956.

Werbner, Richard, and Terence Ranger, eds. *Postcolonial Identities in Africa.* London: Zed, 1996.

Wexler, Philip, ed. *Critical Theory Now.* London: Falmer, 1991.

Whiteside, Alan. *Labour Migration in Southern Africa.* Johannesburg: South African Institute of International Affairs, 1988.

Whitworth, Sandra. "Gender, Race, and the Politics of Peacekeeping." Paper presented at the International Studies Association Annual Meeting, San Diego, April 16–20, 1996.

Williams, Paul. "Intellectuals and the End of Apartheid: Critical Security Studies and the South African Transition." Unpublished Ph.D. thesis, Department of International Politics, University of Wales, Aberystwyth, 2001.

————. "South African Foreign Policy: Getting Critical." *Politikon* 27, 1 (2000).

Williams, Raymond. *Keywords: A Vocabulary of Culture and Society.* London: Fontana/Croom Helm, 1983.

Williams, Rocky. "Peace Operations and the South Africa Armed Forces: Prospects and Challenges." *Strategic Review for Southern Africa* 17, 2 (November 1995).

Wilmsen, Edwin N., and Pat McAllister, eds. *The Politics of Difference: Ethnic Premises in a World of Power.* Chicago: University of Chicago Press, 1996.

Wilson, Francis. *Labour in the South African Gold Mines, 1911–1969.* Cambridge, UK: Cambridge University Press, 1972.

————. "Minerals and Migrants: How the Mining Industry Has Shaped South Africa." *Dædalus* 130, 1 (2001).

Worden, Nigel. *The Making of Modern South Africa: Conquest, Segregation, and Apartheid.* Oxford, UK: Blackwell, 1994.

Wright, Mercia. "An Old Nationalist in New Nationalist Times: Donald Siwale and the State in Zambia: 1948–1963." *Journal of Southern African Studies* 23, 1 (1997).

Wyn Jones, Richard. "'Message in a Bottle'? Theory and Praxis in Critical Security Studies." *Contemporary Security Policy* 16, 3 (1995).

Yap, Melanie, and Dianne Leong Man. *Colour, Confusion, and Concession: The History of the Chinese in South Africa*. Hong Kong: Hong Kong University Press, 1996.

Year Book and Guide to Southern Africa. Ed. annually by G. Gordon-Brown for the Union-Castle Mail Steamship Company Limited. Cape Town: Howard Timmins.

Index

243

About the Book

In this analysis of South Africa's postapartheid security system, Peter Vale moves beyond a realist discussion of interacting states to examine southern Africa as an integrated whole.

Vale argues that, despite South Africa's manipulation of state structures and elites in the region for its own ends, the suffering endured under the apartheid regime drew the region together at the popular level; and economic factors, such as the use of migrant labor, reinforced the process of integration. Exploring how the region is changing today—as transnational solidarity and a single regional economy remove the distinctions between national and international politics—he asks whether South African domination can finally be overcome and considers what sort of cosmopolitan political arrangement will be appropriate for southern Africa in the new century.

Peter Vale holds the Nelson Mandela Chair in Politics at Rhodes University in Grahamstown, South Africa. He has served as deputy vice-chancellor of the University of the Western Cape, South Africa, where he was senior professor of government, professor of social theory, and sometime professor of southern African studies. He has also been a fellow of the International Center for Advanced Studies at New York University. An influential commentator on foreign policy, he has also contributed to such journals as *International Affairs*, *Foreign Affairs*, *Survival*, and *Alternatives*. During South Africa's transition to democracy he served on the African National Congress's foreign policy advisory group. He is coeditor of *Bridges to the Future: Prospects for Peace and Security in Southern Africa*, *Out of Conflict: From War to Peace in Africa*, and *Theory, Change, and Southern Africa's Future*.